Praise for

The **Politically Incorrect Guide**™ to
<u>REAL</u> AMERICAN HEROES

"Forgetting the builders of our nation will lead to the collapse of our nation. Brion McClanahan's *Politically Incorrect Guide*™ *to Real American Heroes* can help us avoid collapse and extend American civilization to future generations."

> —**Leo Thorsness**, colonel USAF (retired), Medal of Honor recipient, POW in Vietnam for six years

"Ronald Reagan reminded us in his first inaugural address, 'Those who say that we're in a time when there are no heroes—they just don't know where to look.' Now they can look here! *The Politically Incorrect Guide*™ *to Real American Heroes* helps us distinguish true heroes from mere celebrities. As Calvin Coolidge said, 'Great men are ambassadors of Providence sent to reveal to their fellow men their unknown selves.' This book is an overdue reminder of this timeless truth."

> —**Steven F. Hayward**, author of *The Politically Incorrect Guide*™ *to the Presidents* and *The Age of Reagan*

"Brion McClanahan is on a mission to revive traditional American virtues. One way to do so, he thinks, is by restoring traditional American heroes to their lost place in our consciousness. Rather than focus solely on a panoply of victims, officials, and people who are famous for being famous, we ought to admire people for whom faith, devotion, duty, self-reliance, ingenuity, and sacrifice served as beacons on the path to their contributions to their communities and the broader society. His choice of explorers, statesmen, military leaders, business tycoons, and authors is not meant to be exhaustive; rather, McClanahan offers us an implicit challenge to ponder the lives of additional admirable Americans of our own choosing. To help us, he throws in a few tales of lionized people who deserve to be knocked off their pedestals."

> —**Kevin Gutzman**, author of *The Politically Incorrect Guide*™ *to the Constitution* and *James Madison and the Making of America*

"You have to read a book that explains why well known men like Robert E. Lee and little known women like Augusta Jane Evans are American heroes, and why PC favorites like the Kennedys and Margaret Sanger should never have been given the title in the first place."

— **Clint Johnson**, author of *The Politically Incorrect Guide™ to the South*

"Brion McClanahan's *Politically Incorrect Guide™ to Real American Heroes* answers a crying need. American kids are growing up ignorant of both the principles and the people that made America great. McClanahan reintroduces the explorers, founders, frontiersmen, soldiers, underdogs, and inventors that every child used to learn about in school, until the curriculum was gutted by the Left. These real American hero stories are an entertaining read—and a valuable education in American ingenuity, self-reliance, and self-government."

— **Marybeth Hicks**, author of *Don't Let the Kids Drink the Kool-Aid: Confronting the Left's Assault on Our Families, Faith, and Freedom*

"Collectivists are fond of claiming that 'it takes a village' for big or good things to happen. Baloney! The strength of the village depends on the character of the unique individuals who drive it forward, often overcoming barriers the village idiots put in their way. With this book, Brion McClanahan helps us celebrate some notable heroes even as he reveals that others thought by many to be heroes shouldn't be in that category at all."

— **Lawrence W. Reed**, president of the Foundation for Economic Education

"'To the victor belong the spoils' is an adage that relates perfectly to Brion McClanahan's *Politically Incorrect Guide™ to Real American Heroes* as McClanahan engages us in a fast-paced account of those heroes purged by the forces that have claimed political victories in the United States. Readers will be inspired by the final frontier escapades of Buzz Aldrin as by the adventures of his colonial frontier counterpart Daniel Boone. Equally inspiring is McClanhan's vivid revival of America's first historian and original misanthrope Mercy Otis Warren. The demigod FDR and classical-education-slayer Dewey are returned to their proper stations in American history's cellar. In an age that features hero worship of the laughable and decadent, McClanhan saves us by providing an exciting restoration of the heroic stories that tamed a continent with republican virtue."

— **Mike Church**, writer-director of *The Road to Independence* and host of Sirius XM's *Mike Church Show*

"McClanahan is one of the best historians of his generation and this may be his finest book. His portrayal of real American heroes like Daniel Boone, Booker T. Washington, and Buzz Aldrin is sure to encourage Americans. Here are people worthy of our admiration and emulation, not superficial celebrities. *The Politically Incorrect Guide™ to Real American Heroes* should appeal especially to parents who recognize the shallowness of public education and the popular media. Read this book. And share it with your children."

—**Sean Busick**, professor of history at Athens State University and author of *The Founding of the American Republic* and *A Sober Desire for History*

"Unless one is intoxicated by the scourge of political correctness, there can be no argument as to who the good guys are and who the bad guys are. Self-evident truth remains common and sensible to those of us honest enough to genuinely scrutinize and study history, thereby identifying when good things happen and when bad things happen and just who the perpetrators are. Brion McClanahan identifies some of the long forgotten American heroes who helped shape the greatest quality of life the world has ever known in his book *The Politically Incorrect Guide™ to Real American Heroes*. Enormous upgrade will occur if this book is made an integral part of the education process for America's youth so we never forget who the real heroes were and how to keep the dream alive."

—**Ted Nugent**, rock 'n' roll legend, outdoorsman, and author of *God, Guns, & Rock 'n' Roll*; *Kill It & Grill It*; and *Ted, White, and Blue*

The Politically Incorrect Guide™ to

<u>REAL</u> AMERICAN HEROES

VOID

The Politically Incorrect Guide™ to
REAL AMERICAN HEROES

Brion McClanahan

Since 1947
REGNERY
PUBLISHING, INC.
An Eagle Publishing Company • Washington, DC

Cataloging-in-Publication data on file with the Library of Congress
ISBN 978-1-59698-320-5

Published in the United States by
Regnery Publishing, Inc.
One Massachusetts Avenue NW
Washington, DC 20001
www.Regnery.com

Manufactured in the United States of America

10 9 8 7 6 5 4 3 2 1

Books are available in quantity for promotional or premium use. Write to Director of Special Sales, Regnery Publishing, Inc., One Massachusetts Avenue NW, Washington, DC 20001, for information on discounts and terms, or call (202) 216-0600.

Distributed to the trade by
Perseus Distribution
250 West 57th Street
New York, NY 10107

*To those who fight for and live traditional
American principles and values—
you are real American heroes*

CONTENTS

Introduction   **1**

Part I   THE REAL HEROES

Chapter 1   Explorers   **9**
The Hero of Jamestown
The Quintessential American

Chapter 2   Founders   **23**
The Original American Hero
The Conservative Conscience of America

Chapter 3   Sailors   **39**
Indomitable Captain
Intrepid Hero

Chapter 4   Frontiersmen   **53**
King of the Wild Frontier
Old Hickory

Chapter 5   Southerners   **71**
The Last Gentleman
The Christian Soldier

Chapter 6   Northerners   **87**
The Lion of the Round Top
The Cavalier

Chapter 7   **Traditional Women**   **101**

A Heroine and a Patriot

A Beacon of Traditional Womanhood

The Girl Scouts' Misunderstood Founder

Chapter 8   **Captains of Industry**   **115**

Titan of Industry

Pioneer of Philanthropy

Chapter 9   **Inventors**   **129**

Mechanical Genius, Benefactor of the Human Race

The Dynamo

Chapter 10   **Underdogs**   **141**

A Classic American Success Story

A Great American Entrepreneur

Chapter 11   **Soldiers**   **153**

Classic American General

"Old Blood and Guts"

Chapter 12   **Aviators**   **169**

The Lone Eagle

Man on the Moon

Part II   **THE FRAUDS**

Chapter 13   **Progressive Frauds**   **187**

The Educator

The Utopian

Chapter 14   **Democratic Frauds**   **197**

The Idealist and the Conspirator

The Evolving Constitution

Chapter 15   **Fascist Fraud**   **207**

                The American Aristocrat

                The American Dictator

                The Warmonger

Chapter 16   **Feminist Frauds**   **217**

                The Birth Control Crusader

                The Feminist

Chapter 17   **Family Frauds**   **229**

                The Sins of the Father

                Jack

                Bobby

                Teddy

Conclusion   **241**

Notes   **243**

Index   **255**

INTRODUCTION

Americans need heroes. Perhaps our heritage mandates that. Americans have tamed a vast wilderness, plowed fields, built companies, won wars in the face of insurmountable odds, spread liberty and civilization across thousands of miles of territory—and accomplished most of this on our own hook. We are a fiercely independent, proud, hardworking, and, yes, heroic people. Yet, as the historian Frederick Jackson Turner lamented decades ago, the closing of the frontier in 1890 may have augured an end to this rugged individualism, this most truly American trait. Urbanization has made many Americans decadent. We have become dislocated from the heroic deeds of our ancestors and as a result look for "heroes" among the artists, musicians, actors, and politicians that dominate modern American life. It hasn't always been this way.

There is a calendar from the year of my father's birth, 1940, on the wall of my parents' home. It was a freebie from an insurance company based in the North, but I noticed several years ago that the birthdays of both Robert E. Lee and "Stonewall" Jackson were included as holidays. There were no asterisks by their names setting them apart as slave-owners or "traitors." This Northern insurance company considered two Southern heroes to be American heroes, too—worthy of celebration, no less. Americans of earlier generations would have been able to discuss the heroics of men such as Captain John Smith, Winfield Scott, Daniel Boone, Stephen Decatur, Davy Crockett, and Lee; and the accomplishments of contemporaries like George S. Patton and Charles Lindbergh would have rolled off their tongues. These genuine heroes were once as much a part of American life as baseball and apple pie. Unfortunately, the same reverence for the heroes of our past is missing from contemporary America. Neither students nor adults remember them.

In 2005, AOL and the Discovery Channel produced a show entitled *The Greatest American*. Among the top one hundred were close to forty entertainers, including such "greats" as Hugh Hefner, Tom Cruise, Arnold Schwarzenegger, Dr. Phil, Madonna, Marilyn Monroe, and Michael Jackson. Ronald Reagan did top the list, and George Washington and Benjamin Franklin were among the top five; but traditional heroes such as Crockett, Boone, and Lee were absent. And then there were the fraudulent heroes, those on whom Americans heap considerable undeserved praise, not knowing much about them other than platitudes and half-truths. The Kennedy family and Franklin D. Roosevelt, for example, were on the list. Americans, it seems, are so starved for people to emulate that they turn to actors, professional athletes, and musicians—most of whom have led less than stellar lives (they certainly would never have been considered "great" by previous generations)—and make demi-gods out of men of questionable character who despised and worked to undermine America's founding documents. As a matter of fact, leaning so far to the Left is a point in their favor. Had they been conservative, politicians and ideologues such as Woodrow Wilson and John Dewey would never have gained the respect they enjoy today.

Our modern education system (thank John Dewey!) is largely responsible for this state of affairs. A study conducted between 2004 and 2005 revealed that Americans, both high school students and adults, consider women and minorities to be more heroic than traditional American icons such as Paul Revere and Patrick Henry. In the survey, conducted by Sam Wineburg and Chauncey Monte-Sano, students were asked to select the top ten most heroic Americans. They could not choose a president or the wife of a president, and they were not prompted with possible answers. Among students, the top ten were Martin Luther King Jr., Rosa Parks, Harriet Tubman, Susan B.

Anthony, Benjamin Franklin, Amelia Earhart, Oprah Winfrey, Marilyn Monroe, Thomas Edison, and Albert Einstein. Adults chose the same top ten "heroes," except that Betsy Ross and Henry Ford replaced Einstein and Monroe. Wineburg and Monte-Sano concluded that decades of "multi-cultural" education have led to a shift in what Americans consider heroic, and they applauded the change, noting that minorities have now found their rightful place in American history.[1] But what about the cost to our shared remembered past—to American history as it has been traditionally understood?

Wineburg and Monte-Sano have correctly identified a cultural shift, but they have missed its significance. "Multi-cultural" education has placed a disproportionate emphasis on women and minorities at the expense of our traditional heroes. They've now been demoted to the dreaded racist, slave-holding, Indian-hating, polluting, land-grabbing, greedy, manly, white male American villains of our past. According to this history, Thomas Jefferson was a slave rapist, a bigot, and a hypocritical demagogue; Robert E. Lee was a slave-owning traitor; George Washington was not only a slave-owner but a dim-witted dunderhead, a sort of eighteenth-century Calvin Klein with a flair for designing uniforms; Daniel Boone was an Indian-killer who stole land from its rightful owners; John D. Rockefeller was a money-grubbing polluter who wrung his wealth from the broken backs of the penniless workers he abused; and Charles Lindbergh was nothing more than an anti-Semitic Nazi sympathizer. There's a classic scene in the iconic teen film *Dazed and Confused* when the feminist history teacher urges her students to remember that "this summer when you are being inundated with this American bicentennial Fourth of July brouhaha, don't forget what you're celebrating, and that's the fact that a bunch of slave-owning aristocratic white males didn't want to pay their taxes." Today, reality has caught up with satire—that type of rhetoric is now common on high school and college campuses.

A greater emphasis on the "forgotten" people of American history may have added "complexity" and "texture"—two terms very popular among professional historians in America—to our understanding of the past, but the purpose of American history should not be to denigrate or replace the men who were the driving forces in the making of America. If leftist American historians are going to attempt (often successfully) to ruin the character of people like George Washington or Thomas Jefferson in their students' eyes, then their heroes—minorities and women included—should be subject to the same harsh scrutiny. They are not.

How many Americans know that Franklin D. Roosevelt, the patron saint of the modern Left, assumed the role of an elected king during his unprecedented four terms of office in the executive branch (the fourth cut short only by his death), goaded the Japanese into war in 1941 (and possibly knew about the attack on Pearl Harbor beforehand but refused to stop or even effectively prepare for it), trampled the Constitution during the Great Depression, and at one time admired Mussolini's Fascism? With Roosevelt consistently ranked as one of the best presidents in American history, probably not many. How many Americans realize that one of the heroes of the modern feminist movement, Margaret Sanger, spoke at at least one Ku Klux Klan rally, and considered religion nothing but a "bugaboo"? Judging by the fact that Sanger has been labeled one of the greatest women in American history, probably not many. How many Americans know the seedy history of the Kennedy clan, starting with John F. Kennedy's father Joe and his ties to organized crime, and trickling down to two generations of adulterers? If they do, they overlook it because the Kennedys are, according to leftist historians, American heroes. How many Americans know that our modern education system, designed by John Dewey, was an attempt to take parents out of the educational equation? We keep shipping our kids to government schools—apparently ignorance is bliss. The seeds of our societal and political destruction have been sown by these frauds, but they are all considered "heroes" or "great men and women." It's tragic.

At one time in the twentieth century, every boy wanted to be David Crockett or George Patton. George Washington was "the man", and more boys had fun playing Confederate soldiers—particularly Lee and Jackson—than even their illustrious Union counterparts. George Custer was a tragic but heroic figure, astronauts like Buzz Aldrin were household names, and businessmen still strove to be like Rockefeller and Carnegie. Excellence had not lost its place in American culture. These men represented an American ideal that society found intoxicating. They would not be found at a nail salon or spending hundreds of dollars on a haircut. Traditional American heroes were honorable, independent, principled, and spirited men, not politicians or actors. They didn't just exploit their talents to achieve a selfish success; they served a cause—a country—bigger than themselves. Traditional heroines embodied sacrifice and devotion to others. They were guides, moral compasses—strong-willed and principled, but not selfish. Family came first. The "Real American Heroes" in this book exemplify all of these traits.

Fortunately, traditional American heroes have not completely disappeared from American history courses, but it seems that celebrations of their merits and accomplishments are few and far between. Saving traditional American heroes from the dustbin to which the historical profession has relegated them should be a top priority—if only to re-connect Americans today with our heroic patrimony and disperse the black clouds of political correctness that obscure it. We stand on the shoulders of giants; our society and political system were forged by the accomplishments and traditions of our ancestors. Connections with these heroes are necessary to preserve our continuity with a distinctive American past. If we continue to ignore them, America will crumble under the false rhetoric of "Progress," "Hope," and "Change."

Part I

THE REAL HEROES

Chapter 1

EXPLORERS

Captain John Smith and Daniel Boone

America is often mislabeled "a nation of immigrants." Certainly the massive waves of migrations throughout America's history, first from the British Isles and northern Europe and later from virtually all over the world, have placed an indelible stamp on our country, making it, even in the colonial period, something different from a nation in the traditional sense. Yet America's course—as an enduring republic, an astoundingly prosperous experiment in self-government, and a beacon of liberty to the world—was set at the time of the founding of the United States. And at that time America was hardly dominated by immigrants. Many of the important men of the founding generation were third- or fourth-generation Americans who were more attached to their native land than to England. The men and women who created the United States were a people of independent spirit, a spirit forged by the trials of the wilderness, in cutting a path in an untamed world. They were bold adventurers, entrepreneurs, pioneers, and explorers. These are the best traits of early America, and no one represented them better than Captain John Smith and Daniel Boone.

Did you know?

★ John Smith left England as a runaway apprentice with just ten shillings in his pocket

★ At one point Smith owned only two books—the Bible, and Machiavelli's *Art of War*

★ Daniel Boone was tortured and forced to join an Indian tribe, but escaped and raced back nearly 200 miles to warn the settlers of a planned attack

The Hero of Jamestown

John Smith made the title "Captain" important before "Captain" Jack Sparrow made it funny in *Pirates of the Caribbean*. Smith's life is shrouded in mystery, and there is perhaps no more polarizing figure in early America. He is both admired and reviled—historians generally either believe his wild tales of adventure or regard him as little more than a self-aggrandizing liar. Either way, there is little doubt that America, particularly the South, would not have been the same without him. He was the first American hero, a trailblazer, statesman, pioneer, soldier of fortune, historian, and explorer. Smith saved Virginia and named New England. His life is a bold, romantic tale that makes even the greatest feats of the modern age seem small in comparison. Such a man is deserving of a prominent place in the pantheon of great Americans.

Smith was born around 1579 in Lincolnshire, England. His family had prominent origins, and when his father died, Smith inherited a small estate, enough to make him believe he could afford fine adventures. He spent little time in school, preferring a life of action to one of study. His guardians apprenticed him to a local merchant when Smith was a teenager, but a career bound to terra firma did not suit him; he heard the call of the sea and the sword. Smith soon broke his apprenticeship, becoming a legal fugitive, and with ten shillings in his pocket from his estate, set forth on the grand adventure of life.

He fled to France and found a role in the French army, fighting in the French wars of religion on the side of the Protestants. This is where he learned the craft of the sword. When those wars ended, Smith served for several years on an English ship battling the Spanish in the fight to control the Netherlands. Four

A Book You're Not Supposed to Read

The Life of Captain John Smith: The Founder of Virginia by William Gilmore Simms (New York: A. L. Burt Company, 1902). Old, but still the best single biography by the great Southern man of letters.

years on the Continent ended with a stop in Scotland in the hope that he could gain influence with the Scottish crown. But the life of a courtier was not for him, and Smith eventually retired to the woods of England and cultivated his independence. He wrote, read, hunted, and practiced his martial skills. He was a hermit in a "pavilion of boughs" who became a famous curiosity to the local peasantry. But this solitary life did not suit a man of his nature, and Smith was soon bound for the Continent again in search of adventure.

His second tour in Europe was less creditable than the first. Smith acted as a thief—in his defense, he had been duped by men who later stole from him. He lived as a pirate, albeit briefly. His wanderings left him cold and hungry. Smith eventually found his calling as a soldier of fortune. The knowledge of military strategy he had gleaned from a thorough reading of Machiavelli's *Art of War* (the only book Smith owned besides the Bible, at one point) impressed several European nobleman, and, in addition to his skill with the sword, earned him a role in the so-called Long War between the Christian Hapsburgs in Hungary and the Muslim Ottoman Turks. He was again a soldier in a war of religion. In honor of his service and performance on the battlefield, Smith received a promotion to captain, a title that added dignity to his name for the rest of his life.

Smith reportedly killed and beheaded three Turkish commanders in duels, a feat that earned him a knighthood and a coat of arms from a Transylvanian nobleman. His skill as a soldier, however, did not make him invincible, and in 1602, Smith was wounded in battle, captured, and sold as a slave to a Turkish nobleman. According to Smith's own account, he was later given as a gift to his master's Greek mistress. The two fell in love and she helped Smith escape his captivity (with Smith "bashing his master's brains out"), in circumstances not unlike those he would face in the New World several years later. He then wandered through Africa and Europe before returning to England in 1604.

Smith was already a hardened, battle-tested soldier when he became involved in plans to organize a permanent English settlement in the New World in 1606. This opportunity suited his personality and ultimately made him a hero and a legend on both sides of the Atlantic. The Virginia Company of London procured ships, supplies, and emigrants, with Smith working to promote the enterprise. In December 1606, three ships set sail for the New World with 144 colonists. The expedition did not lose sight of the English coast for more than six weeks, as the wind did not cooperate with their plans. The colonists became mutinous, and Smith was deemed the leader of the discord. He was arrested and held in chains for the remainder of the voyage—a slow, plodding struggle to the North American coast that took four months.

Smith was facing execution, but when the fleet made landfall at present Cape Henry, Virginia, in April 1607 and the sealed orders from England were opened, the colonists discovered that Smith was to be included in the new government as a member of the council of seven. One hundred and five colonists disembarked, and in May a site was chosen for their settlement. Smith, however, had not yet been permitted to take his seat on the governing council, so he demanded a trial. After the first democratic election on American soil (democracy in America predated the Mayflower Compact by thirteen years) and the first trial by jury in the New World, Smith was acquitted of all charges.

Jamestown, the first permanent English colony in North America, was surrounded by a swamp (and hordes of mosquitoes), was isolated from the best hunting and agricultural land, did not have suitable drinking water, and was established too late in the season for the colonists to plant food crops. An additional disadvantage was that because most of the settlers were gentlemen and their body servants, they cared little for hard work. They were there to find gold, and they expected that it should be simply covering the ground. Smith knew better. He was charged with finding food for the colonists. He developed a solid relationship with the local Indian tribe, but on one excursion he was taken prisoner, carried through the Indian villages as a trophy, and sentenced to death by the Indian chief Powhatan.

Smith regarded Powhatan as a noble figure. His countenance commanded respect, and Smith recounted that he was seated "upon a throne at the upper ende of the house, with such a majestie as I cannot expresse, nor yet have often seene, either in pagan or Christian [courts]."[1] Smith was in a precarious position, and he genuinely feared for his life. The tribe had initially displayed fear over the black-powder weapons of the English, but after several skirmishes and the death of Powhatan's son at the hands of some Virginia settlers, they were bent on revenge. Smith needed a miracle, and according to his tale, he got one.

Powhatan's daughter, a tender-hearted ten-year-old girl named Pocahontas, watched Smith's trial carefully, unobserved by either Smith or her father. When the tribe determined to execute Smith, Pocahontas raced in and threw her body on Smith's head, thus preventing the warriors from mauling his skull with their clubs. Smith and other contemporary historians give bare-bones accounts of the event, with not much in the way of detail. This type of action was quite common in the culture of the tribe, and there is speculation that Pocahontas's intervention was simply a show, a symbolic event to signify the rebirth of John Smith in the tribe. Regardless, Smith was spared and gained newfound respect among the tribe by the intercession of Pocahontas.

Colonial Virginia, No Welfare State

"You must obey this now for a Law, that he that will not worke shall not eate (except by sicknesse he be disabled:) for the labours of thirtie or fortie honest and industrious men shall not be consumed to maintaine an hundred and fiftie idle loyterers."

—John Smith in *The Generall Historie of Virginia, New England, and the Summer Isles*

He returned to Jamestown in 1608 to find the colony on the verge of disaster. The government was in the hands of the men who had sought his execution on the voyage from England, and there was little food and even less hope. Smith was again arrested and sentenced to death by hanging. And again, fate intervened. Shortly before his date with the gallows, Christopher Newport arrived with fresh supplies and new settlers. Smith was acquitted and restored to his position on the council. It seemed that Jamestown had turned the corner. But the colony would soon be in trouble again.

Smith spent his summer exploring the Potomac and Rappahannock rivers, something he preferred to life in the fort, but when the colony faced extermination from disease and starvation, Smith was called upon to save Jamestown. He led a coup and as a result was elected president by the council. Half the population of Jamestown was dead, and Smith needed to turn things around quickly or the colony would fail. He divided up the remaining settlers and instructed them to find food. Smith secured some corn from the Indians but at the same time informed the settlers that those "that will not worke shall not eate." (2 Thessalonians 3:10) This has often been described as harsh administration of justice, but Smith knew the score. The only way to save Jamestown was though initiative and enterprise. The communal plan adopted by the early leaders had failed to produce results, and Smith, cognizant of the effects a lack of discipline and independence had had on the colonists, turned the colony in a new direction. It would not be a stretch, then, to proclaim that Smith and free enterprise saved the English in America.

A fresh batch of supplies and settlers arrived in 1609. Smith's administrative skills had saved Jamestown from certain destruction, but the leadership under the new colonial charter did not see things that way. A power struggle ensued and Smith, wounded in an accidental explosion, finally relinquished control of the colony and headed back to England. In spite of his remarkable accomplishments, Smith was vilified both in Jamestown and in London. He went on the offensive in a stinging rebuttal of the Virginia Company, its leadership, and its methods, and about two years after his arrival in England published a brief account of life in Virginia entitled *A Map of Virginia. With a Description of the Countrey, the Commodities, People, Government and Religion.*

The attempted assassination of Smith's character did not succeed. He was sent back to America in 1614, this time to explore the area north of Jamestown and to find gold. But Smith brought back something more valuable to the English: fish, furs, and an accurate description and map of what he called "New England." Smith poured much of his energy into a potential settlement of New England. He believed the region suitable for settlement and insisted on the necessity of utilizing its abundant natural resources. Before the Pilgrims famously settled in Plymouth, Smith put the location on the map.

An American Soul

"But with his soul ever in America, his body remained in England. If he could not go forth himself, he encouraged all who could do so...."

—William Gilmore Simms[2]

On a return trip to New England in 1615, Smith was captured by the French and held as a pirate. His papers clearly indicated that Smith was on official English business, but maritime laws were often disregarded in the early seventeenth century. Smith finally escaped in the fall of 1615 and returned to England, never again to set foot in the New World. He spent his remaining years as an author, publishing his most famous work in 1624, *The Generall Historie of Virginia, New England, and the Summer Isles.* The Pilgrims made use of his maps and descriptions but never considered an invitation to the hero of Jamestown. He was too old and did not conform to Pilgrim theology. Smith died in 1631, the recognized expert on the early English settlement of North America. His humane treatment of the American Indian tribes, expert administrative abilities, penchant for heroism, and fearless leadership have earned him his rank as a first-rate American legend. If only he were still remembered as such.

A Book You're Not Supposed to Read

The American Democrat by James Fenimore Cooper (Washington, DC: Regnery, 2001). Though Cooper is better known as an author of fiction, his political writings are his best stuff. In *The American Democrat* he aptly defines what it means to be an American.

The Quintessential American

Perhaps the only man more neglected than Smith in modern American history texts is the early pioneer and American hero Daniel Boone. Other American pioneers lived similar tales of adventure and were, perhaps, more successful—at least in regard to financial and legal matters. But what made Boone famous and what has always endeared him to Americans is his honest, sincere approach to life. He was a common man who achieved great things in the rugged world of the American wilderness, carving out a place for the self-confident and self-reliant American.

In the early nineteenth century, nothing said "America" like Daniel Boone. Thomas Cole, the famous founder of the Hudson River School of art, dedicated a canvas to him. James Fenimore Cooper, the great American author and political critic, modeled his Natty Bumppo (otherwise known as Hawkeye), the famous character in his *Leatherstocking Tales*, after Boone. The great Romantic poet Lord Byron made Boone an international celebrity by featuring him in Canto XVIII of his famous *Don Juan*. And in the modern era, Daniel Boone was the star of a popular television show in the 1960s and 70s. Critics charge that such acclaim is unwarranted, that Daniel Boone is more myth than reality—a figment of the vapid American imagination, a two-dimensional character. Perhaps, but Boone and his admirers did much to solidify the American spirit. At one time, Americans of all stripes could testify that Daniel Boone was "one of them." To Europeans, he was "America." To Americans, he was what every man should be.

Boone was born around 1734 near Reading, Pennsylvania. He was descended from Quakers who settled in Philadelphia around 1717. His father was a weaver, blacksmith, and small farmer. Boone had little or no formal education, but by twelve he was an accomplished hunter. He provided money for the family by hunting and trapping furs and also worked on the family farm. The luxury of schooling was out of reach for many frontier families. Historian Avery Craven has called the American frontier the region of sweaty people.[3] The Boones fit that description.

A Book You're Not Supposed to Read

Frank Miniter, *The Politically Incorrect Guide to Hunting* (Washington, DC: Regnery Publishing, 2007).

The family relocated to North Carolina in 1750 in search of better land and better opportunities. This kind of move became part of the Boone—and more importantly, the American—legacy. Whenever Boone needed a little more "elbow room," he simply went farther west, as many adventurous American families did until the frontier "closed" in the late nineteenth century. At twenty, Boone, around 5'8" with light eyes and light hair, signed up as a teamster and blacksmith for the British army in the early phases of the French and Indian War. (Contemporaries often remarked on his physical strength and quiet demeanor.) He participated in the Edward Braddock campaign that resulted in the terrible defeat at the Battle of the Wilderness in 1755. He escaped with his life and his horse, and his brief time with the army allowed him to meet John Finley, a fellow hunter who had traveled to the untamed lands of Kentucky and who spoke of the tremendous opportunities available on the American frontier.

Boone married, started a family (he eventually had ten children), and spent the next several years on the farm in North Carolina and later in

Virginia. But Boone never lost sight of his desire to relocate for better opportunity. He went broke after the war because his hunting grounds were being overrun with more settlers and there was less game for him to shoot. The family struggled. Boone traveled to Florida in 1765 and thought about settling in Pensacola, but his wife objected. Boone was finally able to travel to Kentucky in 1767. He made it to present-day Floyd County and then returned the following spring.

Moving his family west was a difficult decision. Boone was no stranger to unrest on the frontier. Following his return after the Battle of the Wilderness, the entire western region of the British colonies had been subject to Indian war parties. Because the British had not yet constructed adequate fortifications to protect American settlers in the region, removing to the wilds of Kentucky would subject his young family to great danger. Boone, ever the adventurer, left his family behind, disregarded the potential perils, and struck out to explore Kentucky again in 1769 on a long hunting expedition. He had some experience as an Indian fighter during the French and Indian War, and the horrors of frontier warfare did not faze him. Boone wanted land and space, the same as any other man on the frontier, and he was willing to take risks to acquire both.

This expedition proved to be difficult. The hunting party traversed the Cumberland Gap and set up camp at Station Camp Creek on a tributary of the Kentucky River. They spent long days hunting in perhaps the best hunting land east of the Mississippi at that time. But the good hunting at Station Camp Creek was well known to everyone on the frontier—including the various warring Indian tribes. Boone and his companions were treading in "a dark and bloody ground," where there was no guarantee of safety. In December 1769, Boone was captured by a Shawnee hunting party and forced to reveal the location of his hunting camps. All of his own hunting party's supplies and possessions were plundered, and Boone and his friends were warned that this land belonged to the Shawnee. They were told to leave or face death. Boone was undeterred. He and a partner tracked the party and secured several of the stolen horses. The Shawnee, however, recaptured Boone several days later and, though they treated him kindly, they stripped him of all supplies. Boone returned to Station Camp only to find it abandoned. The rest of his party, assuming Boone had been killed, had started back for North Carolina. Boone caught up with them later, and the group re-established a hunting camp in safer territory. He finally returned to North Carolina in 1771, but by that point Boone had decided that he wanted to permanently settle in Kentucky.

Boone left with several settlers in 1775, led them to what became Boonesborough, Kentucky, and helped construct a fort there. Boone is often regarded as the founder of Kentucky. Even if that lofty claim is untrue, he at least had a hand in opening the area to settlement. Boone in fact helped cut the road—called the Wilderness Road—that

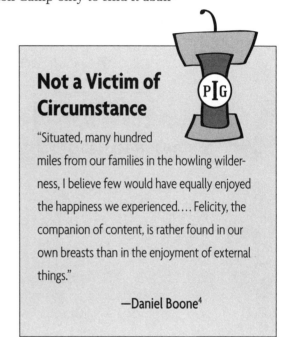

Not a Victim of Circumstance

"Situated, many hundred miles from our families in the howling wilderness, I believe few would have equally enjoyed the happiness we experienced.... Felicity, the companion of content, is rather found in our own breasts than in the enjoyment of external things."

—Daniel Boone[4]

later settlers would use to enter the territory through the Cumberland Gap. He brought his family later that year and spent the next several years engaged in defending Kentucky, Virginia, and the larger American West from the British and their Indian allies.

The American War for Independence interrupted his hopes of wealth and prosperity, but his service in the war enhanced his reputation as a hero. Boone said late in life, "Many heroic actions and chivalrous adventures are related of me which exist only in the regions of fancy. With me the world has taken great liberties, and yet I have been but a common man." Boone's exploits may have been exaggerated, but still, to comfortable modern

Americans living in the confines of suburbia, his efforts in the cause for independence are a refreshing departure from the mundane. Boone was a man in a time of men.

In July 1776, Boone's daughter and two other girls were captured by a Shawnee war party. Boone and a group of Kentuckians tracked them and later rescued the girls after ambushing the Indians when they stopped to eat. This was the most celebrated event of Daniel Boone's life and, to be sure, a manly feat in defense of his family, but his exploits during the war did not end there. He was later wounded by the Shawnee while defending the fort at Boonesborough in 1777 and, after recovering from his wounds, was captured by the Shawnee while attempting to secure salt for dwindling meat supplies. Boone persuaded the Shawnee that Boonesborough would surrender to the Indians the following spring, thus preventing the capture of the fort, but in the several months he was held prisoner, Boone was subjected to torture and forced adoption into the tribe as a warrior.

A Book You're Not Supposed to Read

Robert Ruark, *The Old Man and the Boy* (New York: Holt Paperbacks, 1993). A tale of becoming a man, non-PC style—the Daniel Boone way.

Boone used his time in the tribe to gather information, and when he learned that another expedition had been planned against Boonesborough, he escaped and raced the nearly two hundred miles to Boonesborough in five days to warn the town. His horse gave out from exhaustion, and Boone was forced to make much of the journey on foot. When he arrived, he found that his family had given him up for dead and returned to North Carolina. And to add to his troubles, the residents of Boonesborough doubted his loyalty. They could not understand how Boone had handled his time with the Shawnee with such aplomb, while several of their family members remained captive. In an attempt to prove his loyalty to Kentucky and his home, Boone led a daring raid against the Shawnee and then helped defend

Boonesborough after it was laid siege. No matter. Following the battle, Boone was court-martialed for disloyalty. He was found not guilty, and though the court-martial had vindicated him, Boone considered it an insult for the remainder of his life.

He collected his family in North Carolina in 1779 and returned to Kentucky, where he founded a new settlement called Boone's Station. In the meantime, Virginia had established Kentucky County, thus invalidating the land claims of all of the initial Kentucky settlers. Boone was placed in charge both of procuring supplies for the new settlers and of collecting funds to purchase land claims from the Virginia government. According to Boone, he was robbed of over $20,000 while sleeping at a tavern on the trip to Williamsburg to buy the claims in 1780. This was the first of several major financial setbacks in his life. Out of honor, Boone repaid those who insisted on getting their money back. It took him several years to do so, but his financial difficulties did not affect his reputation.

Boone returned to Kentucky and served with George Rogers Clarke in the western theater of the American War for Independence for two years. He saw action at the Battle of Piqua and the Battle of Blue Licks, where both his brother and son were killed. Though the war technically ended in 1781, Boone continued to serve with Clarke in the Ohio territory until 1782. During this time he was appointed lieutenant-colonel of Fayette County, and later elected a delegate to the Virginia state legislature and then sheriff and deputy surveyor of Fayette County.

Like many Americans on the frontier, Boone understood that land was the most valuable commodity. He began speculating during the War for Independence but quickly ran into financial trouble. By 1798, Boone had lost all of his land holdings in Kentucky, had been sued in court, had been rejected by the governor of Kentucky for a contract to widen the Wilderness Road, and had had a warrant issued for his arrest after he failed to appear in court. Success as a hunter, soldier, and explorer had not translated into material wealth. He removed to what is now West Virginia, where he had a small trading store, and then to Missouri, presumably to start life over. And though Boone had been financially wrecked in Kentucky, the people named Boone County in his honor in 1798.

He was able to secure a land grant in Missouri and was appointed magistrate of St. Charles County in 1800 by the Spanish governor. He held that position until 1804. When Missouri was annexed by the United States in 1803, Boone's land titles were again abolished, but after a prolonged legal battle, Boone was able to reacquire his titles in 1814. In the meantime, he traveled to Kentucky to pay his debts, an undertaking that left him with only fifteen cents to his name but that relieved him of any lingering financial burden. Until his death in 1820, Boone spent his time in the woods, hunting. He apparently traveled as far west as Wyoming in his seventies, with an official report having him in Kansas in 1816, when he was eighty-two. Boone, of course, shared his adventurous spirit with many Americans. All memory of most of them has been lost to time. But Daniel Boone reminds us of the independence and ability to regroup after failure that once marked the American spirit.

Both Smith and Boone suffered defeat and hardship in their lives. In their own time, contemporaries attempted to destroy their reputations, minimize their accomplishments, and undermine their success. But they persevered. That, if nothing else, made them heroic. Americans would do well to remember Smith and Boone. If our modern society still had their enterprising, unconquered spirit, the United States would be drastically different today.

Chapter 2

FOUNDERS

George Washington and John Dickinson

The founding generation is without question the greatest in American history. In fact, the entire generation could be classified as "heroic." Our founders faced down the greatest military in the world, won independence, framed a central government and thirteen state governments, and wrote a federal Bill of Rights and several state bills of rights—establishing a lasting republic the likes of which the world had never before seen. Their "manly firmness," as Thomas Jefferson called it in the Declaration of Independence, was evident from the beginning. Any book on real American heroes must include representatives from this generation.

Two founders stand above the others as examples of the American spirit and the American heroic tradition: George Washington and John Dickinson. Washington is the most famous and important man in American history, the American Cincinnatus, the personification of American heroism, but modern portrayals do not do him justice. Dickinson is an often neglected hero, "the Penman of the Revolution," the conservative conscience of America. Until the twentieth century, Washington was *the* man everyone in America sought to emulate. Dickinson quietly provided countless examples

Did you know?

★ No victorious general in the modern age gave up so much power as Washington did on returning to Mount Vernon

★ Washington believed it was not the president's job to propose legislation

★ John Dickinson was the only founder to be present at every significant political event from the 1765 Stamp Act Congress to the 1788 Constitutional Convention

of American statesmanship and duty to the American tradition. Both deserve our attention.

The Original American Hero

George Washington was a man among men. Standing over six feet tall and weighing around two hundred pounds, he was a giant in the eighteenth century. He had an athletic build and an agreeable countenance. He was a superior athlete and horseman, a graceful dancer, a fine conversationalist with a good sense of humor, a loyal husband, a man who considered duty and honor to be the highest personal qualities, and possessed of a solid though not spectacular intelligence. He was a gentleman who believed in the traditional norms of Virginian society. Washington thought of himself as a planter first, a soldier second, and a statesman third and understood service to be a duty rather than a station.

George Washington was born in 1732 in Westmoreland County, Virginia, as a fourth-generation American. His father, Augustine Washington, owned a small planation but died in 1743, leaving his son George to spend much of his youth with his half-brother Lawrence at Mount Vernon, his brother's Potomac River plantation. Here Washington would be introduced to Virginia society. (Lawrence's wife Ann was a member of the Fairfax family, perhaps the most powerful in Virginia in the mid-eighteenth century.) Most of George Washington's education was what Americans today call "homeschooling." His mother taught

Books You're Not Supposed to Read

The Presidency of George Washington by Forrest McDonald (Lawrence, KS: University of Kansas, 1974).

George Washington: A Biography by Douglas Southall Freeman (New York: Charles Scribner's Sons, 1951), 7 vols.

The McDonald study is excellent and concise; the Freeman is the most comprehensive—and least politically correct—biography of Washington.

him discipline, morals, and the proper etiquette for a gentleman, while his father and Lawrence instructed him in history, theology, mathematics, map-making, and drafting. Washington was naturally bright, not studious, but a solid, well-rounded young man—what used to be called a "Renaissance Man."

Washington's independent spirit was evident from an early age. He befriended George William Fairfax while at Mount Vernon, and at sixteen the two young men left the trappings of high society for the unregulated and wild unknown of the Virginia frontier. They spent a year hunting and exploring in the heart of the wilderness. Washington was no soft-palmed bureaucrat. One year later he was appointed county surveyor for Culpeper. This job led him to the frontier again, where for three years he worked establishing private land plots, mostly at the behest of the Fairfax family. The frontier gave restless young men the opportunity to be men, to discover and hone their masculine traits. Even in polite Virginia society, a man was expected to be a good shot, to know how to survive in the wild, and to be self-sufficient. Washington mastered all those skills.

He inherited Mount Vernon in 1752 and at twenty-one was commissioned major in the Virginia militia. Unlike men in modern American society, all men in colonial America were required to do their part for the militia, to protect hearth and home. The founding generation reasoned that universal service in the militia made standing armies unnecessary. They were generally proven correct. Washington's first charge as an officer in the militia was to deliver a set of demands from the Virginia governor to the nearest French fort on the frontier. Washington, like everyone else, knew the French would refuse the demands, but duty required him to accept the charge. He had to travel over a hundred miles in terrible conditions to find the closest fort. The French refused to comply, and after Washington's horses gave out on his return trip, he had to make the rest of the trip on foot—nearly dying in the process.

Washington was rewarded with a promotion and served with distinction during the French and Indian War. He commanded and organized the defense of the Virginia frontier during the war with little supply or ammunition. After the British secured the frontier in 1758, Washington resigned his command, married, and retired to Mount Vernon. This was the life he preferred, one of peace and prosperity. Soldiers who witness the horrors of war first hand are often the first to gladly accept the benefits of peace.

Unfortunately, Washington's peaceful civilian life, along with those of others of this generation, would be shattered by the tumultuous events of the 1770s.

Washington's generation was defined by the American War for Independence, and yet Washington's character determined the progression of the war, not the other way around. When the war began, he was already a well-respected man with a fine plantation, a solid military reputation, and political appointments. Had the war never occurred, Washington would still have been remembered as a pillar of Virginia. Initially, he was counted among the members of American society who *resisted* confrontation with Great Britain—not out of fear, but out of respect for tradition and custom. Most Americans were not radical revolutionaries bent on remaking society in a new utopian image. (They were not the French.) Washington did, however, recognize that the colonies had legitimate grievances with the crown and, along with other Virginians, demanded redress. As Englishmen, they had a right to do so, or so they believed.

Washington was a delegate to the First Continental Congress in 1774, a body dominated by the conservative element of American society. At the

The Secret of His Success?

PIG

"Discipline is the soul of an army. It makes small numbers formidable; procures success to the weak, and esteem to all."

—George Washington, July 29, 1759[1]

same time, he was charged with organizing several militia companies in Virginia. No other man in his state inspired the same respect for his military capabilities. He was a natural leader of men. Should compromise fail, and Washington hoped it wouldn't, he—and Virginia—would be prepared to defend their rights against tyranny. To the founding generation, talk had to be reinforced by action if necessary.

He took his seat in the Second Continental Congress amidst a cloud of uncertainty. By the time it convened, shots had already been fired in Massachusetts, and Washington was put in charge of organizing the defenses of New York City. There were still some, such as John Dickinson, who clung to the prospect of compromise. By this point, Washington was not among them.

A Display of Manly Firmness

"I think I can announce it as a fact, that it is not the wish or interest of that government, or any other upon this continent, separately or collectively, to set up for independency; but this you may at the same time rely on, that none of them will ever submit to the loss of those valuable rights and privileges, which are essential to the happiness of every free state, and without which, life, liberty, and property are rendered totally insecure."

—George Washington to Robert McKenzie, October 9, 1774[2]

He wore his uniform to every session of Congress, and also a black armband to show support for Massachusetts. John Adams nominated him to command the Continental Army. He accepted the appointment without pay. This was quintessential Washington. He did not wish to receive a salary when he was elected president in 1788 either. To a man bound by duty and imbued with republican principles, compensation was unnecessary. Washington regarded himself as the American Cincinnatus, the stoic Roman general who answered the call of his people but returned to his plow when the war was over. It was no coincidence that Washington was sculpted in a Roman toga or that his favorite play was Joseph Addison's *Cato*, a piece dedicated to the republican principles of liberty, honor, and virtue.

Washington's accomplishments during the American War for Independence are legendary, and had his career ended there, he would still have been in the running for the most important and heroic American. He took command of a badly equipped and poorly organized band of militia and turned it into a fairly effective army, albeit after experiencing more defeats than victories. If nothing else, his ability to keep the army in the field was superhuman. No modern American army has suffered as much as Washington and his men did. They were always short on supplies (including such life-saving essentials as food and clothing), were almost always numerically overmatched and outgunned, and faced problems of mass desertion when the money to pay the soldiers ran out (one of his subordinates, "Light-Horse Harry" Lee simply chopped off a deserter's head and mailed it to a shocked Washington; no more desertion). Washington knew that keeping the army in the field kept the flame of liberty alive, and so he became an expert at slipping away with his army whenever defeat seemed certain to envelop it and crush independence. His strategy of attrition finally paid off, and after six years of painful, bloody, and miserable war and a smashing victory at Yorktown, Washington was able to resign his commission and return to Mount Vernon—broke, but happy to take up the plow again.

This selfless act did more to prove his dedication to republican government and liberty than any other. No victorious general in the modern age gave up so much power. Washington marched into Annapolis, Maryland, the seat of the Congress in 1783, to throngs of jubilant Americans and

Republican Modesty

"But, lest some unlucky event should happen, unfavourable to my reputation, I beg it may be remembered, by every Gentleman in the room, that I, this day, declare with the utmost sincerity, I do not think myself equal to the Command I am honored with."

—George Washington, June 16, 1775[3]

willingly took "leave of all the employ-ments of public life," including even the office of vestryman in his parish church. Washington understood that American liberty required his retirement from the public stage. If the military seized the government, then all of the blood and tears shed during the war would be wasted. The founding generation knew tyranny, both from historical example and as participants in a long, violent contest against George III. Lasting liberty could only be ensured by sheathing the sword, and Washington was happy to do so.

Washington's retirement would be brief. He was called to serve as a delegate to the Philadelphia Convention in 1787, an appointment he at first refused but then reluctantly accepted out of a sense of duty. The Framers of the Constitution almost certainly crafted the executive branch with him in mind, and his name was frequently invoked

Washington's Greatest Act of Heroism?

"The great events on which my resignation depended having at length taken place; I have now the honor of offering my sincere Congratulations to Congress & of presenting myself before them to surrender into their hands the trust committed to me, and to claim the indulgence of retiring from the Service of my Country.

"Happy in the confirmation of our Independence and Sovereignty, and pleased with the oppertunity [*sic*] afforded the United States of becoming a respectable Nation, I resign with satisfaction the Appointment I accepted with diffidence—A diffidence in my abilities to accomplish so arduous a task, which however was superseded by a confidence in the rectitude of our Cause, the support of the Supreme Power of the Union, and the patronage of Heaven."

—George Washington, December 23, 1783[4]

as the model for the ideal executive: disinterested, honorable, virtuous—qualities that are extraordinarily rare among the political class today. Washington supported the Constitution because he did not want to see the Union torn asunder, but he expected that the federal government would retain many of the characteristics of the original Union under the Articles of Confederation. It was not to be a dictatorship or monarchy. Though

Washington believed in a strong central authority, his conception of authority was an eighteenth-century American one, not a modern one. The central government could never have assumed the amount of power it possesses today under Washington's leadership.

A President Who *Wasn't* Power-Hungry

"I assure *you*, with the *world* it would obtain *little credit*, that my movements to the chair of Government will be accompanied by feelings not unlike those of a culprit who is going to the place of his execution: so unwilling am I, in the evening of a life nearly consumed in public cares, to quit a peaceful abode for an Ocean of difficulties, without that competency of political skill, abilities and inclination which is necessary to manage the helm."

—George Washington
to Henry Knox,
April 1, 1789[5]

He arrived in New York in 1789 after being unanimously elected president the previous year. His two terms in office established several precedents; some were followed for many administrations afterward while others were quickly discarded by men of lesser ability and character. After several days of comic deliberation by the Congress on the proper way to address the new executive, Washington insisted on the republican "Mr. President" in lieu of more outrageous titles such as "His High Mightiness." He carefully implemented executive powers, often deferring to Congress rather than taking authority to himself. Washington wanted to avoid even a whiff of monarchy, and though detractors (yes, even Washington had them) seized upon every bold move by the president as a sign of descent into a military dictatorship, it can be said that Washington's administrations, particularly the first, were models of statesmanship, executive restraint, and service.

As a man who firmly believed the government was charged with protecting the life, liberty, and property of its constituents, Washington immediately, and successfully, sought to end the almost decade-long Northwest Indian War. He crafted a foreign policy that maintained American neutrality amid belligerent actions by both Great Britain and France. Today, this policy would be called "non-interventionist." Washington's administration opened the Mississippi to American commerce and solidified American interests in the southwestern Indian territories.

Washington was the glue that held competing factions together in the early days of the federal republic. No other president would have the same success in that regard. He viewed the president as a man above politics, warned of the potential problems of political parties, and though he gravitated toward Alexander Hamilton, the leader of the Federalist Party, during his time in office, was not a "party man" in the modern sense. Washington let Congress legislate, took seriously the constitutional requirement to let the Senate give him "advice and consent" on treaties, and stayed aloof from internal faction. When possible, he refereed disagreements—helping close the deal to bring the federal capital to "Washington City," for example—but he did not initiate legislation. This was the way he believed a president should conduct domestic and foreign affairs. To the detriment of the American people, few presidents have followed his prescription.

He left office after two terms, feeling his age and exhausted by the growing political strife in Philadelphia. This two-term precedent served as an unwritten rule followed by every president until 1940. Washington could have served for life, but as in 1783, he chose to resign, thus displaying his adherence to republican principles. He was called back into military service in 1798 during a threat of war with

★ ★ ★ ★ ★ ★ ★ ★ ★ ★ ★ ★ ★ ★

Executive Restraint

As president, George Washington determined never to veto a piece of legislation unless it violated the Constitution. His veto was not a hammer to be used for partisan purposes.

A Book You're Not Supposed to Read

The Politically Incorrect Guide™ to the Founding Fathers by Brion McClanahan (Washington, DC: Regnery, 2009).

France that never materialized. Washington died suddenly in 1799 of a throat infection, but his heroic legacy endured long after. Even into the early nineteenth century, it was not uncommon for Americans to decorate their homes with his portrait. If any American is to be emulated, it should be Washington.

The Conservative Conscience of America

At first glance, John Dickinson should not be in such lofty company as George Washington's, particularly if his portrayal in the HBO miniseries *John Adams* is anything close to reality. In that film, Dickinson is shown as a man of principle but on the wrong side of history, almost a coward who will not accept the inevitable and charge the British with his guns blazing. He was intractable, disagreeable, contentious, and weak. But the portrayal is inaccurate and dishonest, as those who have studied his life and career know. Like Washington, Dickinson was a fine example of the disinterested statesman, the reluctant patriot, and the ideal American hero.

Dickinson was born in 1732, the same year as Washington, on the family tobacco plantation in Talbot County, Maryland. His parents were Quakers, and opponents often charged Dickinson with adhering to his "Quaker sensibilities" in the months leading to the War for Independence, but being a Quaker had little to do with his reluctance to break with Great Britain.

Dickinson eventually called both Delaware and Pennsylvania home. His family moved to a new plantation near Dover, Delaware, when he was young. After receiving a private education—again, what modern Americans would call "homeschooling"—Dickinson

A Book You're Not Supposed to Read

The Political Writings of John Dickinson, Esquire by John Dickinson (Wilmington, DE: Bonsal and Niles, 1801), 2 vols. Dickinson has been largely neglected by professional historians.

studied law in Philadelphia. At twenty-eight he was elected speaker of the Delaware legislature, and two years later Pennsylvania sent him to its legislative body. (Delaware, the "Lower Counties on the Delaware," was considered part of Pennsylvania until 1776 when the state, in essence, seceded from Pennsylvania.)

As the conflict with the British heated up in the 1760s, Dickinson took an active role in denouncing "unconstitutional" parliamentary acts. He was nicknamed "the Penman of the Revolution" for good reason. His pamphlets were widely read and circulated, even in London, and Dickinson became the face of the conservative resistance to unjust legislation. His attack on the Stamp Act of 1765 led to his participation in the Stamp Act Congress of 1765, where he wrote the Stamp Act Resolutions. In fact, Dickinson was the only Founding Father to be at every significant political event from the Stamp Act Congress through the Philadelphia Convention in 1787. He was that well regarded.

Dickinson's masterpiece was his 1767 *Letters from a Farmer in Pennsylvania to the Inhabitants of the British Colonies.* Before Thomas Paine's *Common Sense*, there was Dickinson's *Letters from a Farmer.* Both were important, but Dickinson's appeal was a conservative—often called "sober"—plea of resistance. The *Letters* called for the American people to have a "sedate, yet fervent spirit, animating them to actions of prudence, justice, modesty, bravery, humanity and magnanimity."[6] Dickinson was not attempting to spark rebellion or violence, though he ultimately believed such a course might be necessary. He warned Americans, "I hope, my dear countrymen, that you will, in every colony, be upon your guard against those, who may at any time endeavour to stir you up, under pretences of patriotism, to any measures disrespectful to our Sovereign and our mother country. Hot, rash, disorderly proceedings, injure the reputation of a people, as to wisdom, valor and virtue, without procuring them the least benefit."[7] Princeton granted him an honorary doctorate for the *Letters*, and Boston publicly thanked him for his dedication to the cause of liberty. Dickinson, though, worried that his moderate tone would fall on deaf ears.

He was elected to serve in both the First and Second Continental Congresses and participated in most of the important debates. In 1775, he penned the *Declaration of the Causes of Taking up Arms*, a more belligerent tome than his earlier work. He argued that the colonists had a right to resist the "aggression" of the British by force in order to preserve their ancient rights, but he also insisted that the colonists would lay down their weapons if the British ceased their unconstitutional violations of the rights of Englishmen. He then extended the olive branch to George III in the hope that the king would arrest the tyrannical acts of Parliament. This was quintessential Dickinson and the model of American resistance in the years leading to the American War for Independence.

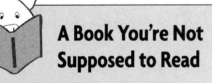

A Book You're Not Supposed to Read

The Politically Incorrect Guide™ to the Constitution by Kevin Gutzman (Washington, DC: Regnery, 2007).

Modern interpretations of the conflict often portray hot-headed patriots violently pursuing their objectives despite the cost. Not true. Dickinson, with his brand of conservative resistance, was representative of most Americans in 1775, including George Washington. While both Dickinson and Washington had determined that military action might be necessary—Dickinson was a member of the Philadelphia militia and a participant in the Philadelphia committee of public safety—each would gladly have accepted conciliation and compromise. This was the more heroic course. Irrationally advocating violence without exhausting all means for achieving compromise and peace is never in the best interest of a people, and the situation in 1775 was no different. Had the British been willing to concede and lighten their demands on the American colonists, the American people might never have pursued independence. Dickinson certainly would have avoided the break with Britain *if the rights of Englishmen could have been maintained.* This does not make him cowardly. On the contrary, this course of action would have saved lives while preserving ancient liberties. That is the true mark of a statesman and a hero.

Dickinson voted against the Declaration of Independence in 1776 because he did not believe the American people were prepared for war. They had no allies, and in his mind did not have the resources required to fight a foe as powerful as the British. He had long been in the vanguard of the cause against the British, and he claimed it was not independence but the timing of independence he was voting against. Nevertheless, Dickinson retired from the Continental Congress the next day and took up arms to defend his state against British invasion. Few other members of the Continental Congress did so. Though he did not want independence in 1776, he was willing to fight and die for it once the die had been cast. His Philadelphia home, Fairhill, was burned by the British in retaliation to his pre-war activities, and he participated in the Battle of Brandywine in 1777. Like other members of the founding generation, Dickinson suffered financial hardship.

Dickinson took part in drafting both governing documents of the United States—the Articles of Confederation and the Constitution. He personally wrote the Articles and was one of the wise sages who helped resist the designs of those who wanted to build a new powerful centralized "national" government on the ruins of the original federal republic during the Philadelphia Convention of 1787. Dickinson favored a stronger central government, but only for specific purposes. As the man who wrote the Articles of Confederation, a document that explicitly recognized the power and sovereignty of the states, Dickinson did not think a new Constitution should obliterate the states or consolidate all power in a central authority. His blessing of the Constitution was a limited one.

Moreover, his resolute defense of the "ancient" tradition of the established rights of Englishmen was nothing short of heroic. As Dickinson stated during the Philadelphia Convention, "Experience must be our only guide. Reason may mislead us." He was grounded in the history of Rome and Great Britain and wanted to avoid the extremes of both artificial aristocracy and excessive democracy. The solution was a balanced government that allowed for democracy in one house (the House of Representatives) while maintaining the role of the states in another (the Senate). The executive would be limited, Congress would have the most authority, and Dickinson hoped that the Supreme Court would not be able to "set aside law," that is, declare legislation unconstitutional. Most important, he rejected the "innovations" of men like James Madison, Alexander Hamilton, James Wilson, and Gouverneur Morris. History provided examples of efficient government compatible with liberty, and there was no reason, in his mind, to veer off the well-lit path provided by ancestral custom and convention.

He signed the Constitution in September 1787 because he thought it was the best government the states and the people would accept: it maintained the role of the states while providing greater central authority. Dickinson, writing as "Fabius" to outline his support for the Constitution, penned a series of nine essays that matched the more famous *Federalist Papers* in cogency and influence. Pamphleteering was his specialty, and Dickinson hoped to persuade wavering delegates to the state ratifying conventions that the Constitution should be adopted. He insisted that the powers of the general government under the Constitution were limited and would not be abused, and he contended that the chief executive was bound by constraints that would make it impossible for him to become a dictator or king. The states, he argued, would not lose their sovereignty; and liberty, the most valuable principle of the American founding, would be preserved.

A Book You're Not Supposed to Read

The Founding Fathers Guide to the Constitution by Brion McClanahan (Washington, DC: Regnery History, 2012). Discusses Dickinson's role in crafting the Constitution in more detail.

Dickinson retired to his Delaware plantation after the Philadelphia Convention. In the last years of his life he became convinced that the so-called Federalist Party of the early federal period had distorted the original meaning of the Constitution by enlarging the powers of the central government at the expense of the states. He died in 1808. Upon hearing the news of his death, Thomas Jefferson fittingly wrote, "A more estimable man or truer patriot could not have left us. Among the first of the advocates for the rights of his country when assailed by Great Britain, he continued to the last the orthodox advocate of the true principles of our new government, and his name will be consecrated in history as one of the great worthies of the Revolution."[9]

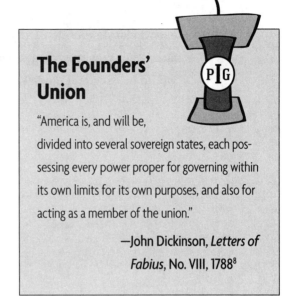

The Founders' Union

"America is, and will be, divided into several sovereign states, each possessing every power proper for governing within its own limits for its own purposes, and also for acting as a member of the union."

—John Dickinson, *Letters of Fabius*, No. VIII, 1788[8]

Washington and Dickinson should be regarded as true American heroes. Both preferred peace to war but accepted their duty to fight for liberty and independence when called to do so. Both were cognizant of the vital importance of historical precedent and "prescription" to the founding of America and sought the ancient order as a "better guide than reason." Both resisted rash and "hot-headed" action until the last. Both were statesmen, important not only because of what they accomplished but because of who they were as men. Their character and rearing, their culture, determined how they reacted to the events of the

A Prescient Warning

"Nothing is more certain than that the forms of liberty may be retained when the substance is gone. In government, as well as in religion, 'the letter killeth, but the spirit giveth life.'"

—John Dickinson[10]

early federal republic. If any Americans of the founding period should be emulated, Washington and Dickinson, the conservative revolutionaries, would be excellent models.

Chapter 3

SAILORS

John Paul Jones and Stephen Decatur

There is something beautiful in the danger of the ocean, a song that men throughout history have found hard to resist. Americans have long been attracted to the sea. From Columbus and Sir Walter Raleigh to those commoners who, on their own blood and hook, took the chance to sail to the New World and start over on the *Susan Constant* and the *Mayflower*, the United States was built on the backs of those who were willing to risk all on the open ocean. Perhaps it is fitting, then, that two of her greatest heroes were sailors. John Paul Jones and Stephen Decatur were at one time etched in the pantheon of American heroes. Their lives and deeds still deserve our attention.

Indomitable Captain

No American sailor reached the height of fame that John Paul Jones attained. John Paul (he assumed the "Jones" only later) was born in Scotland in 1747. His father was a gardener for a well-respected landowner in the parish of Kirkbean. Jones was the fifth child of seven in the family, but because his younger two siblings died in infancy, he was considered the youngest for

Did you know?

★ "I have not yet begun to fight" were the words of John Paul Jones to a British captain who assumed that the outgunned Jones would surrender his sinking ship

★ Horatio Nelson, the hero of Trafalgar, called Stephen Decatur's burning of the *Philadelphia* "the most bold and daring act of the age"

most of his childhood. As a young man, Jones would launch his imaginary "fairy frigate" on the waters around Kirkbean and give commands to his unseen crew. The sea was already calling. He received a brief formal education at the local parish school in Kirkbean and at twelve was apprenticed to a local ship-owner and merchant. He poured himself into navigational theory in what Jones called his "midnight studies"—when the grind of the day's work subsided and Jones had time to devote to books. This was a not-uncommon way for a boy from a modest family to get a leg up in life. Many successful early Americans were largely self-taught or taught at home. Despite the brevity of his formal education, Jones was fluent in French, with a good grounding in mathematics and a firm grasp of grammar—all before John Dewey invented the modern education system.

America called Jones to her shores early in his life. He had contact with American merchants around Dumfries near his father's property and was only thirteen when he took his first voyage to the New World, arriving in Fredericksburg, Virginia. His older brother William had married and settled there, and Jones spent his shore leave at his brother's house. This was around 1760, years before the American War for Independence, but Jones's time in the American colonies led him ultimately to conclude that their cause was his cause. He had a love for America's people, her land, and the spirit of liberty, and like a good Scotsman he detested the heavy hand of the British.

Financial difficulties led his employer to terminate his indentures, leaving Jones to fend for himself when still a teenager. In this regard, Jones was in good company. Early American history is brimming with accounts of young men facing the uncertainties of life virtually alone. For example, long before he became the "American sage," Benjamin Franklin faced a similar situation; he broke his indentures as a young man and was on his own in Philadelphia and later in London. To those with an enterprising spirit and sharp mind, the limitless opportunity of the New World was easy to grasp.

Jones eventually found work on a slaver, the *King George*, and later, at nineteen, was hired as chief mate on another slave ship, the *Two Friends*. Most people regarded the slave trade as the vilest element of the institution of slavery, and Jones, exposed first hand to the realities of life on a slave ship, developed a firm abhorrence of slavery. Shortly after arriving in the West Indies he resigned his position on the *Two Friends* and headed back to Scotland. After that he found only sporadic work, and in 1773 he was charged with murder for killing the ringleader of a mutiny against his command of the ship *Betsey*. Jones fled to America, assumed the surname "Jones" in order to conceal his identity, and eventually befriended several leading members of American society, including Robert Morris of Philadelphia, Joseph Hewes, and Willie and Allen Jones of North Carolina. Rumor had it that Jones took his famous surname to honor the North Carolina Jones family, but there is no conclusive proof. Either way, though, Jones had a difficult time finding work, and, in his own words, once lived for twenty months "on fifty pounds only."

In contrast to many Americans who supported the American War for Independence tepidly, Jones was an enthusiastic supporter of independence from the beginning. What he wanted most was to be part of the new Continental Navy. Jones arrived in Philadelphia in 1775, just a few short months after Lexington and Concord. He took part in fitting out the USS *Alfred*, the first ship to fly the Continental flag in the cause of independence. (Jones himself hoisted it on 3 December 1775.) He was then commissioned a lieutenant in the American navy. Even before his famous command of the *Bonhomme Richard*, Jones made a name

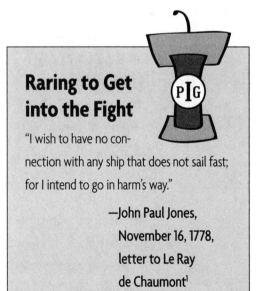

Raring to Get into the Fight

"I wish to have no connection with any ship that does not sail fast; for I intend to go in harm's way."

—John Paul Jones,
November 16, 1778,
letter to Le Ray
de Chaumont[1]

for himself sacking British shipping and creating havoc among the British merchant fleet. His command of the *Providence* in 1776 resulted in the capture of almost two dozen prizes and the sack of the British fishing posts of Canso and Isle Madame. Jones was perhaps the most aggressive commander in the American navy, and his flamboyant and daring style won him a reputation unmatched in early American naval history.

Congress had ranked Jones eighteenth on the list of American captains primarily for political reasons. After several protests Jones was given command of the USS *Ranger* and sent to France to assume the command of the frigate *Indian*, still under construction. When Jones arrived he found that the *Indian* had been transferred to the possession of the king of France, leaving Jones with only his little sloop and his big ambition. No matter. Jones quickly set out to prove his worth, and in short order sacked the fort of Whitehaven, captured nearly half a dozen British ships, and became infamous along the British coast as an American pirate. It must be noted that prior to the American War for Independence, Jones's maritime career had been confined to merchant duties. He was wholly untrained in the art of naval warfare but had brilliant natural talents for leadership, maneuver, and engagement. His commonsense approach to battle was matched only by his willingness to take risks. No man has ever won fame, fortune, or honor without risk.

The French rewarded his stunning success with the command of a small fleet and the *Duras*, an old forty-gun French tub that Jones renamed the *Bonhomme Richard* in honor of Benjamin Franklin's *Poor Richard's Almanac*.

The Savior of the American Navy

PIG

"It is singular that during the first years of the American navy, with the exception of Paul Jones, no man of any talent is to be found directing its operations. Had it not been for the exertions of this individual, who was unsupported by fortune or connexion, it is very probable that the American naval power would have gradually disappeared."

—R. C. Sands[2]

His seven-ship group set sail in August 1779, determined to take the fight to the British. This would be the most important naval mission of his life; it made him a household name in both Europe and America.

After just over one month at sea, Jones's squadron, having already taken seventeen ships, met a British convoy led by the HMS *Serapis* in the most famous naval engagement of the war. The *Serapis* and her commander Richard Pearson were quite a match for Jones and his *Richard*. Pearson had a fine reputation in the British navy, Jones was outgunned, and after early action it appeared that the *Richard* would be heading to the bottom of the ocean. It was only through extensive use of her pumps that the ship did not sink. But Jones had a brilliant plan. He maneuvered the *Richard* into close proximity of the *Serapis*, locked the ships stern to stern, and waged a boarding war. At first Jones was repulsed, and Captain Pearson asked his counterpart, "Has your ship struck?"—meaning had Jones given up—to which Jones famously responded, "I have not yet begun to fight!"

His marines fought bravely in bloody, hard-nosed hand-to-hand combat. Both ships were on fire, and Jones wrote that the battle was "dreadful beyond the reach of language." Jones personally commanded two of the *Richard*'s deck cannon and persistently raked the deck of the *Serapis* with terrible effect. The situation appeared desperate. The *Richard* was burning and sinking; his men were captured or asking for quarter; his batteries—except those he personally commanded—were silent; his own consort ship, the *Alliance*, was sending friendly fire into the *Richard*, causing both damage and casualties; but Jones kept up the pressure. At ten o'clock, three hours after the action started, the *Serapis* surrendered. The American victory was due entirely to the stubborn courage and leadership of Jones. Had a lesser man been in command of the *Richard*, she certainly would have capitulated.

Following his great victory over the *Serapis*, Jones was treated to parties and honors on both sides of the Atlantic. King Louis XVI presented him

A Biographer Gives Credit Where Credit Is Due

"The achievement of the victory was, however, wholly and solely due to the immovable courage of Paul Jones. The *Richard* was beaten more than once; but the spirit of Jones could not be overcome. Captain Pearson was a brave man... but Paul Jones had a nature which never could have yielded. Had Pearson been equally indomitable, the *Richard*, if not boarded from below, would, at last, have gone down with her colors still flying in proud defiance."

—A. S. Mackenzie[3]

with a gold-hilted sword inscribed with "reward of Louis XVI to a strenuous defender of the rights of the sea." The women of Paris fawned over the great American hero. Once Jones was back in Philadelphia, the Congress put on record their "high sense of the distinguished bravery and military conduct of John Paul Jones." The French ambassador threw a lavish party, and with congressional approval presented him with the French cross of the Institution of Military Merit. This allowed Jones to be called the "Chevalier," a title usually reserved to French knights. After the war was over, Jones was the only naval officer of the War for American Independence to be awarded a gold medal by Congress.

Jones spent much of the last years of his life trying to rekindle his fame. The adulation he had received in the late years of the war proved to be fleeting. He accepted a commission in the Russian navy as rear admiral to fight the Turks in 1787, and though Jones fought bravely and expertly in this struggle, he was constantly undermined by those jealous of his famous past and eventually run out of Russia. He did, however, receive the Order of St. Anne for his service to the Russian crown. He died in Paris in 1792, just two years after leaving Russia, dispirited and almost forgotten in the United States. He was buried in Paris, but in 1905 his remains were brought back to the United States. They rest today at the United States Naval Academy at Annapolis.

Intrepid Hero

If there was any American naval man who matched Jones's reputation in the age of sail, it was Stephen Decatur. Jones helped win the United States her independence, and Decatur helped secure it. Both men displayed the qualities that make men heroes: bravery, integrity, toughness, honesty. Both men commanded respect, principally because their actions justified it. They were men among men, and sailors among sailors (often the heartiest and most rugged of American adventurers).

Decatur was born in 1779 to seafaring stock on the Eastern Shore of Maryland. His father had served with distinction in the U.S. Navy during the American War for Independence and later owned two fine merchant vessels. Decatur spent most of his youth in Philadelphia, and though his father was often away on extended trips across the Atlantic, Decatur developed a love of the sea mostly through his father's tutelage. He attended a private academy in Philadelphia and spent a year at the University of Pennsylvania. Decatur was an intelligent young man, but a classical education didn't suit him. He wanted adventure, and the sea always called him.

When the "Quasi-War" with France broke out in 1798, Decatur was commissioned a midshipman at the insistence of Commodore John Barry, often called "the Father of the American Navy." He sailed for the West Indies on the frigate *United States*, and though twenty years old—an advanced age for a midshipman—he quickly learned the trade of a sailor. He impressed Barry, and by the end of the conflict he was promoted to acting lieutenant. His selfless devotion to service impressed those under his charge, and it quickly became apparent that, like his father before him, Decatur was destined for his own command.

Decatur earned that command in 1803, just before the conflict with the Barbary Pirates and the events that made him famous. The War with Tripoli was sparked by demands for bribes from the United States by the pirates

The Measure of a Hero

"In Decatur I was struck with a peculiarity of manner and appearance, calculated to rivet the eye and engross the attention. I had often pictured to myself the form and look of a hero, such as my favorite Homer had delineated; here I saw it imbodied [*sic*].... On being released from a kind of spell by which he had riveted my attention, I turned to the gentleman to whom I was indebted for the introduction, and inquired the character of Decatur. The inquiry was made of a person, to whose long experience and knowledge of human nature the inward man seemed to be unfolded. 'Sir,' said he, 'Decatur is an officer of uncommon character, of rare promise, a man of an age, one perhaps not equalled in a million!' ... It was under such circumstances I first saw the generous and chivalrous Decatur; a man more unique, more highly endowed, than any other I ever knew; to whom, perhaps, the country is most indebted for that naval renown, which is the admiration of the world; a renown so associated with the name of Decatur, as to render them indissoluble."

—Captain Robert T. Spence[4]

who controlled the Mediterranean. Conceding to the demands would have amounted to paying tribute, and the Jefferson administration refused. As a result, the pirates began sacking American merchant vessels. Jefferson, with the authorization of Congress, sent the navy to protect the American merchant fleet. The *Philadelphia*, perhaps the most powerful American frigate in the Mediterranean, ran aground in uncharted waters and soon came under fire from Tripolitan shore batteries. Unable to float off the reef and facing heavy fire from both the shore and onrushing ships of war, she surrendered. Her crew was enslaved and the ship displayed as a prize by the local bandits.

An effort was soon launched to either retake or destroy the *Philadelphia*. Decatur would play a major role. As captain of the schooner *Enterprise*, he captured an enemy ketch, renamed it the *Intrepid*, and on the night of

February 16, 1804, used it in a ruse to work his way close to the stranded American vessel. By the time the enemy realized the trick, Decatur and eighty-one men had already moored alongside the stranded ship, jumped aboard, and swept most of the occupiers into the water. They placed charges, fired them, and with only one man wounded, were back aboard the *Intrepid* in twenty minutes and sailing out of the harbor—though now under heavy fire from the Tripolitan shore batteries—by the light of the burning *Philadelphia*.

While Decatur was given the credit for the raid with a promotion to post captain, he graciously commended his men for his success: "Permit me also, Sir, to speak of the brave fellows I have the honor to command, whose coolness and intrepidity were such as I trust will ever characterize the American tars."[5] Decatur was never a glory-seeker.

Decatur also took part in subsequent action against Tripoli. He personally led several boarding raids on enemy ships, and as he was typically outnumbered and outgunned, continued to enhance his already stellar reputation. His promotion led him to command first the *Constitution* and then the *Congress*, but with the cessation of hostilities, he returned to the United States, married, and took charge of the American naval defense of the southeastern coast. He commanded the *United States*, and when war again called him to service against the British in 1812, he answered the call with his usual vigor.

> ★ ★ ★ ★ ★ ★ ★ ★ ★ ★ ★ ★
>
> ## A Hero Lauds Decatur's Deed
>
> The great British Admiral Horatio Nelson, soon to win immortal fame at Trafalgar, called the burning of the Philadelphia "the most bold and daring act of the age."

Early American success in the War of 1812 depended on the American navy. They had been battle tested and were the first line of defense, both on the open ocean and in the Great Lakes, against a British invasion of the American mainland. Many of the navy's ships needed repair or were at sea when the war began, and crews were sparse, yet the U.S. Navy answered the call, thanks in large part to the skilled leadership of her upper brass. It would not be a stretch to say that had the American navy not performed admirably in the early phases of the war, the United States might have lost. This was the war that made the American navy a well-respected international force. Jones had almost single-handedly brought it early fame, and the navy's performance in the Quasi-War and against Tripoli had forced the French and the Barbary Pirates to recognize its tenacity, but to most of the British, the American navy was still a rag tag gang of pirates who could not match the skill of her seasoned professional sailors. They would learn better.

Again in this war, Decatur played a key role. He merged his three-vessel fleet with that of Commodore John Rodgers and set sail from New York just days after the official declaration of war in June 1812. In October, Decatur broke away from Rodgers and engaged the British frigate *Macedonian*, commanded by his good friend and frequent dinner guest John Surman Carden. They had once wagered a beaver hat on the outcome, should the two of them ever meet in combat. Regardless of their friendship, the two men were professional sailors bent on winning the engagement. The *United States* was the superior ship, outgunning its opponent almost two-to-one. Decatur ordered a broadside from her large 24-pound cannon that completely stripped the *Macedonian* of her rigging and masts. He then jogged the ship a short distance to give Carden an opportunity to contemplate his next move. When Decatur came about to deliver another blow, Carden ordered the Macedonian to strike her colors. This was a great victory for the United States Navy during the first year of the War of 1812, and when Decatur arrived in New London, Connecticut, and later New York with the *Macedonian* in tow, he was treated to a hero's welcome.

By this point, the British blockade of New York and New England had virtually shut down naval operations in the Northeast. As a result, Decatur was forced to stay in New York for almost two years. He was charged with organizing the coastal defenses of the city, but then in the spring of 1814 was given command of the *President*. When a heavy nor'easter raked the coast in January 1815, forcing the British to sea, Decatur attempted to use the opportunity to get the *President* out of New York, but he ran aground (not through his own fault, but because of a poorly marked channel), sustaining heavy casualties and extensive damage to the ship. After freeing the ship the following morning, he ran into a British blockade squadron of four ships, each equal or superior to the *President*.

But Decatur showed superior seamanship. Though his ship was severely damaged, he was able to out-run three of the ships and focus on one of the smaller British frigates, the *Endymion*. He directed fire at her rigging, stripping the ship of her sails, but the British policy of "raking the deck" with their deck cannon had a dreadful effect on the *President*, her crew, and Decatur himself. He was painfully wounded in the action. Though he achieved victory over the *Endymion*, it was short-lived. The rest of the British squadron caught up with Decatur later that evening, and he was forced to surrender. The war was almost over, a peace treaty had already been signed but not ratified by the Congress, and Decatur reasoned that no more American sailors needed to bleed for the cause. They had done their duty, and Decatur, as a man of honor and always mindful of his men, conceded the first and only defeat of his splendid career.

Given his choice of duty following the war, Commodore Decatur assumed command of a nine-ship squadron charged with resolving the now almost ten-year dispute with the Barbary Pirates and Tripoli and a conflict with Algiers that had developed during the War of 1812. He performed his duties expertly, taking the flagship of the Algerian navy and forcing the Barbary Pirates to concede to American demands without bloodshed. Decatur was as good at diplomacy as he was at war. He again returned to the United States and was treated to dinners and parties in his honor. At Baltimore, he honored the people for the spirited defense of the city in the War of 1812 with the following toast: "The citizens of Baltimore! Their patriotism and valor defeated the veteran forces of the enemy, who came, saw, and fled."[6] Though praise was heaped upon him in every city he visited, Decatur remembered that he had not been alone in the great struggle with the British. His own glory always came second to his respect for those who had bled in the cause of liberty.

Decatur spent the last years of his life working for the Board of Navy Commissioners. He had become wealthy, having invested his prize money in real estate. He married in 1806 but remained childless. Decatur met his demise in a duel in 1820. He had engaged in his first duel in 1799 and served as a second in several other contests. Dueling had been an integral part of the life of gentlemen for centuries, and once a challenge was issued, a gentleman had to accept. In this particular contest, Decatur intended to avoid giving a mortal blow, but the feeling was not mutual. Decatur was mortally wounded by the first shot, while his opponent suffered only a wound to the leg. Reporting the news of Decatur's demise, the National Intelligencer said of him, "Mourn Columbia! for one of thy brightest stars has set, a son without fear and without reproach."

The Good Soldier

"Our country! In her intercourse with foreign nations may she always be in the right; but our country, right or wrong!"

—Stephen Decatur, 1816[7]

Both Jones and Decatur earned the respect of the men who served with them and the grateful Americans they helped defend. They have both been largely forgotten—not because their deeds have been overshadowed by greater examples of American heroism, but because their brand of heroism has gone out of fashion. In a time when American men have been reduced to mere caricatures, the lazy buffoons of television sit-coms, Jones and Decatur provide a welcome and refreshing contrast to that image.

A Splendid Example

"It will not be forgotten, either abroad or at home, that a country which once produced a Decatur may produce others like him. In this view also he still survives to animate the youthful aspirant for naval honors, by the splendor of his example. Let the youth of our navy keep this high mark steadily before them, aiming to be like Decatur in all things but his end, and, undismayed by the perfection of their model, find encouragement in the assurance contained in the familiar ancient motto, 'He will reach the highest, who aims at the summit.' Let them approach as near as they may to their high mark, treading after him, though with unequal steps, even if they reach not the lofty eminence which he attained, who revived in our days much of what was best in chivalry, and won for himself the proud titles of 'Terror of the Foe'; 'Champion of Christendom'; 'Bayard of the Seas.'"

—A. S. Mackenzie[8]

Chapter 4

FRONTIERSMEN

David Crockett and Andrew Jackson

The frontier long defined America. The ability of men to move west, start over, and carve a new life out of the wilderness attracted thousands of settlers to American shores. The ruggedness of the frontier made men and heroes. It was an unforgiving life, and only the toughest made a success of it. Andrew Jackson and David Crockett exemplified this manly spirit. During their lives, neither man cared much for the other, but they shared an experience on the frontier that hardened their characters and made them men. In an era when masculinity was well-represented in American society, Jackson and Crockett were head and shoulders above the rest.

King of the Wild Frontier

The modern actor Billy Bob Thornton once said David Crockett in the film *The Alamo* was one of his favorite roles. John Wayne played him, too. Every boy who grew up before the 1970s wanted to be Crockett. He was the "king of the wild frontier," the man who wrestled bears and jumped rivers, the man with the sharpshooter's eye who tamed the wilderness. He was larger

Did you know?

★ Fewer than 200 men at the Alamo held off a force of thousands for several days by superior marksmanship

★ Andrew Jackson fought 13 duels, killed one opponent, and carried a bullet in his shoulder for more than 20 years

★ The U.S. government was debt-free for the first and only time during the presidency of Andrew Jackson

than life. As one historian wrote, "His life is a veritable romance, with the additional charm of unquestionable truth. It opens to the reader scenes in the lives of the lowly, and a state of semi-civilization, of which but few of them can have the faintest idea."[1] Crockett was so popular because he was one of us, a common man without advantages who achieved great things on his own merit. He was the classic American.

Crockett was born in 1786 in Hawkins County, Tennessee. His father's family had emigrated from Ireland and settled in the expansive and untamed wilderness in the mid-eighteenth century. Their cabin was little more than four walls made of small logs, a bark-covered roof, and a dirt floor. They could hunt, and like many Scots and Irish who settled on the frontier, they eked out a life of subsistence—until they eventually fell under the knife of a marauding Indian tribe. Life on the frontier was not for the weak.

Crockett's father, John Crockett, avoided the massacre because he had been hired out as a day laborer in Pennsylvania. John Crockett served in the American War for Independence and took part in the Battle of King's Mountain in North Carolina. After the war was over, he married a woman from northern Maryland and settled for a time in western North Carolina. Neither had an education, and like their predecessors, they struggled to survive on the fringes of civilization. After three years, they pulled up stakes and moved to Tennessee. This was a common occurrence for the Crocketts. They seemed to move every few years, always looking for more land and a better life, free of the confines of civilization. John Crockett owned a tavern, a mill, and on several occasions tracts of land as large as four hundred acres, but he was never wealthy. The family farmed and hunted but had little in the way of creature comforts. Their log cabins were simple, usually one room, with home-made furniture from local wood and animal skins, but this was the way of life on the frontier, the only life David Crockett knew.

Until he was a teenager, David Crockett never had an education. His parents were illiterate, and Crockett himself said that he didn't see a use in books. A book could not provide food or shelter. Living was hard, and simple tasks that modern Americans take for granted, such as acquiring food, required strenuous effort. Those who lived on the frontier were a hearty, independent stock. Dangers from wildlife, hostile Indian tribes, and poor weather made the immediate more important than the future, and the faster a young man could contribute to the struggle to survive, the more valuable he was to the family. David Crockett became an excellent shot because he needed the skill to survive. Marksmanship meant you could eat.

David Crockett had a difficult childhood. His parents showed him little love or tenderness. When he was twelve, Crockett was sent on a four hundred-mile cattle drive with a Dutch stranger, on foot. He had to find his own way home, traversing the unforgiving countryside, often in the snow. When Crockett finally made it back to his father's tavern, he did not receive a warm welcome. After he skipped school for several days, his father threatened to beat him severely, and Crockett again left home, this time of his own accord. In a journey similar to the one he had just undertaken, Crockett made it to Baltimore, Maryland. He was only thirteen.

Crockett spent two years away from home and after returning was forced to go to work to settle several family debts. According to the law at the time, boys were required to work for their parents and help support the family until twenty-one. Crockett did so, but at sixteen his father graciously released him from his obligations. He was already an independent man, having lived in the wilderness for three years, working to provide his own subsistence. His trials as a young teenager had made Crockett a

★ ★ ★ ★ ★ ★ ★ ★ ★ ★ ★ ★ ★ ★

Predestination, David Crockett-Style

After narrowly escaping death as a young man, Crockett wrote, "If a fellow is born to be hung he will never be drowned; and further … if he is born for a seat in Congress, even flour barrels can't make a mash of him."[2]

student of human nature. Though he didn't have a lot of book knowledge, he had a quick wit and plenty of street smarts—or, more accurately in his case, wild frontier smarts. Crockett was also able to use his skill as a marksman to acquire needed money in "shooting matches." But he had no property, save a poor horse, and had to depend on others for work. This lack of assets presented a problem for a young man looking for love.

The people in his community thought well of Crockett, but he nevertheless had trouble finding a wife. He was rejected once, jilted the day before his wedding on another occasion, and almost run off from his future bride by her mother. Modern young men scorned in love may find solace in the fact that the great Davy Crockett was once a forlorn and heartbroken lover. Once married, Crockett attempted to settle into the routine of a frontier farmer. His wife brought a small dowry with her, and as a man of his word who always paid his debts, he was afforded a small loan from a friend. Crockett was thus able to establish a homestead, but he did not have the resolve to be a farmer. Restless, he moved his young family west in search of better land and a better opportunity. Fate intervened.

Crockett fought in the Creek War of 1813–1814, insisting it was his duty to serve his country. He served as a scout early in his enlistment and took part in several small skirmishes and a raid on a Creek village that forever seared into his memory the horrors of war. He returned home and settled down, but

★★★★★★★★★★★★★★★

Marriage Advice from a Real Man

"A man's wife can hold him devlish uneasy, if she begins to scold, and fret, and perplex him, at a time when he has a full load for a rail-road car on his mind already."[3]

The Young and the Brave

"I didn't think that courage ought to be measured by the beard, for fear a goat would have the preference over a man."

—David Crockett[4]

his wife died one year later, leaving Crockett with three small children. He then married the widow of a soldier fallen in the Creek War, and had two more children. Crockett determined that his large family needed better pasture, so he pulled up stakes again and headed farther west. As he had said around 1810, before his first relocation west, "I found I was better at increasing my family than my fortune."[5]

Crockett had already earned a fine reputation as a scout and rifleman by his exploits during the Creek War. Everyone trusted him, and his honesty and work ethic placed him among the first rank of the people of Tennessee. It was no surprise, then, that after settling into Giles County, he was elected first as a magistrate and then as a justice of

The Benevolent Hero

"Whenever I had any thing, and saw a fellow being suffering, I was more anxious to relieve him than to benefit myself. And this is one of the true secrets of my being a poor man to this day. But it is my way; and while it has often left me with an empty purse, which is as near the devil as any thing else I have seen, yet it has never left my heart empty of consolations which money couldn't buy,— the consolations of having sometimes fed the hungry and covered the naked."

—David Crockett[6]

the peace. Crockett had no legal training. He could barely read, but the people respected his commonsense approach to law and politics. To elitists in his own day, Crockett was an example of the backwardness of America. Simple men, they thought, did not belong in government. This, of course, is the same scorn that is leveled at hard-working Americans today by the self-appointed American intelligentsia. But hard-working people recognize bravery and honesty, and Crockett had plenty of both. As a result, he was sent to the state legislature in 1821.

Shortly thereafter, Crockett again moved his family west, settling near the Obion River. He hunted bears, killing over 105 in less than a year, a statistic that must send P.E.T.A. into cardiac arrest. This was the happiest time of his life. Though his closest neighbor was seven miles distant, the people again sent him to the state legislature. Crockett could not escape his reputation. His independence as both a man and a statesman was evident in his opposition to the election of Andrew Jackson as a senator from Tennessee in 1825. He refused to wear the collar of "Jackson's dog." He lost his re-election bid and spent two years dabbling in commerce. In 1826 he decided to run for a seat in the United States House of Representatives. His humorous home-spun stories won over the public, and he was elected to the Twentieth and Twenty-first Congresses (1827–1831).

Crockett quickly displayed his statesmanship. He had supported Andrew Jackson for president in 1828, but, just as in 1825, refused to blindly follow every decision Jackson made. Crockett said he "would sooner be honestly and politically [damned] than hypocritically immortalized."[8] He voted against Jackson's "Indian Bill" because he thought it immoral and unjust. The people of his district turned on him and even drew up papers charging Crockett eight dollars for every vote he missed while in Congress (this was the per diem amount congressmen were paid at the time). This money, they contended, had been swindled from the public treasury and should be returned. Crockett was defeated in his re-election bid in 1830, but won again in 1832 and spent one more session in Congress, from 1833 to 1835. On his trip back to Washington, Crockett reportedly made the following toast at a dinner party, in obvious reference to the growing power of President Jackson, "Here's wishing the bones of

Beware the Cult of Personality

"I voted for Andrew Jackson because I believed he possessed certain principles, and not because his name was Andrew Jackson, or the Hero, or Old Hickory. And when he left those principles which induced me to support him, I considered myself justified in opposing him. This thing of man-worship I am a stranger to; I don't like it; it taints every action of life; it is like a skunk getting into a house—long after he has cleared out, you smell him in every room and closet, from the cellar to the garret."

—David Crockett[7]

tyrant kings may answer in hell; in place of gridirons, to roast the souls of Tories on."[9]

He took a tour of the North and received praise for his manly, independent streak at every stop, from New York to Boston. People asked to shake the hand of an honest man, to hear the stories that made Crockett famous, to soak up the atmosphere of the frontier. To Northern city-dwellers, Crockett was a curiosity. But he was American in the purest sense, cut from the rough-hewn cloth of independence and hardened by the ax and rifle. While Crockett was famous during his lifetime, his greatest glory would be his last.

Crockett lost his re-election bid in 1834. Crowds greeted him at every stop on his return trip to Tennessee, and hunting and the woods no longer had the same appeal as parties and stump speeches. Crockett had been civilized, and perhaps wanted to be president. Crockett famously and bitterly told his constituents that "you may all go to hell, and I will go to Texas." Thus the die was cast. If the United States would not have him, then perhaps Texas would. He left his wife and children behind and set off for Texas in 1835, just months after returning from Washington.

This last adventure included hunting buffalo on the prairie, competing in sharpshooting contests, almost dying after a cougar attack, and enjoying the exotic territory west of the Mississippi. He arrived at the Alamo in February 1836,

★★★★★★★★★★★★★

Political Accountability, Crockett-Style

After receiving a tongue-lashing from one of his constituents for voting for a bill that was clearly unconstitutional, Crockett responded, "Well, my friend, you hit the nail upon the head when you said I had not sense enough to understand the Constitution. I intended to be guided by it, and thought I had studied it fully. I have heard many speeches in Congress, but what you have said here at your plow has got more hard, sound sense in it than all the fine speeches I have ever heard. If I had ever taken the view of it that you have, I would have put my head into the fire before I would have given that vote; and if you will forgive me and vote for me again, if I ever vote for another unconstitutional law I wish I may be shot."[10]

just days before Santa Anna determined to lay siege to the fort surrounding the mission. This battle would make him more famous than ever—forever a hero.

Crockett understood that the way a man died often defined his life. When the Mexican army began their assault on the Alamo in late February, Crockett and the 150 or so men who manned the fort held off their foes (perhaps as many as 3,000) for several days with superior marksmanship. Crockett himself reportedly killed over twenty men. He wrote in his final journal entry dated March 5, 1836, "Liberty and Independence Forever!" The next day, the Mexican army overran the fort and slaughtered every man there. Crockett reportedly fought bravely and died well, perhaps as one of the last men to meet his fate. "Remember the Alamo!" has since been recognized as a rallying cry for all Americans. Crockett died as he lived, bravely and manfully fighting for principle and independence.

Old Hickory

Though Crockett referred to Andrew Jackson as an elected king during Jackson's presidency, the two men shared a common background and had mutual respect for one another until the poisonous atmosphere of Washington politics spoiled them both. Crockett was never defined by his political career, and though Jackson is typically regarded as one of the best presidents in American history, it was the years leading to his time in Washington that made him a hero.

Jackson was born in 1767 on the border between North and South Carolina. He claimed South Carolina as his native state, but several biographers believe that Jackson was born in Union County, North Carolina. His family had emigrated from Ireland in 1765, following a familiar path for those of Scotch-Irish descent. Most of the people of Celtic descent who landed in America were poor, and they moved to the Piedmont region of the United

States looking for land and opportunity. Jackson's father died just three weeks before his birth, leaving his mother alone to care for three boys. Life was hard on the frontier. Jackson had no education and cared little for books, but he learned independence, perhaps the most important trait a young man can have.

He also had a legendary temper. As president, Jackson would yell and bang his fists on tables to make a point. After such an outburst, he might turn to the man next to him and say, "They probably thought I was angry." His stubborn courage and will to fight were fostered at a young age. His Celtic heritage, the frontier, and the warrior caste system prevailing there probably all contributed to the sense of honor that made Jackson a man to be respected. He was always near the top of the pecking order in a society that valued manly independence.

But Jackson possessed other qualities that made him an attractive figure. He deplored debt and did everything possible to avoid incurring any of it—whether public or private—his entire life. In fact, during his presidency the United States was debt-free for the first and only time in its history.

Jackson also had a chivalrous regard for the opposite sex. Though not a refined gentleman along the lines of a Lee or Washington, Jackson was, nevertheless, a gallant man. He cherished his wife. When she died shortly before his inauguration in 1829, Jackson held Henry Clay personally responsible. Clay had circulated terrible stories about Jackson's wife during the presidential campaign through a newspaper surrogate in Cincinnati. Jackson never forgave him; he believed his wife's heart attack had been induced by shame.

★ ★ ★ ★ ★ ★ ★ ★ ★ ★ ★ ★ ★ ★

Don't Mess Around with Andrew

One time when Jackson was a boy, his friends wanted to have a little fun with him. They packed a musket to the muzzle and gave it to Jackson to fire. The weapon discharged with an unexpected kick, knocking Jackson to the ground. He got up, quickly dusted himself off, and in a rage thundered, "If one of you laughs, I'll kill him!" No one laughed.

Jackson's temper and keen sense of honor, the fierce independence that made him hate debt, and his chivalry were all honed in his frontier upbringing. By the time he was a teenager, war had reached the Carolina upcountry. Jackson's two brothers enlisted in the cause for American Independence, and though Jackson himself was too young to fight, he was captured and along with his brother sent to prison for their support of the American effort. His mother organized a prisoner exchange which freed her two sons, but fate would not allow any of Jackson's family to live through the war. His brothers died in battle, and his mother succumbed to "ship fever" in Charleston, South Carolina, while serving as a nurse for American prisoners of war. Jackson was left an orphan. He carried both emotional and physical scars from the war: his mother was buried in an unmarked grave, and Jackson received a terrible head wound from a British officer for refusing to shine his boots. It is little wonder that Jackson hated the British and inflicted as much damage as possible on the British Empire as a soldier.

Jackson spent his late teenage years doing very little. Finally in 1784 he determined to study law. This may have seemed an improbable career for a young man with little education, but he was able to find a job in a North Carolina law firm and in 1788 was admitted to the North Carolina bar. He was then appointed public solicitor for western Tennessee, a job that suited him perfectly. In 1788, Tennessee was the frontier (it did not become a state until 1796), and Jackson, being of frontier stock, excelled in dealing with the people of his adopted home. His ten years in that job were marked by honesty and the ability to prosecute the law even in an area that was known for lawlessness. Jackson was a natural leader with a firm hand, but, like Crockett, he understood human nature—in particular, the nature of frontiersmen. He treated the hard-nosed, intrepid, and often belligerent people of his district with respect, something a man from a softer rearing might not have done.

Jackson took part in the state constitutional convention in 1796, the people of Tennessee elected him to the House of Representatives in that same year (the first from his state), and the legislature sent him to the United States Senate in 1797 (the first of two appointments to that body). He resigned that seat in 1798 to take a seat on the Tennessee Supreme Court. After he left the court, he spent several years working on his plantation, the Hermitage.

In retrospect, Jackson was probably always better suited to be a soldier than a statesman, but as a man who commanded such enormous respect among the frontier people of his state, he was bound to end up in the highest circles of government. The great men of the founding generation regarded Jackson as little more than a country bumpkin attempting to play the part of an august legislator. He did make friends with Robert Livingston of New York, but Thomas Jefferson had few kind words to say about him. Everyone commented on his quick temper.

That famous temper and his unwillingness to forget an insult made Jackson one of the most famous duelists in the United States. Thomas Hart Benton, often called the "Champion of the West," engaged in a famous frontier brawl with Jackson in 1813, one that almost resulted in Jackson's death. Benton was in good company. Jackson fought thirteen duels in his life, killing one man, Charles Dickinson, after Dickinson had insulted Jackson's wife and quarreled with Jackson over a horse race. Yet Jackson's reputation as a duelist would be surpassed by his fame as a soldier. In both cases, Jackson's affinity for brawling led to more victories than defeats. Perhaps Jackson was so successful as a politician because no one wanted to cross him. Certainly, the British and the Creek Indians learned how dangerous that could be during the War of 1812.

Jackson commanded the Tennessee militia and offered it in the service of the United States on several occasions. As tension among the United

States, Spain, and Great Britain mounted between 1810 and 1812, Jackson consistently urged that the United States go to war with Great Britain. His attitude was not uncommon on the frontier. Most of the West viewed British instigation (and Spanish supply) of the American Indian tribes with disdain. America declared war in 1812, and the situation on the frontier reached a boiling point in August 1813 when a Creek war party ambushed Fort Mims near Mobile and killed over five hundred men, women, and children. The massacre sent shockwaves across the South, and militia regiments were immediately raised in Tennessee for the defense of the frontier.

Jackson, recovering from a gunshot wound to the shoulder he had received in his fight with Thomas Benton, left his sickbed to march the West Tennessee militia into Alabama. He was pale and weak and could not move his arm, but Jackson was determined to extinguish the Creek threat. All did not go smoothly. Jackson faced problems of supply; for much of the conflict, his men starved. Their misery, coupled with conflicts over terms of enlistment, sparked dissension in the ranks and led to quarrels between the generals. Jackson had to use his superior skills of leadership to keep the army together and coordinate attacks.

Quick, punishing victories at Tallushatchee and Talladega raised the morale of the men for a moment, but their empty stomachs were hard to appease. They demanded food, and Jackson, sympathetic with his men, ordered that officers would eat no better than enlisted until provisions were secured. In one instance, a hungry soldier came to him begging for a meal. Jackson reached into his pocket, pulled out a few acorns and told the man they could share his supper. Like Washington at Valley Forge, Jackson was fighting off desertion through his will alone. When the men finally scored provisions, the militia began marching home. Jackson rode to the front and implored them to keep fighting for the cause. But his words fell on deaf ears. Word came from the governor shortly thereafter for Jackson to allow the men to disband. Jackson refused, and in little time another five hundred men arrived from West Tennessee to augment his force.

By March 1814, Jackson was in command of a force of five thousand men. He had an insubordinate general arrested and sent back to Tennessee and ordered a man charged with mutiny to be shot in front of his army. He had no further problems with discipline. Jackson then planned his final strike. The Creek had massed at a place they called Tohopeka, now known as Horseshoe Bend, near the fork of the Tallapoosa and Coosa Rivers. They had built a breastwork of earth and logs, perhaps three hundred yards long, across a peninsula jutting into a bend in the Tallapoosa River. Six hundred braves, along with several hundred women and children, were prepared to defend the position. Jackson, with about three thousand men, determined to make a frontal assault. He sent a detachment of cavalry and several hundred friendly Creek across the river to sweep in from the rear and turned his artillery on the breastworks. This pincer movement had the desired effect. Jackson's superior firepower in the front decimated the Creek defense, and the push from the rear cut off those trying to flee. The Tallapoosa ran red that day. Over six hundred Creek braves were felled by Jackson's relentless assault. This was the greatest loss of life by any Indian army in a single battle with the United States. Only two hundred of Jackson's soldiers died that day. It was a tremendous victory, and Jackson received warm accolades from Washington for his service, yet his greatest victory, one that would make him a household name across the United States, was yet to come.

As a result of Horseshoe Bend, Jackson was appointed a major-general in the United States Army in 1814 after William Henry Harrison

A Manly Resolve

"By the Eternal, they shall not sleep on our soil!"

—Andrew Jackson on the British occupation of New Orleans[11]

resigned his command. He was in charge of the southwestern district, which included Mobile and New Orleans. Jackson hoped that the War of 1812 would not end before he had an opportunity to take the fight to the British. Without waiting for authorization, Jackson invaded Florida and sacked Pensacola. Florida was controlled by the Spanish, who, though not at war with the United States, were allowing the British to use Pensacola as a base of operations in the Gulf of Mexico. Jackson finally received word from the Madison administration *not* to attack Pensacola, but no matter. Jackson had decided on a course of action and acted. This type of independence made him both successful and at times a liability for the United States government.

Jackson arrived in New Orleans in December 1814. He declared martial law in the city but realized that it would be a difficult to defend his position. It was easily assaulted from three sides, and his army consisted of little more than militia and pirates, many without weapons. Jackson would need every skill he possessed as a commander. He quickly organized a line of defense and repulsed the British in a night attack. Jackson then retrenched in a better position and waited. The British finally charged across the open plain of marshy, sandy soil in front of Jackson and his men. The attackers suffered severely. The Americans were relentless in their use of artillery and musket, and the British fell in the face of the withering attack. "Old Hickory" had his revenge on the British. Over two thousand British soldiers were killed, captured, or wounded during the Battle of New Orleans. The American side lost fewer than twenty-five. It was perhaps the

★ ★ ★ ★ ★ ★ ★ ★ ★ ★ ★ ★ ★ ★ ★

Jackson and the Nuns

On the night before the Battle of New Orleans, nuns at the Ursuline convent in New Orleans prayed for an American victory. The next morning, Mass was celebrated with a statue of Our Lady of Prompt Succor placed at the altar. During communion, news of the great American victory reached the convent. Ever since, a yearly Mass of Thanksgiving has been held by the convent, and for several years after, whenever Jackson was in New Orleans, he made it a point to stop by and pray with the nuns.

greatest victory in American military history, and, as a result, Jackson ascended above a mere local legend. He was now a national hero.

Jackson spent the next three years settling old disputes, mainly in Florida. He showed the same independent disregard for orders that had created problems in his occupation of Pensacola during the War of 1812. When a band of Creek Red Sticks and Seminole Indians began stirring up trouble in Florida, Jackson wrote to President James Monroe that he could secure the territory in sixty days for the United States and end the Indian uprising. Monroe, who preferred acquiring the territory through peaceful means, did not respond to Jackson's letter for nearly a year. Jackson equated silence with approval. He personally raised an army, marched into Florida, again captured Pensacola, and routed the Seminoles, suffering no casualties in the process. He also ordered the execution of four men, including two British subjects, for inciting war against the United States. This created an international problem. Jackson, by invading a Spanish territory and executing two British subjects, had violated the sovereignty of two nations not at war with the United States. The Monroe administration smoothed things over (and ended up purchasing Florida from the Spanish), but Jackson's actions led Henry Clay to call for his censure in the House of Representatives. The censure vote failed, but Jackson developed a bitter hatred for Clay that lasted for the rest of his life.

Jackson retired to the Hermitage in 1821, seeking the peace he had missed since departing for Alabama in 1814. He was tired, his military campaigns had taken a toll on his body (as had the bullet still lodged in his shoulder from the duel with Benton), and Jackson enjoyed the quiet comfort his plantation and family provided. He was a frontiersman and had waged war in the fiercest way possible, but Jackson was a different man at home. His short temper and penchant for violent reprisal melted away around his wife and children, all ten of whom were either adopted or under Jackson's guardianship. At the Hermitage he was as peaceful as a lamb, and though

Jackson did not become a Christian until late in life, he graciously built a chapel on his plantation for his wife.

Politics called him out of retirement in 1823. He was appointed to the United States Senate by the Tennessee legislature and was a candidate for president in 1824. He won the popular vote—this was the first time it was tallied—but he did not have the majority in the Electoral College. The election was thrown to the House of Representatives where Henry Clay, as speaker, held sway. Clay orchestrated the election of John Quincy Adams, and Jackson, enraged by this second insult from the Kentuckian, swore revenge. He resigned his Senate seat in 1825 and continued to campaign for president. It paid off. He trounced Adams in a rematch in 1828 and took office in 1829 as the seventh president of the United States. As president, Jackson did everything possible to thwart Clay's political ambitions.

His political career is well known, and politics rarely makes men heroes. Jackson was a fine military man who bravely faced the enemy and made the correct decisions on the battlefield. The same cannot be said for his all political decisions. Jackson did, however, represent a new spirit in Washington. He was the first man elected president who did not hail from Virginia or Massachusetts. His frontier persona did not mesh with Washington society, and Jackson is often credited with bringing a leveling, democratic spirit to Washington politics. Most of the founding generation had either died or retired by the time Jackson became president, and the new blood that had aggressively pushed for war with Great Britain in 1812 and had favored expansion in the name of American "nationalism" was now in power. Historians have called this era "the Age of Jackson." America was changing, and Jackson personified that change.

Jackson served two terms as president. He waged a political war against the Bank of the United States (a war he won, though at some cost to the American economy), faced down what he considered "treasonous" nullifiers from South Carolina, refused to enforce a decision of the Supreme

Court, and generally forced his will upon the American government. It would be no stretch to suggest that Jackson and the government were synonymous during his two-term stint in office. No man since Washington had commanded so much respect. His opponents recognized his enormous stature and formed a party based on a loose coalition of those who deplored "King Andrew" for his aggressive actions in office.

Jackson retired in 1837 and died in 1845. Upon leaving office, he reminded the American public "that eternal vigilance by the people is the price of liberty, and that you must pay the price if you wish to secure the blessing." Jackson was always willing to pay the price. He was, as his nickname suggested, tough as old hickory wood, fierce as an enraged bear when challenged, and stubborn as a mule in his positions. He was a free man in the tradition of the American frontier: independent, unrefined, and fiery. There has never been another Andrew Jackson.

The historian Frederick Jackson Turner lamented that the closing of the frontier changed American society. The restless energy that defined Americans had been bottled up and replaced with the decadence of urban life. Perhaps this is why young men today find it difficult to cope in modern America. They can no longer head into the wilderness with their gun and knife and carve a niche for themselves. Their sense of adventure, their independence, has been stolen by concrete and steel. America may never be able to produce a Crockett or Jackson again, at least not until young men rekindle their manly spirit of adventure and enterprise. They could learn from the man in the coonskin cap and the hero of New Orleans.

Chapter 5

SOUTHERNERS

Robert E. Lee and Thomas "Stonewall" Jackson

efore the wave of "political correctness" rolled over the United States in the late 1980s and 1990s, Robert E. Lee and Thomas J. "Stonewall" Jackson were thought of as real American heroes. They were considered the personification of the American—not just Southern—man: dignified, heroic, honorable, just, intelligent, sincere, brave, Christian. Of course, they were Southern men, but Southern men often defined what it meant to be an American, from the colonial period on. The South, and thus the Southern gentleman, dominated the general government of the United States for most of its early history. The Lees of Virginia had long played prominent roles in that history, from signatories to the Declaration of Independence, to heroes on the battlefield, to statesmen at both the state and federal level. Robert E. Lee is just the most conspicuous, not the only important member of the clan. "Stonewall" Jackson did not have quite the same pedigree, but because of his exploits during the War Between the States, he became a recognized representative of the independent American spirit. Unfortunately, in modern America their names have often been made synonymous with "hate" and "treason." This equation is unjust. The American people should know and remember their stories.

Did you know?

★ Robert E. Lee earned the nickname "the indefatigable Lee" in the Mexican War

★ Lee recommended freeing slaves who were willing to enlist in the Confederate Army as part of "a plan of gradual and general emancipation"

★ Jackson marched his infantrymen so fast they were known as "foot cavalry"

A Book You're Not Supposed to Read

The Politically Incorrect Guide™ to the Civil War by H. W. Crocker III (Washington, DC: Regnery, 2008).

Both men were physically impressive. Lee was described as the handsomest man in the Army, and Congressman Samuel Hays recommended Jackson for West Point in part because of his "fine athletic form [and] manly appearance."[1] Each man was near six feet tall with a solid, rugged physique. They commanded the respect of both their friends and their foes. Lee was a refined gentleman who understood the rules of formal society, but like other Southern gentlemen—including his hero George Washington—he was a pillar of physical strength as well as virtue. Jackson, having grown up in the backcountry regions of Virginia, was not as polished, but he knew and appreciated the societal norms that made the culture of the Old Dominion the accepted standard of the South. Both were men in a place and time when men were measured by intelligence, honor, and courage. Such is not the case in modern America.

A Book You're Not Supposed to Read

R. E. Lee: A Biography by Douglas Southall Freeman (New York: Charles Scribner's Sons, 1934), 4 vols.

The Last Gentleman

Robert Edward Lee was born in 1807 at the Stratford Plantation in Westmoreland County, Virginia, the third son of Henry "Light-Horse Harry" Lee and Ann Hill Carter Lee. His father had been governor of the state and a member of the Continental Congress, but was better known as the gallant and daring cavalry hero of the American War for Independence. His mother, Henry Lee's second wife, was a member of the prestigious Hill Carter family from Shirley Plantation in what is now Charles City, Virginia, bordering the James River.

Lee counted several famous individuals among his distinguished ancestors, from his maternal grandfather Charles "King" Carter, who was perhaps the wealthiest man in Virginia at one point, to the several Lees who played dominating roles in Virginia politics. It must be noted that the Carter family produced three signers to the Declaration of Independence, three governors of Virginia, and two United States presidents, along with generations of principled soldiers and statesmen, including Robert Lee. The men of the Carter family took pride in their disinterested statesmanship, anchored in the traditional values of the English aristocracy.

"Light-Horse Harry" Lee was described as "a gentleman of impeccable manners and flashing conversation," but he was a man torn between his natural abilities as a soldier and his desire for fame and fortune.[2] He speculated too much and ran into terrible financial difficulties while Robert was still a young boy. After he was severely beaten and mutilated by a mob, Light-Horse Harry Lee left Virginia in 1813 only to die broke and dispirited five years later. Robert Lee did not dwell on his father's troubles. Instead he remembered his military legacy, his wit and charm, and his statesmanship. Robert's own character was molded in part by his father's instruction and guidance—not in person, but by way of the letters he wrote his son. His father's maxims, along with the rigid Carter traditions of family, church, and God, grounded Robert E. Lee's moral compass.

★★★★★★★★★★★★★★

"Light-Horse Harry" Lee's advice to his son Robert

"Fame in arms or art, however conspicuous, is naught, unless bottomed on virtue."

"Self command … is the pivot upon which the character, fame and independence of us mortals hang."

"The rank of men, as established by the concurrent judgment of ages stands thus: heroes, legislators, orators, and poets. The most useful, and in my opinion, the most honorable is the legislator…. Generally, mankind admire most the hero; of all, the most useless, except when the safety of a nation demands his saving arm."[3]

Young Robert Lee was a fine student. He received a classical education but excelled in mathematics. Later in life he lamented that he had not carried his studies in the classics further, as he enjoyed the scholar's life more than the soldier's. Lee followed his father's footsteps into the military by seeking an appointment to West Point. He received his appointment in 1825 and was graduated four years later, number two in his class and without demerit.

Lee modeled his military career after those of two men: his father and his hero George Washington. While at West Point, he studied a new edition of his father's *Memoirs of the War in the Southern Department*, along with the campaigns of Washington during the American War for Independence. "Light-Horse Harry" Lee's use of discipline, reconnaissance, and tactics made him perhaps the finest commander, save Washington, in the Revolutionary War, but it was his attention to his men that made him famous. He insisted that his men be meticulously appointed and outfitted, and he rewarded them for bravery in combat. Their respect for him was little short of veneration. The same can be said for his son's men during the War Between the States.

Washington, of course, was the most admired man in all of America, if not the world, in the eighteenth century. But he was also a Virginian, and as a Virginian, Lee viewed him as the ideal Southern gentleman. Lee married into Washington's family (his wife, Mary Anna Randolph Custis, was the daughter of George Washington Parke Custis, the step-grandson whom Washington loved and reared as his own son at Mount Vernon), named his first son after Washington, and shared Washington's views on politics, society, and slavery.

Most of the Lees were Federalists who supported the ratification of the Constitution as a way to strengthen the central government. "Light-Horse Harry" Lee wrote Washington's eulogy in 1799, and his nearly fatal beating at the hands of a Democratic-Republican mob was on account of his opposition to the War of 1812 (Federalists generally opposed the war). Robert Lee followed in his father's footsteps. He served with distinction in the Mexican War, earning the nickname "the indefatigable Lee," and as a good solider welcomed this opportunity to do his duty to his country. He complained of politics but loved the Union and was identified with the Whig Party, the Federalists' political heirs. While in South Carolina during the early 1830s, Lee wrote that all the people spoke of was "Nullification! Nullification! Nullification!!" and that "Congress is doing nothing but hammering on the tariff."[4] Lee defended the Union during the "Secession Winter" of 1861, but from the beginning he determined to side with his state. Virginia and her traditions had been in his family since the 1600s, and Lee was not going to buck two hundred years of family history and heritage and fight his own kin—the fellow Virginians Thomas Jefferson had called his own "countrymen."

Like Washington and many other Virginians, Lee considered slavery to be a moral evil, and, as a good Christian, he believed that slavery would one day be extinguished from Southern society—peacefully, as had been done in countries around the world in the nineteenth century. The institution was, however, part of Southern life, and it was a difficult question how to end it effectively with as little social upheaval as possible. Lee despised abolitionists, believing their insistence on immediate emancipation would only spark violence. Manumission had been the Washington tradition. George Washington had freed his slaves upon his death, and Robert E. Lee, as the executor of his wife's father's estate, was charged with manumitting all of George Washington Parke Custis's 150 slaves within five years of Custis's death. Lee did so in 1862. During the War, Lee also recommended that the Confederacy should consider

A Book You're Not Supposed to Read

The Politically Incorrect Guide™ *to the South (and Why It Will Rise Again)* by Clint Jackson (Washington, DC: Regnery, 2007).

abolishing slavery and enlisting the former slaves into the service of the South. He was no pro-slavery ideologue.

By the late 1850s, Lee was spending much of his time near home caring for his ailing wife and managing his family affairs. But he was in Texas in late 1860 and early 1861 when the Deep South began seceding from the Union. On April 18, 1861, Robert E. Lee was offered command of the United States Army, but knowing that Virginia was in deliberation on the secession question, he declined the appointment. Lee, with a heavy heart, resigned his commission in the Army two days later. Lee was not a Constitutional scholar. But as a man steeped in tradition, he believed that Virginia (and the South) should have adopted a declaration of independence rather than an ordinance of secession. Southerners were, after all, fighting for independence, exactly as their fathers had done just eighty years before. Washington became their symbol and the cause of '76 their rallying cry. Lee was reluctantly defending his state and his people from a Union he had loved and hoped he would never have to leave. But as a good soldier and an honorable, duty-bound man, he accepted his fate and poured his considerable skill and energy into the defense of Virginia.

Without Robert E. Lee, the South would probably have lost the War well before 1865. Lee had served primarily as a scout in the Mexican War, had never led an army the size of the Army of Northern Virginia, and certainly had never been in the position he was confronted with in 1862 after Joseph E. Johnston was wounded and relieved of his command in Richmond. Lee was always outgunned, out-supplied, and outmanned, typically three to two but often three to one, yet he won victory after victory at the helm of the Confederate war effort in the Eastern theater. He was the George Washington of the Confederate army and, like Washington, Lee understood that winning entailed perfectly planned offensive strikes, the ability to retreat when needed, and—at bottom—the capacity to keep the army in the field and inspire devotion to the cause. Lee was a gentleman, but he understood the terrible business of war and was a better commander than almost any general officer in American history.

Lee's accomplishments during the war are legendary. He relieved Johnston of command while the federal army was creeping toward Richmond in 1862 and proceeded to force their retreat during the Seven Days Battles. He then went on the offensive, something most in the Confederate ranks did not think could be done, and was stopped at Sharpsburg, Maryland, only by chance. But Lee, like Washington, was able to retreat south and avoid capture. In heroic fashion, he followed this defeat with a smashing victory over the Union army at Fredericksburg in December 1862, a battle that resulted in over twelve thousand Union casualties, compared to five thousand for the Confederate army. Union dead were piled high on the approach to the Confederate ramparts, forcing the living to use them as shields. It was an appalling sight, and Lee, ever mindful of the cost of war, remarked during the battle, "It is well war is so terrible else men would learn to love it too much."

Lee followed up his victory at Fredericksburg with his greatest tactical effort. Planning in conjunction with "Stonewall" Jackson, Lee split his army at Chancellorsville in 1863, and in spite of overwhelming numerical odds, crushed the Union army. The victory was bittersweet, as Jackson was mortally wounded, but Lee determined to invade the North again and in July 1863 met the Union army at Gettysburg, Pennsylvania. His actions during the battle remain the most controversial of his command, though military historians have placed much of the blame for the lack of Confederate success on James Longstreet, not Lee. The Army of Northern Virginia had early success at Gettysburg, and Lee ordered Longstreet to take the high ground on the second day of the battle. Longstreet was slow to move—almost resistant to his orders—and by the time his men began their assault, the Union army had already occupied the well-protected hills overlooking the Confederate position. Lee ordered what is now considered a futile charge against well-entrenched Union lines on the third day of the battle, but perhaps if his men had been properly supported, as Lee had ordered, the result would not have been the bloody rout known famously as "Pickett's Charge."

Lee slipped away again, and continued to frustrate Union chances of victory. He punished the Union army during Ulysses S. Grant's Overland Campaign in 1864, surprised Grant during the Battle of the Wilderness, and butchered his army at Cold Harbor. Grant, however, was able to rebuild his ranks with fresh draftees, while Lee's forces were quickly dwindling. The final siege at Petersburg in 1864 and 1865 was a testament to Lee's personal leadership and his men's respect, nothing short of love, for their commander. His men fought for him in 1865 knowing the war was lost. They continued to die out of duty to the Army of Northern Virginia and wept when Lee offered his surrender at Appomattox Courthouse in 1865.

Devotion to the Cause and the Man

"As soon as he entered this avenue of these old soldiers, the flower of the army, the men who had stood to their duty through thick and thin in so many battles, wild, heartfelt cheers arose which so touched General Lee that tears filled his eyes and trickled down his cheeks as he rode his splendid charger, hat in hand, bowing his acknowledgments. This exhibition of feeling on his part found quick response from the men whose cheers changed to choking sobs as, with streaming eyes and many evidences of affection, they waved their hats as he passed. Each group began in the same way, with cheers, and ended in the same way, with sobs, all along the route to his quarters. Grim, bearded men, threw themselves on the ground, covered their faces with their hands and wept like children. Officers of all ranks made no attempt to conceal their feelings, but sat on their horses and cried aloud.... One man... extended his arms and with an emphatic gesture said, 'I love you just as well as ever, General Lee!'"

—Colonel W. W. Blackford on Robert E. Lee at Appomattox[5]

This last meeting between Grant and Lee exemplifies the dichotomy between the two. Lee rode to the meeting meticulously appointed in his finest dress uniform. He was dignified to the end. Grant, weary from the war and supposedly suffering from headaches, met Lee in his muddy, disheveled blues. Lee never showed his exhaustion, at least not during the negotiation. Grant was cordial and gave Lee agreeable terms, but even Union men at Appomattox admired Lee's refined nature. He was a living legend.

Lee survived five years after the war was over. His heart was still heavy with defeat, but as he had done while superintendent at West Point, he efficiently and effectively poured his energies into education, serving as president of Washington College—now Washington and Lee University—in Lexington, Virginia. He was working to rebuild the South, and he advised fellow Southerners to bury the resentments of the war. He died in 1870, his last words being "Strike the tent." Perhaps no other man in American history, save Washington, was more important to the American people than Lee. He served his country and his state, both before and after the War Between the States, with honor and dignity.

The Christian Soldier

The Northern essayist and Republican partisan E. L. Godkin wrote, following the death of "Stonewall" Jackson in 1863, that Jackson was "the most extraordinary phenomenon of this extraordinary war. Pure, honest, simple-minded, unselfish, and brave, his death is a loss to the whole of America, for, whatever be the result of this war, the United States will enjoy the honor of having bred and educated him."[6] Godkin claimed Stonewall Jackson because he recognized that Jackson was more than a representative of the South—he was an American hero, pure and simple.

A Book You're Not Supposed to Read

Stonewall Jackson: The Man, The Soldier, The Legend by James I. Robertson Jr. (New York: Macmillan, 1997).

Jackson was born in 1824 in Clarksburg, Virginia. While the Jacksons had a solid reputation, they came from humble beginnings. Both the general's great-grandfather and his great-grandmother had arrived in America as indentured servants, having been convicted of theft. They fell in love on the voyage over and, once they had satisfied their indentures, married and moved to the frontier, where they acquired vast tracts of land. Both Jackson's great-grandfather and his grandfather served with distinction in the American War for Independence, and his great-grandmother opened the Jackson homestead as a refuge for American settlers dislocated during the war.

Jackson's father died when he was a boy—something Jackson had in common with Lee—and his mother, left with crushing debt, sold their farm and moved to a one-room rental. Jackson was only six at the time of his father's death and was left an orphan when his mother died five years later. After bouncing between relatives for a few years, Jackson eventually settled on his uncle's frontier farm. He was largely self-educated and taught one of his uncle's slaves how to read and write.

Though he lacked a formal education and had difficulty with the entrance exams, Jackson was admitted to West Point in 1842, and he applied himself to his studies with the stubborn determination that later became a well-known character trait. Jackson did not choose the military because he longed to be a soldier. What Jackson wanted most was to sharpen his character as a man. The military, in his mind, offered the best opportunity for success and respect. He is known for his military acumen, but his career and the famous decisions he made in battle were shaped by his character. As was true of Washington and Lee, the war he fought in so brilliantly did not define his character; his character defined the war.

Jackson was socially awkward as a young man and exhibited eccentricities throughout his life, often to the amusement of his contemporaries. Unlike Lee and other Virginians from the Tidewater region, he did not have the social refinement typical of Southern gentlemen. But Jackson was the perfect example of what Thomas Jefferson and other members of the founding generation considered the "natural aristocracy." In addition to honesty, integrity, and determination—while a West Point cadet he informed his cousin, "I can do anything I will to do"—Jackson had talent, a keen mind, and the ability to make instantaneous and brilliant decisions on the battlefield. He could have been successful in any endeavor he chose.

Like many generals on both sides in the War Between the States, Jackson got his first taste of combat in the Mexican War. He was commissioned a second lieutenant and saw action as part of the 1st U.S. Artillery Regiment. He was awarded more battlefield promotions than any other American officer during the war and had garnered Winfield Scott's highest regard by the time the conflict was over. Jackson exhibited the calmness in battle that would earn him the nickname "Stonewall" during the War Between the States. He had a cannon ball land between his legs, stood his ground under a hail of lead at Chapultepec, and encouraged his men to fight because, in his words, "See, there is no danger; I am not hit!"[7] His bravery was unquestionable.

If Stonewall Jackson has left any lasting legacy, it is that of the ideal Christian soldier—perhaps even the model Christian man. Jackson's Christian beliefs were

The Religion of the Brave

"Captain, my religious belief teaches me to feel as safe in battle as in bed. God has fixed the time for my death. I do not concern myself about that, but to be always ready, no matter when it may overtake me. Captain, that is the way all men should live, and then all would be equally brave."

—Stonewall Jackson to Captain John D. Imboden on July 24, 1861[8]

reinforced during the Mexican War. His unflinching actions on the battle-field were guided by his resolute Christian faith. He flirted with Catholicism while in Mexico (and became somewhat fluent in Spanish), was baptized in the Episcopal Church, and finally settled on Presbyterianism upon his return to Virginia. A common description of Jackson is that he lived by the New Testament but fought by the Old. He was a warm, tender, dutiful, and faithful husband. His first wife died in childbirth, and his second wife, Mary Anna, wrote that he "was a great advocate for marriage, appreciating the gentler sex so highly that whenever he met one of the 'unappropriated blessings' under the type of truest womanhood, he would wish that one of his bachelor friends could be fortunate enough to win her."[9]

Jackson spent ten years as an instructor of artillery at the Virginia Military Institute. He was not well-liked by the students, who gave him the nickname "Tom Fool." His uncle and mother had been teachers, but Jackson had not inherited their gift for pedagogy. He lectured by rote and answered questions by repeating what he had previously memorized. A follow-up question from a student resulted in punishment. Yet Jackson took his duty as a Christian seriously in regard to both his students and the black population of Lexington, Virginia. He began every lecture with a prayer in the hope that his students would be encouraged by the word of God, and he led Sunday school classes for the black population, both free and slave, of Lexington.

In the course of his adult life, Jackson owned six slaves. Four were given to him as wedding gifts, and two requested that he purchase them so that they could work for a man of Jackson's kind temperament. He honored their request. Like Lee, Jackson never made any statements in support of slavery. He was typical of many Southerners in his belief that slavery was ordained by God, that slaves had been given that burden by the hand of God, and that as a Christian man he was required to be a kind master. His pastor described his relationship to the black population of Lexington: "In their religious instruction he succeeded wonderfully. His discipline was systematic and firm, but very kind.... His servants reverenced and loved him, as they would have done a brother or father.... He was emphatically the black man's friend."[10]

Jackson was not a secessionist. He remained relatively neutral in the events leading to the "Secession Winter" of 1860 and 1861, but once Virginia determined to leave the Union, he supported the cause with a vigor virtually unmatched by anyone south of the Mason-Dixon line. He advised waging an aggressive war on the North, taking the bayonet to the enemy in the enemy's territory, but though his strategic assessment of the military situation in 1861 was probably correct and might have won the South the war, he was overruled by the more conservative members of the military brain trust, most importantly Confederate president Jefferson Davis. The war, they argued, had to be a just, defensive one to preserve the South. Lee shared Jackson's advocacy of an offensive war, but they differed about what the scope of such a conflict should be. The two men, however, would serve as the perfect one-two punch during the early years of the War Between the States. The pugnacious Jackson was the ideal complement to Lee's selectively aggressive style.

"Stonewall" Jackson earned his famous nickname during the first major engagement of the war, the First Battle of Manassas. His early efforts during the conflict had involved organizing and training several companies of Virginia volunteers in the Shenandoah Valley. "Stonewall's Brigade" was perhaps the best trained and disciplined group of men in the Southern army. They were affectionately

How the South Could Have Won the War

"We must make this campaign an exceedingly active one. Only thus can a weaker country cope with a stronger; it must make up in activity what it lacks in strength. A defensive campaign can only be made successful by taking the aggressive [offensive] at the proper time. Napoleon never waited for his adversary to become fully prepared, but struck him the first blow."

—Stonewall Jackson[11]

Great Generalship

"I yield to no man in sympathy for the gallant men under my command; but I am obliged to sweat them tonight, that I may save their blood tomorrow."

—Stonewall Jackson,
May 24, 1862[12]

referred to as the "foot cavalry" for their ability—at their commander's firm insistence—to ignore pain, suffering, and sickness in long and astoundingly quick marches.

These men saved the day at Manassas in July 1861 by standing firm against a punishing Union assault on Henry House Hill. General Bernard Bee of South Carolina said, after seeing Jackson and his men holding the line in the face of the onrushing Union army, "There is Jackson standing like a stone wall. Let us determine to die here and we will conquer. Rally behind the Virginians!" There is some debate as to whether Bee, soon killed in combat, was leveling praise or scorn at Jackson. Either way, the nickname stuck.

This was classic Jackson. The lead was flying, the situation tense, and Jackson steadily and bravely stared down the enemy. Because of Jackson and his men, what looked to be an early victory for the Union turned into an overwhelming one for the Confederacy, and a legend was born.

Jackson's fame only grew. With fewer men (often outnumbered four to one), he harried and tied up the Union army in the Shenandoah Valley in a campaign still studied at West Point today. His penchant for relentless attack struck fear into the hearts of the Union command. At one point a large detachment of Union men evacuated a town on the mere *suspicion* that Jackson was going to attack. He was, but his men were probably too sick and tired to fight. Such was the benefit of Jackson's disorienting, hard-hitting approach to battle. No one knew where Jackson was, and no one could predict what he would do next. His unconventional approach to warfare was pure military genius. Jackson understood human nature—particularly human nature in Karl von Clausewitz's "fog of war"—better than most. Most men did not share his calmness in the face of fire and would shrink when the action was too hot. Jackson always turned up the heat.

His most brilliant strategic plan would ultimately be his last. Jackson orchestrated the Confederate attack at Chancellorsville in 1863. He persuaded Lee to split his army, sending Jackson's corps to assault the Union right flank while Lee held off the Union forces at Fredericksburg. It was a risky maneuver, for they were outnumbered two to one, but making use of expert reconnaissance, Jackson was able to mount a surprise attack that pushed the Union right flank back against the Rappahannock River in a classic double envelopment. He struck quickly, and soon the Union troops were running from the Confederate assault. Jackson was scouting his forward position in the twilight when the 18th North Carolina Infantry mistook him and his staff for a Union detachment. They fired, striking Jackson three times. His left arm was amputated, but it was pneumonia that took Jackson's life one week later.

Master of the Elements of Victory

Jackson was "one of the most remarkable soldiers we have ever known. His mastery of two of the greatest elements for victory in war—surprise and envelopment—never has been surpassed. His magnetic personal leadership, which so dominated and inspired his men, constituted only one of his many attributes of greatness."

—General Douglas MacArthur[13]

He was alert until the end, saying he had always wanted to die on a Sunday. God granted him his wish. His last words, "Let us cross over the river and rest in the shade of the trees," were a fitting end to Jackson's life. He had found peace in war. The Confederate cause, however, would never be the same.

Lee struggled to find a substitute for Jackson's aggressive tactics and claimed later in life that had Jackson had been alive during the Battle of Gettysburg, the outcome would have been different, and the South would have won her independence. Fate intervened. The historian James Robertson has called Jackson "a man of arms surrounded by tenets of faith," and said that Jackson's biography was "the life story of an extraordinary man who became a general."[14] He was more than a master military mind. Jackson, as one of his former students said, was "a soldier of the cross."[15]

There have been few examples of American heroism to match those of Lee and Jackson. For years their names were synonymous with the qualities that all American men, both North and South, aspired to possess. These men have not been forgotten, but most children in the modern American education system would be hard pressed to identify the character traits that made them great. After the war was over, Lee once said, "I look forward to better days, and trust that time and experience, the great teachers of men, under the guidance of an ever-merciful God, may save us from destruction and restore to us the bright hopes and prospects of the past."[17] Lee and Jackson, two great names in the heroic American tradition, demand that restoration.

Hope, Robert E. Lee-Style

"My experience of men has neither disposed me to think worse of them nor indisposed me to serve them; nor, in spite of failures which I lament, of error which I now see and acknowledge, or of the present aspect of affairs, do I despair of the future. The truth is this: The march of Providence is so slow and our desires so impatient; the work of progress is so immense and our means of aiding it so feeble; the life of humanity is so long, that of the individual so brief, that we often see only the ebb of the advancing wave and are thus discouraged. It is history that teaches us to hope."

—Robert E. Lee,
September 1870[16]

Chapter 6

NORTHERNERS

Joshua Chamberlain and George Armstrong Custer

Until 1975, very few Americans outside of Maine had heard of Joshua Chamberlain. (The same cannot be said for George Armstrong Custer.) But because of the best-selling, Pulitzer Prize-winning novel *Killer Angels* by Michael Shaara, Chamberlain, "the Lion of the Round Top," has become the recognized Northern hero of the Battle of Gettysburg, and the 20th Maine has become synonymous with American heroism. Custer is still—unfairly—better known for his defeat at Little Bighorn than for his achievements during the American War Between the States. But both men exemplified Northern honor during the American Civil War. They were different (Chamberlain the reserved, studious, pious college professor and Custer the flamboyant professional cavalry officer) but nevertheless the war—nay, American history—would not have been the same without them. These Northerners placed an indelible stamp on all of America and they should be recognized North, South, East, and West for their heroic contributions to American society.

Did you know?

★ Joshua Chamberlain led his troops to victory at Little Round Top while suffering from malaria and dysentery

★ Despite numerous cavalry charges against great odds, Custer suffered only a minor shrapnel cut, the flu, and some poison oak in the War Between the States

★ When all else failed, Custer charged

The Lion of the Round Top

For the last thirty years, Joshua Chamberlain has been almost a caricature of the noble Northerner in the popular imagination, but from 1863 to 1975, few even knew of his role in the War. A monument dedicated to Chamberlain and the 20th Maine stood at Little Round Top, but it was hard to find and rarely visited. Jeff Daniels (perhaps better known to younger Americans for his role in *Dumb and Dumber*) portrayed Chamberlain in the films *Gettysburg* and *Gods and Generals*, and though he did a nice job, his interpretation made the hero of Maine almost a flawless man. Still, Chamberlain in real life was much as he is represented in *Killer Angels*, *Gods and Generals*, and the film adaptations of those books. Historians, a naturally skeptical lot, have questioned the validity of several of his noble deeds. Yet this makes him no less heroic—perhaps more so. Heroes have to muster courage, and victory, under moral threats to their lives, their men, and their cause. Chamberlain may not have been the flawless hero of historical fiction, but that matters little. He was still a hero.

Chamberlain was born in Brewer, Maine, in 1828, the oldest of five children. He was descended from a line of great Americans. His great-grandfathers had served in the American War for Independence. His grandfather had fought in the War of 1812, and his father took part in the "Aroostock War" (no shots were fired) of 1839. He enrolled in Bowdoin College in 1848, having taught himself ancient Greek in order to pass the entrance exams, and was graduated in 1852. He spent the next three years in seminary and returned to Bowdoin as a professor of rhetoric. He was fluent in ten languages and during his tenure at the college taught every subject offered at Bowdoin except math and science. Chamberlain was a popular and well-respected professor, a family man with two children and a good salary. But he was also a man with firm principles who believed that duty must supersede the comforts of home. Bowdoin attempted to keep him out of the war by appointing him chairman of the new department of modern languages at the college and granting him two years leave—presumably to travel and study in Europe. Chamberlain accepted, but only to gain time to finalize his plans for military service.

In the early years of the war, Chamberlain had encouraged his own students to serve. He considered the war a just cause and thought it was their patriotic duty. "Nearly a hundred of those who have been my pupils," he wrote to the governor when he volunteered in 1862, "are now officers in our army: but there are many more all over our State, who, I believe, would respond with enthusiasm, if summoned by me, and who would bring forward men enough to fill up a Regiment at once." He considered it hypocritical to champion the cause and yet sit idly by while other Mainers shed blood on the battlefield.

Remarkably, in light of his later exploits on the battlefield, Chamberlain had no formal military training (as he himself admitted). But he was a professional student, so he was able to learn. He read everything he could on military matters, and what he could not find in books he found in interviews with more seasoned soldiers. Chamberlain's studious habits bore fruit in the army. He was appointed lieutenant colonel of the 20th Maine in August 1862, and by the end of the war would be brevetted major general. Not bad for a college professor.

Chamberlain's leadership abilities made him great. He never asked his men to do anything he wasn't willing to do himself. He took six bullets or metal fragments during the war and was twice apparently on his deathbed.

No Chicken Hawk

"This war, so costly of blood and treasure, will not cease until the men of the North are willing to leave good positions, and sacrifice the dearest personal interests, to rescue our Country from Desolation, and defend the National Existence against treachery at home and jealousy abroad. This war must be ended, with a swift and strong hand; and every man ought to come forward and ask to be placed at his proper post."

—Joshua Chamberlain[1]

Each time he recovered, though one of the wounds probably did lead to his death, at the ripe age of eighty-five. He had three horses shot out from under him, but his last horse, Charlemagne, survived the war (though damaged, like his owner). Contemplating the prospect of being wounded or perhaps killed in the war, Chamberlain wrote his wife, "Most likely I shall be hit somewhere at sometime, but 'all my times are in His hand'... & no harm can come to me unless it is wisely & kindly ordered so."[2]

Chamberlain fought for the preservation of the Union. He may have been influenced by the writings of Harriet Beecher Stowe while a student at Bowdoin College (he succeeded her husband in his initial appointment as professor), but he was never an ardent abolitionist. He wrote in 1862 that he was fighting for "Nationality—the Law of Liberty.... we fight for all the guarantees of what men should love, for the protection and permanence and peace of what is most dear and sacred to every true heart."[3] He also consistently displayed respect for Southern soldiers. He defied their cause but admired their courage and honor. Chamberlain's largely autobiographical *The Passing of Armies*, published after his death in 1915, is full of praise for his one-time adversaries in gray.

He saw his first action at the Battle of Fredericksburg in December 1862. The cost of war was never more on display than here. Chamberlain wrote that he led the charge of the 20th Maine with the ground "bursting underfoot" and the "very sky... crashing down upon us" while the "bullets hissed like a seething sea." The bodies and limbs of the men who had already unsuccessfully attempted this charge against well-entrenched Confederate lines were stacked "in heaps" on the battlefield. As darkness fell, Chamberlain and the 20th Maine stopped and held their position on the wet, cold, "trampled and bloody field." They used the bodies of dead men for both cover and warmth. They had no blankets and those who stood up to try to find shelter were often cut down.[4] This was hell on earth, and the moaning of the wounded men on the battlefield amplified the suffering. The 20th was relieved the next day, and though Chamberlain had made it through his first battle unscathed, he would not always be so lucky.

Chamberlain happened into glory. He was the right man at the right time for the Union army, and it would not be a stretch to suggest that he saved the Union at the Battle of Gettysburg. On the second day of the battle, Chamberlain and the 20th Maine were charged with defending the hill that has since been called Little Round Top. Of the three days of Gettysburg, this was the best opportunity for the Confederacy to take the field. If not for Chamberlain, they might have. Outnumbered and outgunned, Chamberlain held off several Confederate attempts to take his position, the extreme left flank of the Union line. When his regiment ran out of ammunition, Chamberlain and the other officers led their men down the hill in a spirited bayonet charge. In the process, they captured 101 Confederate soldiers and worked like a hinge, consistently pushing the Confederate line inward. Chamberlain was hit twice in the action, though neither wound was severe. The fact that Chamberlain was suffering from malaria and dysentery during the battle makes his tactical decisions more remarkable.

Thirty years later, Chamberlain was awarded the Medal of Honor for his conduct, but he always said the true credit went to the men of the 20th Maine. They bravely held the line against apparently insurmountable odds and charged without ammunition. When

This Hallowed Ground of Heroes

"In great deeds, something abides. On great fields, something stays. Forms change and pass; bodies disappear; but spirits linger, to consecrate ground for the vision-place of souls.... generations that know us not and that we know not of, heart-drawn to see where and by whom great things were suffered and done for them, shall come to this deathless field, to ponder and dream; and lo! the shadow of a mighty presence shall wrap them in its bosom, and the power of the vision pass into their souls."

—Joshua Chamberlain,
upon returning to
Gettysburg late in life

asked why men would face fire on the battlefield, Chamberlain once wrote that it was "simple manhood, force of discipline, pride, love, or bond of comradeship" that made it possible. An officer, he suggested, acts bravely because he is "so absorbed by the sense of responsibility for his men, for his cause, or for the fight that the... instinct to seek safety is overcome by the instinct of honor."[5] Chamberlain knew better than most. A veteran of twenty battles by the conclusion of hostilities, he had witnessed first hand the effects of combat, both mental and physical. If there was ever an American expert on why men fought in that war or any other, it would be Joshua Chamberlain.

Chamberlain was promoted to brigadier general in 1864 shortly before the Battle of Petersburg began. In the early days of that action, he was shot laterally through the hips, a wound that was presumed fatal in 1864. Believing in Chamberlain's impending doom, Ulysses S. Grant brevetted him to major general so he could die at that rank. Miraculously, Chamberlain survived, though the pain and infections caused by the wound would linger for the remainder of his life. He rejoined the fight during Grant's Overland Campaign but again was wounded, this time shot just below the heart. The bullet was deflected by his leather case of field orders and ended up only breaking two ribs and bruising his arm, yet Chamberlain passed out, apparently in his final minutes of life. New York papers printed his obituary. Thankfully again for the Union cause, they were wrong. Chamberlain wrote his mother after one of his many wounds, "I am not scared or hurt enough yet to be willing to face the rear, when other men are marching to the front." It was "honor and manliness" that kept him in the field.[6]

In the final two weeks of the war, Chamberlain, though he received another grave wound, was responsible for punching a hole in the Confederate defenses around Petersburg, and then later participated in the assault that destroyed Lee's right flank and the attack that dislodged him from his entrenched line in front of Richmond. Chamberlain then marched his men, almost in a run, to block Lee's final attempt at escape. Lee had finally run out of options. Chamberlain received word from one of General John B. Gordon's staff officers on April 9, 1865, that Lee intended to surrender. The war had come to an end, but Chamberlain did one more heroic act.

Chamberlain was chosen to receive the formal surrender of the Army of Northern Virginia on April 12, 1865. This was a solemn event, and an honor for the Lion of Little Round Top. Grant could have chosen any one of several other general officers who ranked Chamberlain, but Chamberlain had served the Union heroically and Grant believed he deserved the duty. The choice was perfect. As General Gordon and his men gravely marched by Chamberlain and the 20th Maine, heads buried in their chests, in some cases tears in their eyes, Chamberlain ordered his men to "carry arms" in salute of the Confederate soldiers. Gordon, realizing the honor, snapped to and reciprocated. This was a final gesture of respect for a defeated but gallant foe, and years later Gordon called Chamberlain the "knightliest man" in the Union army.

Northerners criticized what Chamberlain had done, but he understood that the wounds of the war needed to be healed quickly. He wrote that his salute was not for the Confederate cause, but for Confederate courage. "Before us in proud humiliation stood the embodiment of manhood... thin, worn, and famished but erect, and with eyes looking level into ours, waking memories that bound us together as no other bond;—was not such manhood to be welcomed back into a Union so tested and assured?"[7] This was showing a masculine generosity to a defeated people. If only all Northerners had shown such manly courage and respect.

After an illustrious post-war career—four times the governor of Maine, president of Bowdoin College—Joshua Chamberlain died in 1914 of complications from his 1864 wounds, the last Civil War veteran known to have died from injuries suffered in combat.

The Tide Turns

Mainstream historians have generally overlooked evidence that challenges the traditional narrative about the War Between the States. No longer. These two books by established mainstream historians question the accepted interpretation that the war was simply a test of good versus evil, an anti-slavery North against a pro-slavery South. The second of these books even dares to ask, was the war necessary?

The Union War by Gary Gallagher (Cambridge, MA: Harvard University Press, 2011).

America Aflame: How the Civil War Created a Nation by David Goldfield (New York: Bloomsbury Press, 2012).

The Cavalier

If Joshua Chamberlain was the common man's knight, then George Armstrong Custer was the nobility. He admired all things aristocratic, loved Southern culture, and wanted to be a cavalier. He even looked and often acted the part. His flowing blonde curly locks and cavalier mustache and beard made him seem like a royalist soldier from the English Civil War of the 1640s. Custer had an independent spirit that was difficult to tame. He relished charging headlong into the teeth of the enemy. That is all he was doing at 1876 at Little Bighorn. He was often criticized for his reckless zeal, but that was Custer, and no amount of military discipline could corral him.

Custer was born in Ohio in 1839, the son of a farmer and blacksmith. He spent time in Michigan and was eventually admitted to the United States Military Academy at West Point. He finished last in his class and ended his time at West Point with a court-martial. Custer openly flaunted the rules, and the student body loved him for it. He was the king of demerits. The infractions ranged from "Calling Corporal in a boisterous tone of voice," to "throwing snowballs," to bringing food and utensils into his often "grossly out of order" quarters. Custer was bright, but like other adventurous souls he thought study and discipline got in the way of his fun. He drank and cussed and at times caused general mayhem. Custer was a ball of fire both in life and in combat. He lived and died on the edge.

Custer was graduated in 1861 just before the opening salvos at First Manassas. The "Boy General," as he was often called later in the war, shone in combat, but not because of any real tactical genius. His greatest moves were orchestrated by someone else. No, Custer changed the outcome of battles because when all else failed, Custer charged.

He did little at First Manassas. It was not until the Peninsula Campaign of 1862 that he distinguished himself, and at first not on the battlefield. In the early days of the campaign, Custer bravely conducted reconnaissance for Union General William F. "Baldy" Smith in a hot air balloon. The Confederate army knew he was floating overhead and could have shot him down, but they didn't; and Custer went up in that balloon every day until the Confederate army retreated.

Shortly thereafter, Custer charged into the Chickahominy River to test its depth. The Union needed to cross the river, but the bridge was gone, and General George B. McClellan's engineer needed to know if it could be forded. Custer proved it could. As a reward, Custer was allowed to lead four companies in a surprise attack near New Bridge, Virginia. It was a smashing success that netted fifty Confederate prisoners and may have resulted in the first captured Confederate Battle Flag of the war. McClellan gave Custer a brevet promotion to major and asked him to join his staff.

Custer enjoyed the spotlight and the "hunt" and adrenaline of battle. His first confirmed kill was a large Confederate officer mounted on a thoroughbred. Custer chased him down, told him to surrender, and when he refused, Custer killed him and took his beautiful saddle and sword. He wrote to his sister, "It was his own fault; I told him twice to surrender."[8] Custer had the reputation of being reckless, gallant, and stubborn. He was also perceived as something of a dandy, a frivolous glory-seeker who had Lady Luck—or perhaps God—on his side.

Abraham Lincoln sacked McClellan after he failed to capture Richmond in 1862, and as a result Custer was again reduced in rank to a lieutenant. That did not change his style. He joined the staff of General Alfred Pleasanton; the two men shared a love for flamboyancy and self-promotion. It was under Pleasanton's liberal regime that Custer adopted his trademark "uniform." He wore gold lace on his pants, Confederate boots, and a hat that more closely resembled a Confederate kepi than the Union cavalry headgear.

A Cavalry Commander's Religion

"I have never prayed as others do. Yet, on the eve of every battle in which I have been engaged, I have never omitted to pray inwardly, devoutly. Never have I failed to commend myself to God's keeping, asking Him to forgive my past sins, and to watch over me while in danger.... After having done so all anxiety for myself, here or hereafter, is dispelled. I feel that my destiny is in the hands of the Almighty. This belief, more than any other fact or reason, makes me brave and fearless as I am."[9]

—George Custer

His blue navy shirt, tight jacket with gold loops, and red necktie made him stand out on the battlefield. That was the point. When he was promoted to brigadier general in 1863, he acquired two stars and had them sewn on his jacket as well.

There was more to Custer, however, than image. While Pleasanton often embellished his battlefield exploits, Custer didn't have to. He would charge into the teeth of battle, and yet with the exception of a minor cut by shrapnel, a case of the flu, and a bit of poison oak, Custer was unharmed during the war. He once charged a Confederate force which outnumbered his own five to one. And at the Battle of Aldie, he charged ahead so far and so fast that he found himself well behind Confederate lines. It was only because of his non-regulation uniform that he was able to make it out alive; they thought he was one of them. On another occasion he charged an entire Confederate division with only four hundred volunteers. Eighty-six were killed, but the Confederate advance was stopped. Custer rode out front. This may seem suicidal, but Custer thought it heroic.

This type of mettle was bound to be noticed, and Custer finally had his chance to shine on the big stage when he was given command of the third division of the Cavalry Corps of the Army of the Potomac. He was twenty-three, the youngest general officer in the Union, and he didn't disappoint.

On July 2, 1863, Custer led his first charge at Gettysburg. He had his horse shot out from beneath him and was repulsed by Wade Hampton, but he was cited for gallantry. On the following day, Custer was ordered to protect General George Meade's rear from Confederate General J.E.B. Stuart. He did so with unmatched enthusiasm.

His first order to charge came in the midst of heavy action. Custer took the lead, as he always did, and one-fourth of the mostly inexperienced soldiers who followed him fell to their doom. He regrouped and charged again, this time at the head of his best regiment. To the cry of "Come on, you Wolverines!" Custer blasted into the Confederate line. The clash of the armies was so intense that horses toppled over and the "fog of war" blinded the combatants. This was vicious hand-to-hand combat. When the action cooled, the Confederate cavalry, Stuart's Invincibles, were retreating. Custer had won the day.

For Custer, the rest of the war carried on in similar fashion. War often brought out the worst in men; the intense stress of battle, both mental and physical, broke their spirits. Not Custer's. He throve on the action, which appeared almost fun to him. Men died, lost

"Without Fear and Beyond Reproach"

"These days it is stylish to denigrate the general, whose stock sells for nothing. Nineteenth-century Americans thought differently. At that time he was a cavalier without fear and beyond reproach."

—Historian Evan Connell on George Custer[10]

limbs, and were mutilated (including his brother, who was shot in the face). Custer washed his hands, preened his mustache, oiled his hair with cinnamon, brushed his teeth, danced and sang, and even found time to flirt and marry during the war. The "horrors of war" never fazed him. Life carried on almost as if the war was a distraction, a play in which he was a leading actor, but never a life-and-death struggle. Perhaps it was his youth and boyish enthusiasm, or perhaps it was his firm belief in divine protection. Either way, Custer never worried about his fate. He charged forward into the teeth of battle "with a whoop and a shout,"[11] never thinking of the consequences. He gave up drinking rum only after stumbling home so drunk that his sister prayed for intervention. In the process, Custer became a staunch Christian, but he never abandoned his cavalier ways. Custer could not be tamed.

The last years of the war saw him under the command of General Philip Sheridan, the most notorious Union cavalry commander. Sheridan liked Custer, simply because he charged without orders and took the fight to the enemy with ruthless passion. Custer did not hate Southerners. He thought they deserved to lose, but he had respect for them as a people, admired their courage in battle, and saw them as an able and honorable foe. He had his band play "Dixie" during the Southern surrender and became an Andrew Johnson Democrat after the war because he thought the Republicans were extracting too much pain and suffering from the Southern people during Reconstruction. Like Chamberlain, he favored "resumption" over "reconstruction."

After the war, Custer was assigned by Sheridan to the West. This assignment was dreadfully boring to the adventure-seeking cavalry officer. After being busted to captain, he thought about serving as a mercenary in the Mexican army—President Grant even wrote a letter of recommendation—but that opportunity fell through. Eventually he was promoted to lieutenant colonel of the 7th Cavalry Regiment and dispatched to the Dakota Territory to fight the Sioux. He brought several family members with him, including even his wife. Custer loved her company. If nothing else can be said for Custer's character, he was a loyal and devoted husband.

Custer's wartime heroics are overshadowed by his supposedly igno-minious defeat at the hands of the Sioux at Little Bighorn in 1876. Custer is often por-trayed as the polar opposite of the noble Indian; he is the quintessential American trespassing on the Indians' lands, waging war in a way alien to them, causing mayhem among their people—and he got his come-uppance. The conventional story is a concat-

> ### A Book You're Not Supposed to Read
>
> *Son of the Morning Star* by Evan S. Connell (San Francisco, CA: North Point Press, 1984).

enation of second-hand accounts, conflicting testimonies, and attempts at character assassination by those who considered Custer an impudent glory-seeker or a brutal "iron ass"—as his men sometimes did call him. The truth is that no one actually knows what happened on that fateful day in June 1876, beyond the bare facts. Custer charged and was surrounded, defeated, killed, and mutilated.

It is true that Sheridan and William Tecumseh Sherman, neither man a stranger to total war, advocated a punishing strategy in the West that ulti-mately resulted in terrible atrocities by American soldiers. On the other hand, the Indians responded in kind, and also initiated brutalities. Settlers recounted terrifying encounters with Indian braves on the warpath; their violence knew no limitations of age, sex, or condition. Settlers in the wrong place at the wrong time were shown no quarter. As a result, none was given by them.

Custer did not hate Indians, nor did he always concur with the tactics being used to root them out of the West. He believed the Indians had legit-imate complaints about their often unfair treatment, but he also agreed that they needed to be "civilized" and given a heavy dose of Christianity.

Historian Evan Connell has, in fact, compared Custer to his formidable adversary, Crazy Horse. Both men had an air of invincibility, a dash of recklessness, and a fierce warrior's spirit. They were both heroes to their people.

Regardless of his defeat at Little Bighorn and the circumstances surrounding it, Custer should be remembered for his gallantry in the War Between the States and for his even-handed treatment of Southerners both during and after the war. Those accomplishments alone made him heroic. The other qualities—his brash, intemperate, but often winning conduct on the battlefield; his loyalty; his devotion; his honesty; his manly defense of principle—are simply icing on the cake. In an age when such qualities are often penalized rather than rewarded, Custer serves as a beacon. He was not the best military mind in the nineteenth century—far from it—but he was certainly near the bravest man in the army during his brief life. He should be commended, not despised, for his dedication to his cause.

Several heroes emerged from the War Between the States, both North and South. War tends to have that effect, but one could argue that Chamberlain and Custer were born to be heroes. Their personalities determined that they would find lasting fame and that without them the Union cause and hence American history might have turned out differently. They were not marble statues, and each had personality foibles, but those faults seem almost insignificant when weighted against their positive attributes. Their foes respected them, and perhaps that is their greatest tribute. They fought honorably, won honorably, and served honorably. In the end, one cannot ask for more.

Chapter 7

TRADITIONAL WOMEN

Mercy Otis Warren, Augusta Jane Evans, and Juliette Gordon Low

efore the "women's rights" movements of the twentieth century and the infatuation with suffrage and careers, women, as mothers and wives, molded the future. They reared their children on the history of their clan, community, and country; ran households; helped shape the destinies of their sons and husbands though careful encouragement; and participated in charity and philanthropy. The most astute among them understood their power and carefully guarded these roles for their daughters. They were the backbone of society. They were the guardians of the traditions, the customs, the manners, the morals of America. It would not be a stretch to say that the radical modern change in the roles and habits of women has contributed to a dramatic societal decline.

The traditional woman was not weak or subservient, at least not in the way modern feminists would suggest. She was an intelligent, strong-willed, witty, and supportive companion to her husband, the hub of her family, and an irreplaceable asset to her community. She did not need political office because she held sway in the home, where her job was often more rigorous than any career. Three women, all from different states and different generations, exemplify the spirit of traditional American womanhood: Mercy

Did you know?

★ Mercy Otis Warren called fellow supporter of American independence Tom Paine "blasphemous and without principle"

★ Augusta Jane Evans, best-selling Southern novelist, argued against communism in 1866

★ Juliette Gordon Low, founder of the Girl Scouts, was a proponent of purity and modesty for girls

A Book You're Not Supposed to Read

The Politically Incorrect Guide™ *to Women, Sex, and Feminism* by Carrie L. Lukas (Washington, DC: Regnery, 2006).

Mercy Otis Warren, Colonial Spitfire

"There was always a tang in her words like that of good honest cider or the west October wind. She could not only think and feel, but most emphatically she could speak."

—Alice Brown[2]

Otis Warren of Massachusetts, Augusta Jane Evans of Alabama, and Juliette Gordon Low of Georgia.

A Heroine and a Patriot

John Adams—after a three-month quarrel with Mercy Otis Warren—once wrote that "History is not the Province of the Ladies."[1] He had been enflamed by Warren's criticism of his administration, in particular by Warren's suggestion that his personality made him unfit for the executive office. Warren had never held her tongue, at least not in regard to history and politics. She had the pleasure of being in the inner circle of Massachusetts society during the founding period. Her husband, James Warren, was a famous and well-respected patriot who served both in the Massachusetts government and as paymaster for the Continental Army during the American War for Independence. Because of his positions, she knew not only the wives of various colonial leaders, but also the leading men in the cause for independence. Mercy Otis Warren corresponded frequently with John Adams, Samuel Adams, Thomas Jefferson, John Dickinson, Elbridge Gerry, and Henry Knox.

Mercy Otis Warren was a feminist for her time—though perhaps not quite as much so as Abigail Adams. Warren had five sons and performed her duties as a mother and wife admirably, but she also believed that women deserved an education, and she scoffed at the notion that women were inferior to men. She chided society for placing too much emphasis on the education of boys while neglecting girls: "It is my Opinion that that Part of the human Species who think Nature (as well as the infinitely wise & Supreme Author thereof) has given them the Superiority over the other, mistake their own Happiness when they neglect the Culture of Reason in their Daughters while they take all possible Methods of improving it in their sons."[3] Yet Warren was at least comfortable with the societal constraints of the time, and she often advised women to play along, in relation to men.

She had contempt for laziness and illiteracy in both sexes: "When the Cultivation of the Mind is neglected in Either Sex, we see Ignorance, Stupidity, & Ferocity of Manners equally Conspicuous in Both."[5] Warren herself was no intellectual slouch. She read voraciously on diverse subjects, from philosophy and religion to politics and history. She dabbled in literature as a writer, publishing several plays and political satires and a collection of poetry in 1790 titled *Poems Dramatic and Miscellaneous*. In that volume, the words of her dedication to George Washington drip with patriotism and devotion to republican principles.

Women's Empowerment, Eighteenth-Century-Style

"My dear, it may be necessary for you to *seem* inferior; but you need not be so. Let them have their little game, since it may have been so willed. It won't hurt you; it will amuse them."

—Mercy Otis Warren[4]

Some have described her as "democratic," but Warren considered America a republic in the Roman sense. Her *Poems* included a tragedy on the downfall of Rome, and she believed that in the cause of independence Americans had exhibited virtue and morality comparable to those of the ancients—in contrast to modern European decadence. In fact, Warren was a critic of the "democratic" and anti-religious strains in the thought of her day. She despised the French philosophe Voltaire and the liberal Scotsman

A Prescient Warning

In a poem entitled "Simplicity," Warren laments the day when a future America would fall into the decadence of European society:

"Ocean rebounds, and earth reverberates,
And Heaven confirms the independent states;
While time rolls on, and mighty kingdoms fail,
They, peace and freedom on their heirs entail,
Till virtue sinks, and in far distant times,
Dies in the vortex of European crimes."

—Mercy Otis Warren

A Book You're Not Supposed to Read

History of the Rise, Progress, and Termination of the American Revolution by Mercy Otis Warren, (1805), 3 vols.

David Hume for their stand against Christianity. Warren called the works of Tom Paine, the famous American democratic (and anti-Christian) pamphleteer, "blasphemous and without principle."[6] She railed against threats to American virtue during the crisis of war and thought that every bedside needed a Bible during the dark days of conflict with Britain.

Warren's razor wit, caustic pen, and penetrating intellect produced one of the best works of history of the early nineteenth century. Her *History of the Rise, Progress, and Termination of the American Revolution*, published in three volumes in 1805, was more than a treatise on the War for Independence. It was a sweeping defense of American liberty and the principles of 1776. This was her gift to her sons and their posterity, an American tale told on her knee for future generations of American mothers to give to their children. John Adams may have found fault with Warren's audacity in writing such a history, but history has long been the province of the ladies, and Warren shone at it.

She consistently referred to the American republican spirit and called on Americans to maintain the principles of the War for Independence. In the concluding chapter of volume three of her history of the war, Warren discussed the effects of the Constitution on American republicanism. She feared that the

Constitution granted too much power to the central government, fretted over a consolidation of the states, and virtually wept at the loss of liberty she supposed would continue unabated into the future. Warren opposed the Constitution (before it was amended by the Bill of Rights) not because she was un-American but because she *was* a patriotic American. Her attitude is difficult for modern Americans to understand, and of course in the two intervening centuries the Constitution (now including the Bill of Rights) has proven to be a lasting (if flawed) instrument of government. But Warren, like other opponents of the Constitution, accurately foresaw that it could bring about many of the problems America faces today. She was a heroine of independence and republicanism, a female Cato attempting to hold back the tides of centralization, tyranny, and despotism. That is what angered Adams and endeared her to Jefferson. Her history has been largely forgotten, but Warren was a true American patriot and heroine, a model of feminine virtue, and an inspiration for young American women.

The Principles of 1776 Endangered by the Constitution

"The observers of human conduct were not insensible, that too much power vested in the hands of any individual, was liable to abuses, either from his own passions, or the suggestions of others, of less upright and immaculate intentions than himself."

—Mercy Otis Warren[7]

A Beacon of Traditional Womanhood

Though born almost a hundred years later and over a thousand miles away in Columbus, Georgia, Augusta Jane Evans had much in common with Mercy Otis Warren. Both believed in educating women well, both were successful authors, both were uncomfortable with the direction of feminism in their time, both were patriots who believed in the principles of 1776, and both suffered through terrible wars—though Evans would claim that the

Confederate defeat in 1865 dashed all of her enthusiasm. Warren personified the republican North, Evans the republican South, but both were distinctively American heroines.

Evans's family was from South Carolina. She was the oldest of eight children and was largely educated at home by her mother. The family moved to Texas in the early 1840s but returned east to Alabama in 1849, settling in Mobile. Evans wrote her first novel at fifteen or sixteen while the family was still living in Texas. Every one of her works had a female lead, and Evans lived much of her life through her characters. Her heroines shared her political, religious, and societal views, and they were model women—chaste, moral, intelligent, strong, honest, and dedicated. They were what she intended women to be and what she thought society needed from the fairer sex. "The real woman"—as Evans called her—was to be the spiritual and moral guide of man and the glue that held a people together.

Her two most important works were published during the difficult 1860s. The first, *Macaria; Or, Altars of Sacrifice*, was dedicated to the Confederate soldiers and the women who sacrificed on the home front during the War Between the States. They were fighting, in her words, to "deliver the South from despotism" and win "constitutional republican liberty." She wrote the book by candlelight while serving as a nurse to wounded Confederate soldiers, her mind never far from the horrors of war or the cause for which they bled. She could not serve in the army, but Evans hoped her literary offering would galvanize Southern spirits and help deliver victory on the battlefield. *Macaria* was popular in both the North and South, and was smuggled through Northern lines during the War. One Union general ordered it burned because of the influence it had on his men. Southerners must be reduced to a brood of ignorant, treasonous, rebelling hayseeds; it would be better to have a truer image of them burned than to allow minds to be swayed in the rebels' favor.

Evans understood that the world was watching the Confederacy. She desired that the Southern people become a beacon of artistic and literary achievement. Her character Electra wished for the Confederacy, in the days after victory, to be a "marble-hearted land… which Southern genius can mold into monuments of imperishable beauty. This war furnishes instances of heroism before which all other records pale, and our Poets, Sculptors, and Painters have only to look around them for subjects which Greek or Italian Art would glorify and immortalize."[8] Women, of course, were society's backbone. Left at home during the War, they were working to cultivate an artistic spirit unmatched since the ancient world. Evans saturated *Macaria* and her other novels with references to Greek, Roman, and Egyptian history. Her understanding of political philosophy was second to none, and her accuracy in depicting human nature was superb. Evans was no flirty, weak-minded, giggling girl. She deplored and destroyed that stereotype. Her characters give themselves to romance and to men, but they—relying on a woman's true moral compass—dictate the terms.

She made her view on women's empowerment clear in her masterpiece, *St. Elmo*, published in 1866. Evans held the cause of women's suffrage in low regard and scoffed at

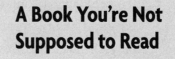

A Book You're Not Supposed to Read

St. Elmo by Augusta Jane Evans (1866).

"bluestockings," educated women who shunned the traditional role of wife, mother, and caregiver for politics and speaking engagements. Her anti-suffrage position puts her at odds with modern society, but she was not alone in the nineteenth century. While the modern reader may laugh at her quaint provincialism, her reasoning, made clear in *St. Elmo*, stemmed from her faith and her dedication to "womankind."

Edna Earl, the main character in *St. Elmo*, is a devout, pious, pure, well-read, beautiful, and intelligent young woman, the model of Christian virtue. She falls in love with an immoral scoundrel, St. Elmo, but does not allow herself to express her interest because he is unworthy of her love. She pities him and prays for him, and though her heart is his, she never betrays her feelings. As a result, she spends much of her young life engaged in study, in nursing sick children, writing critically acclaimed books and articles, and fighting off suitors who boast high social status and money but who cannot win her pure heart. In the end, Edna is able to reform St. Elmo. He returns to Christ, becomes a minister, and marries Edna. While it is a great romance, *St. Elmo* is also a political tale interwoven with social critique.

For example, Evans, through Edna Earl, argued that women should "jealously [contend] for every woman's right which God and nature had decreed the sex. The right to be learned, wise, noble, useful, in woman's divinely limited sphere; the right to influence and exalt the circle in which she moved; the right to mount the sanctified bema of her own quiet hearthstone; the right to modify and direct her husband's opinions… the right to make her children ornaments to their nation… the right to advise, to plead, to pray; the right to make her desk a Delphi, if God so permitted; the right to be all that the phrase 'noble, Christian woman' means." But she cautioned her fellow woman against involving herself in anything that might "trail her heaven-born purity through the dust and mire of political strife."[9]

In *St. Elmo*, Evans described her heroine's writing career in words that could just as easily be applied to her own:

> The tendency of the age was to equality and communism, and this, she contended was undermining the golden thrones shining in the blessed and hallowed light of the hearth, whence every true woman ruled the realm of her own family. Regarding every pseudo "reform" which struck down the social and political distinction of the sexes, as a blow that crushed one of the pillars

of woman's throne, she earnestly warned the Crowned Heads of
the danger to be apprehended from the unfortunate and deluded
female malcontents... and to proud happy mothers, guarded by
Praetorian bands of children, she reiterated the assurance that
"Those who rock the cradle rule the world." Most carefully she
sifted the records of history, tracing in every epoch the sover-
eigns of the hearth-throne who had reigned wisely and content-
edly, ennobling and refining humanity; and she proved by
illustrious examples that the borders of the feminine realm could
not be enlarged, without rendering the throne unsteady, and
subverting God's law of order.[10]

Politics, Evans pointed out, has never proved to be the salvation of the
human race. Women, most importantly mothers and wives, had long been
the calming factor, the guiding hand, and the nurturing vessel of a prosperous and peaceful people. Neither voting nor political office were necessary
when women already held such power over men.

Critics complained that Evans's writing style was too pedantic, that her
heroine seemed to have "swallowed an unabridged dictionary." Admittedly,
St. Elmo is difficult to wade through at times. Evans's use of historical references and religious imagery places a strain on the reader, but the book
was widely popular—what we would call a best-seller. Evans did not marry
until 1868, when she was in her thirties. She spent the next forty years of
her life in Mobile, Alabama, writing several more books, all dedicated to
the virtues of the "noble, Christian woman" and the difficulties women
faced in the modern age. She died in 1909, but well into the twentieth century, Evans's *St. Elmo* was a well-worn handbook for the traditional woman.
Several generations of women read it and then required their daughters and
granddaughters to read it as well. Evans should be respected, if for nothing
else, for her dedication to the hearth and home, to the moral fabric of

America, and—most importantly—to the idea that women should use their strength and intelligence to mold future generations by their actions at home. Women, in Evans's view, set the standard.

The Girl Scouts' Misunderstood Founder

In May 2012 Juliette Gordon Low was awarded the Medal of Freedom. Because the Girl Scouts are celebrating their hundredth anniversary, Low has been a topic of discussion on talk shows, morning news programs, and the Internet. Unfortunately, and incorrectly, the Left (including the current leadership of the Girl Scouts) has claimed her as one of their own and made her out to be a champion of modern feminism. Low had a different message; in fact, the Girl Scouts have strayed so far from Low's vision that she would barely recognize the organization.

Juliette Gordon Low, often called "Daisy," was born in Savannah, Georgia, in 1860, the daughter of William Washington Gordon and his wife Eleanor Kinzie. Juliette's grandmother was reported to have been the first white child born in Chicago. Low's childhood was shaped by the War Between the States. Her father was a captain in the Confederate army, and when William T. Sherman captured Savannah in 1864, the families of all Confederate officers were ordered out of the city. Her mother removed the family to Chicago, and Low spent the remainder of the war there.

Low's mother eventually sent her to several fine boarding schools in Virginia, New Jersey, and New York. Low had all the charm and grace of a "Southern belle." It was said she had a disarming sense of humor and a warmth that could win over the coldest soul. She went partially deaf in one ear in 1885 and in the other in 1886, in both cases because of medical accidents. She married a wealthy cotton merchant in 1886 and for several years split her time among Georgia, England, and Scotland. The marriage was unsuccessful at best and ultimately embarrassing. The couple had no children, and Low's husband, William Mackay Low, was a notorious womanizer. He wanted a divorce, but Daisy refused to grant him one. In an act of desperation, he moved his mistress into their home and evicted Daisy. She then agreed to the divorce, but before it was final her husband died—leaving his fortune to his mistress. Low sued and was successful in retaining at least her home in Georgia.

After her husband's death, Low traveled and spent time in the United States working in convalescent care during the Spanish-American War of 1898. Her father had been commissioned a general in the United States army, and Low focused her efforts on the welfare of soldiers returning from war. She was also an accomplished artist and helped found the Savannah Art Club. Upon returning to England after the war, Low met and befriended Sir Robert Baden-Powell, founder of the Boy Scouts, and his sister Agnes, founder of the Girl Guides. Soon she was hooked. She started three troops in England and Scotland and began making plans to organize a similar group in the United States.

Because Low had no children, the Girl Guides offered her a unique opportunity to teach girls life skills, womanly virtue, and

> ## Low's Advice to Girls
>
> "Throughout our history the emergency seems always to have found the man. And they have been prepared by our great women. For even if a man has not a wife it is seldom that any great thing is done that is not helped on by a woman. Girls, know your places. They are no mean positions that you are destined to hold. The pages of the history of the future may hold your names in a high and honored place. Do well your part today. The work of today is the history of tomorrow, and we are its makers."
>
> —Juliette Gordon Low[11]

independent. The original charge was to create "guides" as the name suggests, female stewards for the betterment of society, working both at home and in the community. The "home" component was always explicit in the mission. Low established the first American troop in 1912 in Savannah, Georgia. The next year, the organization was renamed the Girl Scouts and in 1915, after the organization was incorporated, Low was named president, a position she held until 1920 when her title was changed to "founder."

In 1916, Low wrote *How Girls Can Help Their Country*, a guide to scouting based on the books by the Baden-Powells that were available in England. This was the first Girl Scout handbook in America, and it reflected Low's opinions on scouting and the role of girls and women in society, both at home and in the community.

She listed ten "laws" that Girl Scout captains had to obey and that all girls should strive to learn and live up to: honor, loyalty, usefulness and helpfulness to others, a friendship to all and a sisterhood with all girl scouts, courtesy, cheerfulness, being a friend to animals, obedience, purity, and thrift. Compare her law on purity, "A Girl Scout keeps herself pure in thought and word and deed,"[12] with current statements on the Girl Scouts website, in particular those advanced in a book promoted by the Girl Scouts entitled *Teens before Their Time*. "Family members… should not prevent the girls from growing up."[13] Translation—the Girl Scouts today accept changing societal norms about relationships and reject traditional notions of "purity." By not denouncing the sexualization of preteens, the modern Girl Scouts essentially condone it. Low had a much better approach.

In a section entitled "Self-Improvement," Low emphasized that in the "Great Law of Life," "the influence of women over men is vastly greater than that of men over one another." She believed this imparted "to girls and women a peculiar power and responsibility, for no Girl Scout or other honorable woman—whether old or young—could use her influence as a woman excepting to strengthen

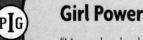

Girl Power

"Many a boy has been strengthened in his character and his whole life made happier by the brave refusal of a girl to do wrong; while the opposite weakness has been the cause of endless misery and wretchedness."

—Juliette Gordon Low[14]

the characters and to support the honor of the men and boys with whom she comes in contact." Girl Scouts were to be guides to the opposite sex, for "there are two kinds of women,—one kind that builds men up, and the other that pulls men down; and there is no doubt as to where a Girl Scout should stand." This did *not* mean that women were to rule men. "On the contrary... [understanding her power to influence men] should make her humble and watchful to be faithful to her trust."

Low, of course, was suggesting that girls exert positive peer pressure. Immorality, she believed, was not likely to be a problem unless girls succumbed to the dual threat of vanity and the *"desire to be admired."* Girls, Low wrote, should be faithful to themselves, be constantly on guard to improve their minds, bodies, and souls, and use their strength "to fight for the right of life in another." She believed it was selflessness that made women strong: "Be prepared, therefore, to do a true woman's full duty to her men by never allowing the desire for admiration to rule your actions, words, or thoughts."[15]

Low cautioned girls to be modest:

> Girls of good feeling should be especially careful to be modest in dress and deportment on social occasions. Unfortunately many girls who are perfectly innocent and unconscious, cause comment and are the cause of improper feelings being aroused among their companions. Girls should not risk, by their manner of dress or method of dancing, bringing temptation to others. It is easily possible for a girl to exert an excellent influence upon her friends by setting a proper example.[16]

While she recognized that most women were homemakers—as she noted, a woman "is sure to have to 'keep house' some day, and whatever house she finds herself in, it is certain that that place is the better for her being there"[17]—she encouraged women to seek employment and a career if that suited them. Either way, Low insisted that women cultivate thrift, economy, and independence. The object was not to supplant men, but to help guide society. Low had no problem with traditional gender roles. On the contrary, she believed that men and women complemented one another. The goal was for them to act as a team, both building on the strengths and remedying the weaknesses of each. That was the model of feminine virtue.

Warren, Evans, and Low personify the traditional woman. All believed in a moral society guided by the fairer sex, all thought that women were the intellectual equals of men, and yet all believed that traditional gender roles kept society properly organized and maintained continuity between generations. Women held society together. In our age, when both sexes seem to be drifting into a self-idolatry of selfish devotion to career and personal pursuits, these women offer a different and refreshing ideal—the nurturing hand of a mother, wife, or grandmother who devotes herself to her family and the community without regard to fame or fortune. This position seems quaint now, but perhaps there will come a time when Americans, looking on our crumbling civilization, realize that traditional morals, values, and even roles for women suited mankind better than the progressive dogmas we have been ingesting for years. After all, the traditional values were built on the wisdom of successive generations, not modern fads and theories. Perhaps by the time we realize their wisdom it may already be too late.

Chapter 8

CAPTAINS OF INDUSTRY

John D. Rockefeller and Andrew Carnegie

n 1934, journalist and historian Matthew Josephson described the leading American industrialists of the late nineteenth century as the "robber barons." According to Josephson, a progressive historian, they had plundered the American people and destroyed the American political and legal system, while their pursuit of wealth drastically offset any good that came from their philanthropic activities. Mark Twain labeled this period in American history the "Gilded Age," for many of the "new rich" were simply gold-plated, unrefined, and corrupt ruffians. This has become the standard interpretation of the period. The demonization of nineteenth-century businessmen serves as propaganda for modern American class warfare. Wealth is simply greed, and the "one percent" who have it now are obvious villains.

This shallow interpretation of American history has produced several generations of Americans who have, at least in part, forgotten the beauty of American free enterprise. Instead of "robber barons," most of the wealthy men of the late nineteenth century should be described as what they were—captains of industry. They were trailblazers, entrepreneurs, innovators, men who made valuable contributions to the achievement of the highest standard of living the world has ever known. Their philanthropic activities did more

Did you know?

★ John D. Rockefeller gave 10 percent of his income to charity from age 20

★ Standard Oil reduced the price of kerosene by 80 percent, raising living standards

★ Steel tycoon Andrew Carnegie's first job was working 12-hour days in a cotton mill

★ By the time Carnegie died, he had given virtually all his millions away to philanthropic causes

for American art, science, education, and medicine than the modern federal government could ever hope to accomplish. They should be admired, not scorned. Two of these industrial heroes stand head and shoulders above the rest: John D. Rockefeller and Andrew Carnegie. Each man exemplifies the limitless possibilities of American free enterprise, for both the individual and the community.

Titan of Industry

John David Rockefeller was born in 1839 in Richford, New York. His father was a traveling salesman who scammed the public with worthless tonics. He was called "Doc Rockefeller," and he abandoned the family when Rockefeller was a teenager. He was later discovered to be a serial bigamist. Rockefeller disowned him later in life. Rockefeller's mother, in contrast, was a devout Baptist who taught him the values of industry and thrift. And though she struggled to keep the family afloat during her husband's long absences from home, she provided a nurturing and loving environment for her six children.

Rockefeller was a good student and as devout a Christian as his mother. The family moved to Cleveland, Ohio, when he was a teenager, and Rockefeller took a short business course at Folsom's Commercial College. He took his first job at sixteen, as a bookkeeper in a local produce firm. He had good business sense, particularly in calculating the costs of transportation, and had learned the art of the deal from his father. At the same time, Rockefeller believed in charity; immediately after finding employment, he began giving away six percent of his wages. By the time he was twenty, he had increased it to ten percent and was tithing to the Baptist Church. For a man so often demonized for his "love of wealth," Rockefeller understood from an early age that those with means had a Christian obligation to help those without. He was as generous with his money as he was shrewd in making it.

He pinched and saved and eventually, with a partner, raised enough capital to start his own wholesale produce company. He had no wealthy benefactors and no government loans for start-up. This was pure individual entrepreneurship. Rockefeller saw the potential growth in the infant oil-refining industry and in 1863 formed a company with five partners and built his first refinery. Rockefeller was of age to fight in the War Between the States, and he was an ardent abolitionist and firm supporter of the Republican Party (he once helped a black resident of Cincinnati purchase his wife's freedom), but he thought his family obligations and business interests necessitated that he buy his way out of the war. Like many wealthy Northerners, Rockefeller paid for a substitute to fight in his place. His produce company did well in government contracts during the war, and Rockefeller gave generously to the cause, though with money, not blood. His older brother Frank, however, served in the War.

When the war ended in 1865, Rockefeller doubled down on his oil interests and bought out his partners for $72,500. This would be, in his words, "the day that determined my career." His vision did not mesh with the views of his partners. Rockefeller thought big. He wanted to dominate the oil-refining industry, which was then starting to take off because of the expansion of the railroads and the increasing demand for kerosene. Within less than a year, Rockefeller controlled the largest refinery

Grow Up and Earn It!

What would Rockefeller say to the spoiled, delusional, "Occupy Wall Street" crowd who expect big salaries and cushy jobs out of college? Get off the street and earn it!

"Nowadays young men—and others—want to have too much done for them. They want to be presented with bonuses and to receive all sorts of concessions. To get on, young men should study their business thoroughly; work carefully, accurately, and industriously; save their money.... They must be self-reliant. They must not expect to have things handed to them for nothing. They must make themselves strong by becoming able, brainy workers, by establishing a credit and by accumulating every dollar they can save after doing their full duty to society."

—John D. Rockefeller[1]

in the Cleveland area, then the center of the American oil industry. In 1866, he brought his brother William into the business and built another refinery. He went into debt but re-invested his profits and quickly expanded his company. His was a plan that called for steady growth and investments.

When prices collapsed and an oil industry bubble burst in the late 1860s, Rockefeller was insulated from the damage by his successful planning.

The secret of Rockefeller's business acumen was his meticulous attention to detail. He had a cost-savings system that went to the third decimal point, and he micro-managed every aspect of his business. He quickly implemented better and more efficient practices to reduce costs, hiring the best-trained workmen he could find and also the best minds in the business, such as partner and railroad magnate Henry Flagler, who negotiated better shipping rates for the company. Labor conditions may have been tough in the late nineteenth century, but without men like Rockefeller, many laborers would not have found employment at all.

★ ★ ★ ★ ★ ★ ★ ★ ★ ★ ★ ★ ★ ★

Divine Intervention

Rockefeller believed that God had given him the gifts to succeed, but only because he was a generous man dedicated to charity. His "life plan" as he called it, followed these words from a favorite minister: "Get money; get it honestly and then give it wisely."[2]

Rockefeller has often been derided for his supposed "illegal" and "unscrupulous" deals with railroad and shipping companies. The oil industry at this time was a highly competitive game, not just among the refineries themselves, but also among the railroad companies fighting for their business and the cities that housed the companies. Rockefeller was simply more innovative and efficient, traits that led to better profits and a larger piece of the pie. That is the goal of all businesses. Those companies that suggest they welcome competition are lying. Rockefeller was forthright in his desire to corner the market.

He and his partners took the first step toward that goal in 1870 when they formed Standard Oil, a joint-stock corporation with 10,000 shares. Rockefeller controlled just over 25 percent. They began purchasing smaller companies (at a fair market price) and absorbing their share of the market. By 1877, Standard Oil controlled 90 percent of the oil-refining capabilities in the United States. They began expanding their overseas market and were the face of the American oil industry in the late nineteenth century. This was all due to Rockefeller's vision. As one of his lieutenants put it, Rockefeller could see further ahead than anyone, "and then see around the corner." But by the 1880s, Standard Oil began taking heat from the American public.

To thwart potential legal challenges to Standard's control of property in several different states, a company attorney devised a business model called a "trust." This allowed for nine members of an executive committee (of course Rockefeller was one of the nine) to hold all the shares of the company and make decisions based on the interests of the trust at large. Thus, all of Standard Oil's holdings in various states now fell under the legal umbrella of the Standard Oil Trust. Critics—particularly progressive legislators—immediately took aim at the overwhelming might of the company. They saw the trust as a danger to American prosperity. But was it?

At the height of its power, Standard Oil had reduced the price of kerosene 80 percent. This made it cheaper for Americans to heat their homes and to buy manufactured products that depended on oil-based manufacturing techniques. The cost of operating machines was reduced; the cost of operating a railroad was reduced; the cost of manufactured goods

A Book You're Not Supposed to Read

Burton W. Folsom Jr., *The Myth of the Robber Barons: A New Look at the Rise of Big Business in America* (Herndon, VA: Young America's Foundation, 1991).

was reduced. In short, Americans enjoyed the benefits of Standard Oil's—and by default Rockefeller's—vision. Standard Oil employed thousands of workers in various industries through its extensive vertical integration (for example, by owning a barrel-making plant that produced the containers Standard used to ship its products). For anyone interested in business, the Standard Oil model should be a starting point. Who better to emulate than the wealthiest man in American history, if not the history of the entire world?

Such success produced jealousy and ultimately a public outcry against Standard Oil, culminating in the Sherman Anti-Trust Act of 1890, a law written by the "Old Icicle," Senator John Sherman of Ohio. The company was broken apart into several regional organizations, and by the late 1890s the Standard Oil Trust had ceased to exist. Even at the time of the passage of the Anti-Trust Act, however, Standard Oil was hardly a "monopoly." Its market share had continually declined, and at its demise Standard Oil controlled seventy percent of the oil refining capacity in the United States, but only 14 percent of the American oil supply. But to the progressives, Standard Oil was the supreme evildoer, the standard by which all monopolies were measured, and it had to be destroyed. Rockefeller's reputation suffered accordingly.

Most of Rockefeller's critics failed to understand the depth of his character. When he retired in 1897, Rockefeller determined to put his considerable energy and resources into philanthropic activities. He had been a lifelong member of the Baptist church, and still shook hands with each member of the congregation after Sunday service, but Rockefeller wanted more, and with his wealth could do more for humanity. He had helped improve the standard of living for the American people through his business ventures; now he wanted to do it through charity. His was a heroic and godly dedication to the human condition.

Rockefeller had an interest in education, the arts, and science. His affiliation with the Northern Baptist Convention led to contributions to educational opportunities for former slaves in the South, including a major portion of the funding for Spelman College in Atlanta, a black women's college named after Rockefeller's abolitionist in-laws. The General Education Board, established by Rockefeller in 1902 with a one million dollar gift, worked for fifty years to provide educa-

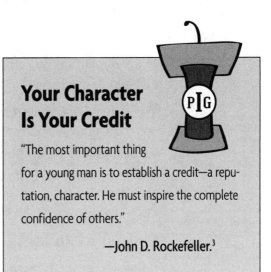

Your Character Is Your Credit

"The most important thing for a young man is to establish a credit—a reputation, character. He must inspire the complete confidence of others."

—John D. Rockefeller.[3]

tional opportunities for black Southerners. This was nothing new. While still a young man, Rockefeller was spreading his then paltry earnings to a variety of causes—from a black church to a Catholic orphanage—in addition to tithing to his own Baptist church. In 1890 Rockefeller endowed the University of Chicago with an eight-million-dollar gift after it had closed four years earlier because of financial difficulties.

Donations to educational ventures were only part of Rockefeller's generous contributions to bettering society. His interest in medicine led to the establishment of the Rockefeller Institute for Medical Research (later changed to Rockefeller University), the Rockefeller Sanitary Commission, and ultimately the Rockefeller Foundation. The eradication of hookworm, a vaccination for yellow fever, and the establishment of international colleges of public health are just a few of the accomplishments of these organizations. By the time of his death in 1937, Rockefeller had donated half a billion dollars to charity. To put that dollar amount in perspective, the total American GDP at the time was less than a hundred billion dollars.

Critics often claimed that Rockefeller engaged in such generous philanthropy to shield himself from charges that he was a greedy, self-serving industrialist. Nothing could be farther from the truth. He donated when he had virtually nothing to give and continued until he drew his last breath. In a time when we hear claims that giving would stop if not for an oppressive income tax, and science and educational grants would dry up without federal dollars, Rockefeller's activities are a reminder that wealthy men do more for the betterment of society than government ever has.

Pioneer of Philanthropy

If Rockefeller set the standard for industrial efficiency and philanthropy,

Smell the Roses

"I know of nothing more despicable and pathetic than a man who devotes all the hours of the waking day to the making of money for money's sake."

—John D. Rockefeller[4]

then Andrew Carnegie was not far behind. The two have similar histories, and though Carnegie never achieved Rockefeller's wealth (he was possibly the second wealthiest man in American history), he was perhaps even more generous than Rockefeller, and his charitable contributions were more eclectic. Like Rockefeller, Carnegie lifted Americans' living standards while making himself a fortune: Standard Oil greased the wheels of progress, but Carnegie Steel provided the firm backbone for growth.

Andrew Carnegie was born in 1835 in Dunfermline, Scotland. His father was a weaver and had little money. The poor Scottish economy forced the Carnegie family to emigrate to the United States in 1848 when Carnegie was thirteen. They settled in the industrial town of Allegheny, Pennsylvania, and as a capable worker, Carnegie went to work in a cotton mill—twelve hours a day, six days a week—to help provide for the family. His father also worked in the mill, and his mother earned a small amount as a cobbler and seamstress. Wealth seemed to be an impossibility for a man with such humble beginnings. But Andrew Carnegie was reared on tales of the great Scottish heroes, and he rightly saw America as a land of opportunity. He determined that mill work and poverty would not be his destiny.

Carnegie eventually landed a job as a messenger boy for the Ohio Telegraph Company. By virtue of his solid work ethic and ability to translate Morse code without scribbling the messages on paper, Carnegie moved up quickly in the company. Just three years later Carnegie was hired by the Pennsylvania Railroad Company as a telegraph operator. He made contacts with important and influential men and used those relationships to advance his financial interests. One of these men, Thomas A. Scott, the president of the company, took an interest in Carnegie and guided him in several lucrative investments. By the outbreak of the War Between the States in 1861, Carnegie was well on his way to becoming a wealthy and important man.

During the war, Carnegie was given the position of superintendent of the Military Railways in the East. It was his task to organize transportation and supply for the Union army in the crucial Eastern theater. The job also included management of the telegraph system, an important responsibility. Abraham Lincoln relied heavily on the telegraph during the war for battlefield reports and news from the front. Carnegie proved to be an efficient asset to the Union cause, but the war was also important for Carnegie. It led him to a crucial insight: he realized that the future depended on the railroad, and that the railroad depended on iron.

Carnegie emerged from the war determined to break into the iron industry. He founded the Keystone Bridge Company in 1865 and began developing more efficient methods for the mass production and use of iron. In the process, Pittsburgh became the center of the iron and later steel industry in the United States. Carnegie was an organizational genius. His vertical integration plans matched and perhaps surpassed those implemented by Rockefeller and Standard Oil. He was also innovative, and it was his constant thirst for improving costs and production that led him to adopt the Bessemer method for steel manufacturing. The improvements in efficiency and quality were fantastic.

Before Carnegie, steel rails cost around $160 a ton; after Carnegie, $17 a ton. Thus began the steel revolution in the United States, with Carnegie supplying most of the product. Other companies could produce at the same rate as Carnegie in the early years of his steel outfit, but by 1892 Carnegie had absorbed most of his competitors into Carnegie Steel Company (founded that year) and through his business expertise had transformed steel production into an art. Carnegie Steel outclassed rival German and English firms and could produce around 2,000 tons of pig metal a day. Steel became the standard in bridge and railroad construction and created the "skyscraper" revolution of the early twentieth century—all in large part because of the vision and entrepreneurialism of Andrew Carnegie.

The well-oiled machine of Carnegie Steel was not yet a decade old in 1901 when Carnegie decided to sell his company and retire. J. P. Morgan made an offer he couldn't refuse, and the transaction was the largest industrial buyout in American history. At sixty-six, Carnegie sold his company and retired with $230,000,000 in bonds (around $6 billion in 2012 dollars). Carnegie had the bonds delivered to a New Jersey vault—he never saw them—reportedly because he did not want them to disappear into the hands of New York tax collectors. Carnegie believed he could do better with the money than corrupt politicians and bureaucrats.

What made Carnegie a real American hero was not his massive wealth. Carnegie was heroic because of his dedication to humanity, the arts, and science. Carnegie was, in many

It's Your Money, Not the Government's!

"Upon the sacredness of property civilization itself depends—the right of the laborer to his hundred dollars in the savings bank, and equally the legal right of the millionaire to his millions."

—Andrew Carnegie[5]

respects, a man of letters. He was a fine example of self-determination, self-discipline, and the limitless possibilities that men with those personal traits can achieve. He was a self-described rags-to-riches story; in many ways he had lived the quintessential American dream. But as Carnegie himself said, "No idol is more debasing than the worship of money." He thus devoted his life after retiring in 1901 to philanthropy.

Carnegie had little or no formal education as a young man, but he decided in his twenties that reading and learning would comprise much of his daily routine. He had a genuine interest in books as a youth, but never had many. That changed as an adult. Carnegie is perhaps the most substantial benefactor to libraries in the history of the world. Between 1883 and 1929, over 2,500 Carnegie libraries were built around the world, including over 1,600 in the United States alone. They were revolutionary. Stacks had to be open, allowing patrons to browse and discover books. Carnegie libraries were free and open to the public—a novel concept—and the librarian had a central desk allowing users access to a knowledgeable person. Before Carnegie, libraries were often located in colleges and universities with restricted access. He opened the world of books to the American public.

The Need for the Rich

"Thus is the problem of Rich and Poor to be solved. The laws of accumulation will be left free; the laws of distribution free. Individualism will continue, but the millionaire will be but a trustee of the poor; intrusted for a season with a great part of the increased wealth of the community, but administering it for the community far better than it could or would have done for itself."

—Andrew Carnegie[6]

This was not surprising, given his penchant for reading and thirst for knowledge. He published several books, and his *Triumph of Democracy* sold around 40,000 copies. Carnegie endowed several institutions of higher education throughout the world, including Tuskegee Institute in Alabama.

He built and owned Carnegie Hall in New York City and donated thousands of organs to churches across the country. His Carnegie Hero Fund, established in 1904, still recognizes the heroic deeds of everyday Americans. Carnegie established a pension fund for his steel workers when he sold his company in 1901—labor historians who lambaste Carnegie as a ruthless labor overlord never mention this—and when he died in 1919, he had given away almost all of his money to various philanthropic activities. He completed that task in his will.

The careers of Rockefeller and Carnegie are typically portrayed as examples of the negative effects of American free enterprise. The truth is quite the opposite. They never took government subsidies or grants, they accomplished tremendous things from their own sweat and perseverance, and they increased American prosperity and affluence in the process—particularly for the average citizen. They were both self-made men, and they proved that wealthy Americans contribute more to the well-being of the American people through business and charity than any government agency. In fact, Rockefeller and Carnegie essentially defined the word philanthropy by giving away nearly half their wealth in their lifetimes. Thousands of Americans' paychecks were due to their business activities. In contrast to the popular notion that wage earners never benefitted from their extensive enterprises, both Carnegie and Rockefeller increased wages as profits increased—just not as steeply and rapidly as aggressive labor

What Makes a Hero?

"The Hero Fund will prove chiefly a pension fund. Already it has many pensioners, heroes or the widows or children of heroes. A strange misconception arose at first about it. Many thought that its purpose was to stimulate heroic action, that heroes were to be induced to play their parts for the sake of reward. This never entered my mind. It is absurd. True heroes think not of reward. They are inspired and think only of their fellows endangered; never of themselves."

—Andrew Carnegie[7]

organizers wanted. (The current state of the American auto industry suggests an answer to the question of whether it would have been wise to give in to those labor organizers' demands.) Americans should be thanking the wizard of Standard Oil and the able Scotsman of Carnegie Steel for their heroic contributions to society.

Chapter 9

INVENTORS

George Westinghouse and Nikola Tesla

here are all kinds of heroes. Many—several in this volume—were masters of the battlefield and earned the title "hero" by their bravery in combat. Others were pioneers, men who tamed the frontier and blazed trails in unknown regions of the globe and beyond. But there is a type of hero that Americans often overlook, particularly today when the enhancement of the mind has taken a backseat to leisure pursuits. It is the inventor, a pioneer of a sort, who has a vision for the improvement of society and the betterment of man. Americans long dominated the world in inventions. The open frontier, the blistering pace of America's economy, and her embrace of the free market both necessitated and facilitated invention. In an age when Americans embraced the bounty and imagination of industry, two American inventors stand out: George Westinghouse and Nikola Tesla. Neither is a household name today, and their status has been eclipsed by a contemporary, Thomas Edison, but their brand of invention was the practical means by which electricity was harnessed for the good of mankind. Without them, we would be living in the dark.

Did you know?

★ Thomas Edison wanted to call electrocution "Westinghousing" to discourage the public from trusting his competitor

★ Brilliant inventor Nikola Tesla was reduced to digging ditches when his first electric company was a failure

★ Tesla claimed to have invented a "death ray," and the FBI confiscated his research materials after his death

Mechanical Genius, Benefactor of the Human Race

Westinghouse could rightfully be called a captain of industry in the great American industrial age of the late nineteenth and early twentieth centuries, but he preferred to be known as an inventor. He was born in 1846 in Central Bridge, New York. His father owned a machine shop that produced agricultural implements and was considered an inventor in his own right. Westinghouse was born for industry. As a young man, he showed natural talent for the family business, but in 1861 war called. The ambitious and adventurous young man, only fifteen, enlisted in the New York National Guard, determined to fight for the Union. His parents called him home, but eventually conceded to his military dreams and allowed him to join the regular army in 1863 at the age of sixteen. He served in the New York Cavalry but saw no action on the battlefield. Westinghouse resigned from the army in 1864 and joined the Union navy, hopeful that his skill at machines might pay off in a different branch of service. He served on the *Muscoota* and the *Stars and Stripes* but again did not experience combat. When the war ended in 1865, Westinghouse returned home, but he was a different young man.

Before he left for the army, he had been intemperate and shiftless, showing little interest in education. The hard discipline of the army—not to mention simply having to first care for his horse before he could rest in the evening—forced Westinghouse to grow up. He was always a bright-eyed, confident, and intelligent youth (at seventeen he had tried to raise his own regiment so he could serve as an officer), but now he had the personal resolve and discipline necessary to achieve success. Westinghouse understood the virtues of patience and of hard work. He had become a man.

This did not translate to academic success. He enrolled at Union College in 1865 and barely attended class. His favorite formal subject was geometry, but Westinghouse spent much of his time in the engineering lab, fascinated by the various experiments. One classmate recalled that Westinghouse was a young man of "definite purpose" who was absorbed in mechanics. His language professor lamented that Westinghouse wasted time making pencil sketches of mechanical objects while other students worried over German or French syntax and grammar. When he did not perform well in classical subjects, the president of the school called him in for an interview. Westinghouse informed him that he would rather be spending his time in a machine shop or working on his various ideas for inventions. The president agreed that those would be better uses of his time and sent him home. The recognition that a classical education did not suit him freed Westinghouse. In an age when practically every American is pushed to get a "higher" education at a college or university, Westinghouse serves as a fine example to those who prefer the mechanical and practical to the theoretical and classical. Not everyone is suited to be a professor.

He went to work for his father and just one month after leaving school had obtained a patent for a rotary steam engine and helped develop the Westinghouse Farm Engine, a machine instrumental in the transition from horse to machine on American farms. But the railroads were his passion. The railroad was the king of American industry in the late nineteenth century. Railroads spurred development of several other industries and fostered American invention. While other men, such as George Pullman, worked on ways to improve passenger comfort, Westinghouse worried over safety. Pullman may have provided "luxury for the middle class" with his famous sleeping cars, but Westinghouse reduced the possibility of death on cross-country trips with his improved braking system.

Westinghouse had witnessed a terrible railroad accident as a young man, one that he thought could have been prevented had a better braking system been in place. The engineers of both trains saw the other train approaching, and each attempted to stop the forward motion of his own train, but at that time trains had to be stopped by hand brakes in each individual car. This was inefficient and dangerous. Before his twenty-third birthday,

Westinghouse had invented an air brake system for railroad cars that could be controlled from the engine and stop a train quickly. His air brake revolutionized railroad safety. He later standardized his invention so that it could be used for all rail cars. The basic concept of Westinghouse's design is still used today. He also invented a device for placing derailed cars back on the tracks, a railroad frog (a switch that improved safety and efficiency in switching trains to different tracks), and several improvements to railroad signals.

By 1881, Westinghouse owned two companies and had become a wealthy man. But it was not wealth that drove him. Invention sparked his imagination and formed his business goals. He began researching and experimenting with natural gas. Within two years, Westinghouse had received over thirty patents for improved natural gas distribution. His "step up" and "step down" system reduced the risk of explosion and led to a natural gas revolution around Pittsburgh, his industrial home. This was an exciting time, and because of his interest in safe and efficient means of energy transmission, Westinghouse was naturally drawn to the virgin field of electrical transmission and generation, then being tested by Thomas Edison around New York.

Westinghouse thought that Edison's low voltage direct current system would prove too inefficient for long distance transmission, and he was correct. Having already worked with "alternating current" in his natural gas delivery systems, Westinghouse was drawn to the work of two Frenchmen in that field, and in 1885 he purchased their transformers and began work on improving their designs. In less than a year, Westinghouse and his team of electrical engineers had developed a new type of transformer and were ready to

> ★ ★ ★ ★ ★ ★ ★ ★ ★ ★ ★ ★ ★ ★
>
> ## "You Didn't Build That"
>
> Before President Barack Obama infamously said in 2012 that "If you've got a business—you didn't build that. Somebody else made that happen...." the press said virtually the same thing about George Westinghouse and his companies. His response: "I suppose all those great works built themselves."[1]

market their product. Westinghouse incorporated his Westinghouse Electric Company in 1886 and began making plans for the widespread sale and distribution of his revolutionary "shell type" transformer. One problem. Edison had already developed a strong following and viewed Westinghouse as a threat to his electrical empire. His propaganda team immediately went to work in an attempt to discredit alternating current.

★ ★ ★ ★ ★ ★ ★ ★ ★ ★ ★ ★ ★ ★

More Than a Man of Money

A friend of Westinghouse once said, "Had he coveted riches for their own sake he could have passed his life making steel rails, cutting them off in thirty-foot lengths, and selling them for cash; but this would have led nowhere."[2]

Edison classified Westinghouse's design as dangerous and alternating current as a killer. Cities passed ordinances against high-voltage wires, Edison publicly railed against them, the mayor of New York said that he would personally strip all the high voltage lines from the city, and a showman named Harold P. Brown went on a personal crusade to demonstrate the harmful effects of alternating current by executing various animals in public with high-voltage charges (he had been financially supported by Edison). In heroic form, Westinghouse attempted to stay above the fray by refusing to criticize Edison. In one of his few public announcements defending his work, he admitted, "The alternating current will kill people, of course. So will gunpowder, and dynamite, and whisky, and lots of other things; but we have a system whereby the deadly electricity of the alternating current can do no harm unless a man is fool enough to swallow a whole dynamo."[3]

The debate reached its crescendo when Brown obtained permission to use a high voltage device to kill a man on death row in New York. This, he and Edison thought, would be the event that would finally prove the danger of high voltage and sink Westinghouse and the other proponents of alternative current. What has since become known as the electric chair was used to kill convicted murderer William Kemmler in 1890. Before the event,

Kemmler and his high-profile team of attorneys (no one knows who paid their salaries; Westinghouse denied that he had) argued that death via electric chair would be a long and gruesome event, similar to torture. In fact his death was quick, and the electric chair became and remained for years the standard method of execution in the United States. Brown and Edison wanted to call it "Westinghousing," but "electrocution" stuck. Regardless, it became clear that the cost and inefficiency of direct current would render it impractical, and Westinghouse's system soon took off. He had the final victory.

By 1907, Westinghouse companies employed 50,000 people in the United States, and his alternating current delivery system was used throughout the world. In 1893, Westinghouse was contracted to provide the power for the World's Columbian Exposition at Chicago and given the rights to develop alternating current generation using the immense power of Niagara Falls. He had turned on the lights for the American people, something his more famous rival Edison had failed to do. A light bulb is no good without the means to power it, and Westinghouse gave it the juice. He had over four hundred patents to his name at the time of his death and had accomplished what he set out to do: improve the lot of mankind through invention.

Though Westinghouse was a great inventor, he was known more for his honesty, integrity, and compassion to those who worked for him. That is what distinguished him from Edison, a man whom few enjoyed working for. In a time when labor strife and substandard factory conditions were common, Westinghouse pioneered solid employee compensation. When he started his first company in 1872, Westinghouse gave his men Saturday afternoons off, a practice that was unique at the time. That Thanksgiving, he invited all fifteen of his employees and their families to dine with him, starting a tradition that eventually required truckloads of turkeys and an army of cooks to meet the appetites of a substantial work force. He developed a pension system; provided good wages and salaries; gave his female employees comfortable eating facilities, coffee on the house, and a climate-controlled working environment; and kept men working even in tough economic times—at his own expense. Westinghouse was the public face of his company, but those who worked for him always received the praise they deserved, albeit quietly, for helping develop the technologies that grew the business. Westinghouse treated his inventors and engineers fairly. When Westinghouse ran into financial trouble himself in the early 1900s, his employees attempted to bail him out. They never forgot that Westinghouse, whom they dubbed "the Old Man," treated them all like family.

Westinghouse's dedication to his employees and his reputation for fair and honest dealings with inventors led to perhaps the most important, albeit

★ ★

Keep 'Em Working

During a severe economic downturn in 1896, Westinghouse faced the possibility of having to lay off hundreds of workers. His response to the problem: keep them working, even if it meant losing money. When confronted about this issue by one of his managers, Westinghouse answered, "I am going away for a while, but I can't leave till I have made some arrangement for continuing those men at work, at least till the cold weather is over. Haven't we anything in the shops that needs overhauling?"

"No, sir," answered the man, "not a thing that I know of now."

"What has become of that load of stuff we put into the loft some time ago to get it out of the way?"

"It is there still, and it's practically all scrap. There's nothing in the lot that we could possibly make use of by repairing it."

"Well, never mind, get it down and do something to it—I don't care much what, as long as these fellows are employed. If that won't answer, bring out some billets and have them shaped into squares or hexagons."

"But, Mr. Westinghouse, it would mean a tremendous waste."

"No, it wouldn't. Nothing will be wasted that keeps the wives and children of all these men from suffering this winter. Do as I tell you."[4]

short-lived, alliance in modern American scientific history. In 1888, Westinghouse hired a young Serbian immigrant named Nikola Tesla because of Tesla's mastery of alternating current delivery. Though Tesla would only work for Westinghouse for one year, that one year changed American science and earned Tesla his reputation as one of the great inventors in American history.

The Dynamo

Nikola Tesla was born in 1856 in Croatia. His father was a Serbian Orthodox clergyman who wanted his son to follow in his footsteps. His mother was illiterate but liked to tinker with household items. Perhaps Tesla inherited the gift of invention from her. He moved quickly through school, showing an interest in mathematics, physics, and mechanics. He ultimately rejected a career in the ministry, and pursued a degree in science. Tesla's father died before he could finish at the University of Prague, so for three years he held various jobs, mostly in mechanical professions, in the hope of improving his lot in life.

He emigrated to the United States in 1884 with a letter of introduction to Thomas Edison. Tesla had been working on a brushless motor design in order to improve the practicability of alternating current. Edison hired him but, because of his own predilection for direct current, put Tesla to work on other projects. The two had a falling-out, with Tesla claiming Edison had reneged on promised compensation. Tesla quit and attempted to form his own electric company in New York. It failed, and Tesla had to resort to manual labor, often as a ditch digger, to stay alive. This may seem incredible to the modern reader, but in a time with no social safety net legislation it was quite possible that a bright, college-educated man without a parent's couch to sleep on might have to dig ditches to earn a living. (Perhaps it's no coincidence that this was also the age in which American invention and industry set our economy up to dominate the world in the twentieth century.) Tesla did not protest his lot in life or complain that he deserved to be chairman of the board while only in his twenties. He knew he had to prove himself, and he viewed America as a land of opportunity. Tesla became an American citizen in 1889.

Tesla saved and with the help of investors at the Western Union Telegraph Company built a laboratory to improve his polyphase alternating current motor design. Over the next two years, he took out a dozen patents on his motor designs and in 1888 Westinghouse bought them and brought Tesla to Pittsburgh to work for his company. Westinghouse paid a premium for Tesla's designs, around $200,000 in 1888, and as Tesla said, "Despite... hard times he has lived up to every cent of his obligation."[5] If not for Tesla, Westinghouse's plans for alternating current expansion might never have come to fruition. Tesla had graduated from ditch-digging to being a sought-after inventor, and in fact had already become a sensation in America. His genius was finally recognized, and Westinghouse was only the first to pay for his talent.

Real Hope and Change

"The scientific man does not aim at an immediate result. He does not expect that his advanced ideas will be readily taken up. His work is like that of the planter—for the future. His duty is to lay the foundation for those who are to come, and point the way. He lives and labors and hopes."

—Nikola Tesla, 1934

Tesla left after one year at Westinghouse Electric, but he never had a bad thing to say about Westinghouse. In contrast to his departure from Edison, Tesla's split with Westinghouse was amicable. He even canceled the royalties Westinghouse owed him at a point when they would have bankrupt Westinghouse Electric. Had he not chosen to do so, Tesla would have become the richest man in the world. Not many men would pass up such an opportunity. That spoke volumes about Tesla's character.

The period of Tesla's life after leaving Westinghouse was the most dynamic and exciting of his career. He was still in his thirties, a tall and attractive man, and he reveled in the opportunity to be the center of attention. He lived in hotels and attended lavish parties and lectures in his honor. He lived as a freewheeling bachelor and enjoyed bringing friends and admirers to his laboratory to showcase his ground-breaking experiments. And Tesla had many friends and admirers, men and women alike. He was truly a Renaissance man. In addition to science, Tesla was a connoisseur of music, poetry, literature, philosophy, chess, billiards, food, and wine. He spoke eight languages fluently, wrote a detailed autobiography, and helped translate Serbian poetry for Robert Underwood Johnson and *The Century* magazine. He required little sleep, stayed awake for days, and once spent almost eighty-four hours straight in his lab, working. He was a man of many talents, a true genius, the American da Vinci. The modern reader may think that this type of lifestyle would tend toward immoral activity, but Tesla was celibate; while not a Christian, he had a solid moral foundation. He claimed his chastity kept his mind clear and enabled him to have a more productive career.

> ★ ★ ★ ★ ★ ★ ★ ★ ★ ★ ★ ★ ★ ★
>
> ## Tesla on Westinghouse
>
> "I like to think of George Westinghouse as he appeared to me in 1888, when I saw him for the first time. A powerful frame, well proportioned, with every joint in working order, an eye as clear as crystal, a quick and springy step—he presented a rare example of health and strength. Like a lion in the forest, he breathed deep and with delight the smoky air of his factories...."

After leaving Westinghouse, Tesla began working with what later became known as X-rays. He invented the radio and received the first patent for a prototype. He demonstrated radio-controlled devices and worked on the wireless transmission of power. His lab burned down in 1895, and Tesla lost all of his models, experiments, and papers. He was in the process of applying for a patent for a device that could liquefy air, but lost the plans in the fire and then lost the patent to a foreign rival. He insisted that aluminum would be the metal of the future and drew designs for aircraft. His work in electricity allowed for the mining and reduction of aluminum ore, a process that would have been too expensive without alternating current. He invented a crude form of radar and in his late seventies claimed to have produced a weapon of mass destruction he called "the death ray" or "peace ray," which has lent to conspiracy theories about man-made disasters and climate distortion. The FBI confiscated Tesla's belongings after his death and classified much of the material. It has since been released, and the government denies any such device exists, but there are still those who believe it is possible.

Tesla died virtually broke in 1943. He spent the last years of his life living in hotels and working on his various theories. He lost much of his fame shortly before World War I after several of his experiments failed to pan out. The most famous of these ventures was the Wardenclyffe Tower in New York, a device that Tesla claimed would be able to transmit power wirelessly from New York to Paris. He ran out of money, time, and friends with capital, and eventually his tower was dynamited by the military. Tesla became an anti-social recluse.

Most true geniuses have quirks, and Tesla was no different. He had obsessive-compulsive disorder, was mysophobic, hated overweight people, and became a vegetarian late in life. He was always meticulously dressed and insisted on cleanliness, both in his personal space and in bodily hygiene. His personal eccentricity led many to label him a "mad scientist." Tesla

★ ★ ★ ★ ★ ★ ★ ★ ★ ★ ★ ★ ★ ★

Tesla on Albert Einstein and His Famous Theory of Relativity

"The theory wraps… errors in a magnificent mathematical garb which fascinates, dazzles and makes people blind to the underlying errors. The theory is like a beggar clothed in purple whom ignorant people take for a king… its exponents are brilliant men but they are metaphysicists rather than scientists.…"[6]

was many things, but no one ever called him lazy. He will always be a model for those visionaries who have a constructive imagination.

American inventors have not disappeared, but perhaps the demonization of industry and free markets has arrested their productivity. Or, perhaps it is the modern education system or government mal-investment in politically driven technologies that has sapped American ingenuity. We still marvel at tech pioneers like Bill Gates or Steve Jobs, but it must be noted that they, like Tesla, dropped out of the mainstream education establishment. Maybe government is the problem after all. Tesla and Westinghouse had tremendous success without government sponsorship, grants, or money. If Americans truly want to revive the heroic accomplishments of the American inventor, maybe the government needs to get out of the way—both in education and investment—and give the ambition of creative individuals like Tesla and Westinghouse free rein.

Chapter 10

UNDERDOGS

Booker T. Washington and S. B. Fuller

Most Americans have heard of Booker T. Washington. The same cannot be said for Samuel B. Fuller. Yet the two men share a common legacy: though they have been criticized by the black American community as being "sellouts" and marginalized in (or completely left out of) black American history, their accomplishments should place both men in the pantheon of great Americans, regardless of race. Washington and Fuller don't fit the leftist paradigm for black leaders: neither man could be considered an agitator, and neither considered himself a victim. Instead they both exemplify the American spirit of ingenuity, creativity, independence, and self-reliance. These two "underdogs" in American society were no different from the Americans who settled on the frontier with little money or prospects, or the inventors, captains of industry, and explorers who blazed trails for future generations in science and commerce. They deserve our attention and admiration.

A Classic American Success Story

Booker Taliaferro Washington was born in 1856 to a slave woman in Franklin County, Virginia. His father was white, probably from a nearby

Did you know?

★ Former slave Booker T. Washington built the Tuskegee Institute up from 40 students in a borrowed church to over 100 buildings, 197 faculty members, and a $2 million endowment

★ S. B. Fuller's company started with only $25, reached $18 million in sales

★ Fuller advised resolving the Montgomery bus boycott by buying the bus company into black ownership

plantation, but he never met him or knew him. In his autobiography, *Up from Slavery*, Washington recounted that life on the plantation was hard, but no worse in his opinion than typical conditions across the South; and while he condemned the institution of slavery, he refused to condemn slave owners. He believed that they were simply products of the system, just as much caught up in the great misery of the institution as the slaves themselves. Washington even recounts how slaves on his plantation felt genuine sympathy for "the white people" during the War Between the States, both for the tremendous personal losses they suffered and for the hardships they endured because of the lack of supplies across the South.

Washington wrote, "One may get the idea, from what I have said, that there was bitter feeling toward the white people on the part of my race, because of the fact that most of the white population was away fighting in a war which would result in keeping the Negro in slavery if the South was successful. In the case of the slaves on our place this was not true, and it was not true of any large portion of the slave population in the South where the Negro was treated with anything like decency."[1] This does not fit with the politically correct picture of race relations before or during the War, but Washington understood complexities of Southern society that modern historians miss.

After the end of slavery, Washington's family moved to near Charleston, West Virginia. He and his brother and sister walked most of the way. This degree of personal resolve marked Washington's life as a young man. His

No Race Baiter

"Not only did the members of my race entertain no feelings of bitterness against the whites before and during the war, but there are many instances of Negroes tenderly caring for their former masters and mistresses who for some reason have become poor and dependent since the war. I know of instances where the former masters of slaves have for years been supplied with money by their former slaves to keep them from suffering."

—Booker T. Washington[2]

mother was able to acquire an old copy of Webster's *Blue Back Speller*, and Washington quickly learned the alphabet. But reading would have to wait. Though a school had been established for former slaves in Charleston, Washington's wages at the local salt furnace were needed at home. Washington decided to work during the day and ask for private tutoring from the local teacher at night. He excelled—because he did more in the few hours at night than most students did during an entire day at school. When he was able to attend regular classes, Washington woke early and worked until 9 a.m. at the furnace. He then went to school for five hours before returning to the furnace for the last two hours of the work day.

It was at school that he adopted the surname "Washington," because every other student had at least two names and he didn't remember ever being called anything but "Booker." (He learned only later that his mother had named him "Booker Taliaferro"

★ ★ ★ ★ ★ ★ ★ ★ ★ ★ ★ ★ ★ ★ ★

Typical American Ingenuity

Washington was often late for class because the furnace where he worked was a substantial distance from the school. So he came up with a solution. He moved the clock at the furnace forward thirty minutes in order to get out of work early. He resorted to the same ingenious plan day after day, until he was finally caught and the clock was locked up. Washington said he did not mean "to inconvenience anybody. [He] simply meant to reach the schoolhouse on time."[3]

at birth.) He chose that name because of its proud heritage—something he had been denied but hoped his posterity could enjoy. Given the economic pressure on his family, Washington's attendance at school was spotty at best, and eventually he had to give up day school and return to work full time. He spent several grueling years in a coal mine, fearful for his life and depressed about the intellectually debilitating environment. Eventually, through his mother's influence, Washington was able to secure a job as the house servant for the mine owner's wife at five dollars a month. The job got him out of the mine and allowed him to continue his education. It also helped him learn to value systematic attention to detail.

At seventeen, Washington left West Virginia and began heading east toward Hampton, Virginia. He had heard of a black boarding school, the Hampton Normal and Agricultural Institute. Washington undertook the five-hundred-mile journey to his future in education with only a few dollars and a little satchel for his belongings. His way would not be easy. Washington did not have enough money for a train or a stage coach, he was denied lodging because he was black, he had to walk or hitch rides, and he slept on the streets ("under a sidewalk" in fact) in Richmond and then begged to work unloading pig iron to earn enough money to eat and to save for the rest of the trip. He finally arrived in Hampton with fifty cents to his name. His clothes were rags, he had not had a bath in weeks, and Washington did not expect that the school would admit such a "tramp."

He was handed a broom and told to sweep a classroom. This was his chance. Washington swept it three times and dusted it four times, moved every piece of furniture and cleaned every crevice, skills he had learned as a house servant in West Virginia. The inspection by the "Yankee" woman who "knew where to look for dirt" was thorough, and in the end she determined that a young man capable of such attention to detail deserved a shot at Hampton. Washington was admitted. He wrote, "The sweeping of that room was my college examination, and never did any youth pass an examination for entrance into Harvard or Yale that gave him more genuine satisfaction. I have passed several examinations since then, but I have always felt that this was the best one I ever passed."[4] Not many college applicants today would "stoop" to sweeping a classroom—nor would they travel five hundred miles almost entirely on foot to reach their selected college. Washington was never one for privilege, and in his view hard work was just as important as natural ability.

His tuition was paid by a Northern benefactor. Washington spent three years at Hampton learning the skill of a mason. He was graduated in 1875, spent time as a waiter, and then began teaching. This was his true calling.

Washington's work ethic was second to none; he showed the same determination in teaching that he had as a student, a salt furnace operator, a coal miner, and a house servant. Late in life he wrote that he never saw a dilapidated house or fence and did not wish to paint it, or a dirty yard and not wish to clean it. The same can be said for education. Washington never saw an educational opportunity he did not wish to exploit or a student he did not wish to help.

In 1881, Washington was given an opportunity that would change both his life and the lives of thousands of black Southerners. He was selected to run a new school for former slaves built and secured with Southern investment and legislation in Tuskegee, Alabama. Washington would spend the next thirty-four years in dedication to both its mission and its students, all the while taking insults from other black leaders for his positions on black education and advancement—positions he had arrived at in working his way up from the bottom in the South.

A Book You're Not Supposed to Read

Up From Slavery by Booker T. Washington (1901).

In its first year Tuskegee had forty students and held class in a run-down old Methodist church building. By the time of Washington's death Tuskegee had over one hundred buildings, 2,000 acres of local land, 25,000 acres in North Alabama, a $2 million endowment, and an annual budget of $290,000, 197 faculty members—all black—and it offered degrees in thirty-eight areas of study. Its board boasted prominent members of both the white and black communities in the North and South. Additionally, Washington had established the National Negro Business League and written or edited twelve books on the value of hard work and technical skills. Tuskegee and these other endeavors succeeded because of Washington, and he hoped that future generations of black Southerners, many of whom could not read or write and were without a proper diet and habits of hygiene, would follow his example of hard work, thrift, and dedication to excellence.

He once wrote, "We have no race problem in Macon County." Washington never had trouble exercising the franchise, and he moved easily in white circles. He attributed this to his work ethic, his economic resourcefulness, and his education. He wanted the same for Tuskegee graduates. He believed that black Americans could achieve success through a technical education and thought that economic power and the willingness among black Americans to "show their worth" would change minds in America. Those things had worked for him.

Washington was a unifier, not a divider. Nothing made that clearer than his words before the Cotton States and International Exposition in Atlanta in 1893, in what his critics labeled the "Atlanta Compromise" speech. He was accused of being an Uncle Tom, but Washington was simply being a realist. He based his message on his experiences. The Atlanta speech made Washington, for a time, the recognized leader of black America. He wrote in *Up from Slavery* that his objective at the Exposition had been to "say something that would cement the friendship of the races and bring about hearty cooperation between them."[6] America could do a lot worse than that kind of compromise.

Before "I Have a Dream"

"I have learned that success is to be measured not so much by the position that one has reached in life as by the obstacles which he has overcome while trying to succeed.... Every persecuted individual and race should get much consolation out of the great human law, which is universal and eternal, that merit, no matter under what skin found, is, in the long run, recognized and rewarded."[5]

—Booker T. Washington

Washington argued, "Ignorant and inexperienced, it is not strange that in the first years of our new life we began at the top instead of at the bottom; that a seat in Congress or the state legislature was more sought than real estate or industrial skill; that the political convention or stump speaking had more attractions than starting a dairy farm or truck garden." He warned against "artificial forcing" of social equality and urged both white and black Southerners, two groups with a fraught 250-year history, to "cast down your buckets where you are," meaning that the two races should work together for industrial progress:

> As we have proved our loyalty to you in the past, in nursing your children, watching by the sick-bed of your mothers and fathers, and often following them with tear-dimmed eyes to their graves, so in the future, in our humble way, we shall stand by you with a devotion that no foreigner can approach, ready to lay down our lives, if need be, in defense of yours, interlacing our industrial, commercial, civil, and religious life with yours in a way that shall make the interests of both races one. In all things that are purely social we can be as separate as the fingers, yet one as the hand in all things essential to mutual progress.[7]

This position, however, ran counter to the idea among many black leaders in the early twentieth century that the only way to achieve political and social equality was through confrontation and agitation. They believed that Washington was simply being used as a token to allow white America to put up a show of interest in the welfare of black Americans, while at the same time whites worked against civil rights behind closed doors. Washington knew the score. He privately donated to causes that advanced civil rights, but publicly called for educational and economic opportunities that would further the prosperity and welfare of black America. As he had argued in Atlanta, "No race that has anything to contribute to the markets of the world is long in any degree ostracized." He dined with the president, mingled with prominent and wealthy white Americans, and spoke across the country about racial tolerance and opportunity, but he never lost sight of his goal. The only way to the top, he emphasized, was to earn it. Such was the case in the racially stratified society of his time. Washington did not want a handout or a hand up. He earned everything he had, and expected nothing less from any American, white or black.

Booker T. Washington died in 1915. A bronze statue in his honor on the campus of Tuskegee Institute bears the following inscription, one of his favorite sayings: "No man, black or white, from North or South, shall drag me down so low as to make me hate him."

A Great American Entrepreneur

S. B. Fuller has much in common with Washington, with one notable exception—very few people have ever heard of him. Fuller was born in a rural Louisiana parish in 1905. He was reared by his mother and because of the family's economic plight—he had six brothers and sisters—was forced to work to help provide for the family. Work and poor educational opportunities hindered his scholastic career, and he received only a sixth grade education. When his mother died in 1922, Fuller and his family were confronted with the choice to accept "relief" or fend for themselves. They chose the latter, for in Fuller's words, "It was something of a shame for people to receive relief in those days.... We did not want our neighbors to know we couldn't make it for ourselves."[8]

He was living in Chicago by this point, his family having participated in the "Great Migration" of black Americans to Northern cities, and there he gained a reputation as an honest, hard-working, and reliable man. He worked in several low-paying jobs before being promoted to manager in a coal field. But Fuller knew that he could not depend on anyone else to create opportunities for him, so he began to hone his skills in business.

He worked as a door-to-door salesman and began making plans to start his own company—seemingly a quixotic dream for a black American in the 1920s. The Northern economic climate for blacks, while slightly better than that in the South, was no paradise. Many black intellectuals had adopted Marxism, some whites (including President Woodrow Wilson) feared that black soldiers returning from World War I might bring Bolshevism

A Book You're Not Supposed to Read

33 Questions About American History You're Not Supposed to Ask by Thomas E. Woods Jr. (New York: Three Rivers Press, 2007). Woods has a nice chapter on S. B. Fuller.

home from Europe with them, and in the infamous "Red Summer" race riots of 1919, blacks were killed, injured, and left homeless in cities across the North, including Chicago. Black leaders, particularly black intellectuals, were considered dangerous. Racial tension continued to increase, and by the 1930s, during the depths of the Great Depression, black Americans were being shut out of jobs in urban America because they were viewed as troublesome labor competition. Fuller saw this as an opportunity.

Fuller opened Fuller Products with only $25 in capital (roughly $500 in 2012 dollars). He sold cosmetics of various kinds, as well as hosiery and men's suits. He also owned two newspapers, the *New York Age* and the *Pittsburgh Courier*. A quarter-century after his $25 start-up, Fuller Products made $18 million worth of sales, and Fuller was probably the richest black man in America. Many Americans did not even realize that Fuller Products was owned by a black American. Fuller's was a rags-to-riches story worthy of a place in the annals of great American entrepreneurs like Carnegie, Rockefeller, Westinghouse, and Tesla. Then the bottom fell out.

Fuller believed in civil rights, but like Washington, he thought that black Americans should gain financial independence before pursuing political and social equality. He had been the head of the South Side

Chicago branch of the N.A.A.C.P., but he thought the war for racial equality would be won in the wallet, not the ballot box. He believed economic opportunity was more important than political success. Washington had said the same thing in his Atlanta Address. When Rosa Parks and Martin Luther King Jr. began the Montgomery Bus Boycott in 1955, Fuller told King that they should buy the bus company to make a social and an economic statement. The company was struggling, and what better way to show that black Americans had power than through economic muscle? King didn't get it, instead pursuing a political agenda that Fuller believed had no long-term prospects for success. If black Americans could not break a cycle of dependency, if they could never be viewed as more than a downtrodden race subject to political handouts, then how could they truly achieve freedom?

Fuller took his case public in 1963, much to the detriment of his own finances and reputation. Speaking before the National Association of Manufacturers, Fuller stated, "It is contrary to the laws of nature for man to stand still; he must move forward, or the eternal march of progress will force him backward. This the Negro has failed to understand; he believes that the lack of civil rights legislation, and the lack of integration have kept him back. But this is not true.... Unfortunately, the Negro believes that there is a racial barrier in America which keeps him from succeeding, yet if he would learn to use the laws of observation, concentration, memory, reason, and action, he would realize that there is a world of opportunity right in his own community."[9]

Like Washington, Fuller thought that if black Americans focused on their own community and sought to improve their own financial lot, they could achieve more. He had done so in the face of withering adversity, and he believed other black Americans could do the same.

Capitalism, not Marxism or social agitation, was the answer. To Fuller, black America could solve its own problems without outside assistance and unnecessary legislation. "Since our capitalistic system is a competitive system, the Negro must learn to compete with his fellowman. He must not only seek jobs, but he must own establishments which will give jobs to others."[10]

Black organizations immediately denounced his speech. The National Urban League, the N.A.A.C.P., and the Congress of Racial Equality all condemned him. Yet, Fuller's positions were not unique. Marcus Garvey, a Jamaican native who spent time in the United States and corresponded with both Washington and W. E. B. Dubois, pushed black enterprise, education, and business in the 1920s. Garvey raised funds to start a school modeled after Tuskegee in Jamaica. Like Fuller he was roundly criticized by mainstream black leaders, including Dubois, as being dangerous to the black community. Garvey, like Fuller, saw prosperity in community action, enterprise, and entrepreneurship, not legislation. Garvey and Fuller had different political views, to be sure. Garvey supported black separatism while Fuller worked within the system, tending to vote Republican. But the two men shared a vision of a world where black Americans helped themselves, took the reins, and plotted their own course. But their ideas ran counter to conventional wisdom among mainstream black American leaders.

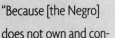

Prescription: Self-Help

"Because [the Negro] does not own and control retail establishments in his own community, he is unable to stabilize his community. For every evening, at the close of business, the substantial citizen leaves that community and goes to another community to live, thus leaving the Negro community impoverished, and the wealth derived from the community through retail sales is transferred to the other community, thus building up that community. These merchants are not to be blamed for this, because the supply and demand must be satisfied. Since the Negro does not supply the demand in his own community, the white man must come in, and he takes advantage of the opportunity. Then the Negro thinks that there is a racial barrier that keeps him from making progress. Therefore, he asks for legislation to remove the barrier which he automatically created himself, due to the lack of action in his own behalf."

—S. B Fuller

Fuller's message was unpopular with those who perceived black Americans as victims who would be able to achieve opportunity only through political solutions.

Fuller Products collapsed after his speech. Facing boycotts from both white and black consumers, the company filed for bankruptcy. Fuller reorganized his company and had some success in the 1970s and 80s, but he never again headed a multi-million dollar company. He died in 1988, a casualty in a war of ideas that had begun long before the controversy of 1963.

Washington and Fuller were more than entrepreneurs, they were American visionaries. Both men found success through their own initiative because they never accepted the mentality that societal obstacles meant certain failure. Both were models of racial tolerance at a time when it was hard to find. Perhaps if more Americans had listened to Washington and Fuller, the decline in so many black American communities might not be as pronounced as it is today, and the racial tension so evident in modern American politics (and so evidently fanned by the Left) might not exist. Of course, racial harmony and prosperity among black Americans would actually be counter-productive from the point of view of the Left's agenda. Victimhood and prosperity don't mix. Washington and Fuller would agree.

Productivity Trumps Skin Color

"It doesn't make any difference about the color of an individual's skin. No one cares whether a cow is black, red, yellow, or brown. They want to know how much milk it can produce."

—S. B. Fuller[11]

Chapter 11

SOLDIERS

Winfield Scott and George Patton

oldiers make great heroes. Every culture in world history has them. And the martial tradition of Western Civilization has made immortals out of a few men, from Leonidas to Wellington. There are partisan heroes—Lee and Stonewall Jackson for the South, Chamberlain and Custer for the North—whom, unfortunately, not all Americans celebrate, though all are American. And there are American soldiers whose glory is easily recognized by all, without the need to set aside sectional biases. Winfield Scott and George S. Patton are foremost among the latter.

Classic American General

Before the War Between the States, a handful of American generals had garnered the respect and admiration of the whole American people. Just below George Washington in this pantheon of heroes was Winfield Scott, a man who is hardly remembered today but who was considered by his contemporaries to be without equal. It was not until later, cataclysmic American wars, from the 1860s to the twentieth century, that his fame was eclipsed. Scott was born in Virginia on his family's plantation, Laurel

Branch, in 1786. His father had served during the American War for Independence and his mother counted the prestigious Mason and Winfield families among her ancestors. Scott's father died when he was six; his mother, when he was seventeen.

Scott was a large man, standing six foot five and weighing around 230 pounds. He was a good student, briefly attending William and Mary College and then studying law in Petersburg, Virginia. He found little scope for his sense of adventure in a stuffy law office, and when the threat of war with the British arose in 1807, Scott immediately joined the Virginia cavalry. For the next few years, Scott bounced back and forth between the law and the army, until in 1810 he was court-martialed on trumped-up charges of making "ungentlemanly" comments about a superior officer—General James Wilkinson, a man now widely regarded as the most corrupt general in American history.

Scott was forced out of the army for a year. He continued his studies, immersing himself in military strategy. The knowledge he acquired at this time would serve him well during his sixty-three-year career, forty-seven of which years he served as a general. When the War of 1812 began, Scott was in New Orleans. He immediately left for Washington, was promoted to lieutenant-colonel, and was transferred to Philadelphia and then to New York to take part in the defense of that state and possibly an invasion of Canada.

Scott was the brightest star in what was a mostly underwhelming American military effort, particularly at the outset of the war. The army was unprepared and unmotivated, lacked quality leadership, and faced dissension within the ranks—a problem Scott experienced first hand. In the fall of 1812, Scott led the American

A Book You're Not Supposed to Read

The Military Heroes of the War of 1812 with a Narrative of the War by Charles Jacobs Peterson (Philadelphia: William A. Leary and Co., 1849). Peterson's book is an unapologetic celebration of the military valor so repugnant to the politically correct Left.

regular army in a daring raid across the Niagara River at the Battle of Queenstown Heights, the first major engagement of the War. The New York militia, however, refused to cross the river. Scott was forced to surrender and became a prisoner of war. This event inspired Scott's life-long disdain for militia. He became a firm advocate of a regular army and relied heavily on regular troops for the remainder of the war.

Once paroled, Scott was promoted to full colonel and participated in the recapture of Fort George in 1813, a feat of tremendous energy and perseverance. He often had to work twenty-hour days, but was able to reclaim the fort as a formidable American stronghold. Without Scott, there is little question that American efforts in New York and Canada would not have been as successful. In fact, they might have failed altogether. He had a dogged determination to succeed, a firm sense of duty, and an unmatched courage. In 1814 he was promoted to brigadier general and participated in the Battle of Chippewa, to that point his greatest victory. Overmatched and without aid, his men pushed the British army in a running panic sixteen miles to the banks of the Chippewa River.

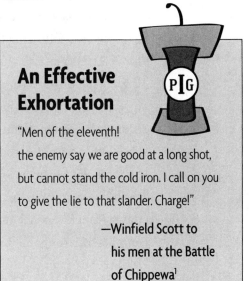

An Effective Exhortation

"Men of the eleventh! the enemy say we are good at a long shot, but cannot stand the cold iron. I call on you to give the lie to that slander. Charge!"

—Winfield Scott to his men at the Battle of Chippewa[1]

Scott was wounded several times during the war, last at the Battle of Lundy's Lane, the bloodiest single engagement of the war. Scott had trained his men hard in the weeks before the battle, and his preparations paid off during the contest. Scott and his men displayed a tenacity that had not been seen before in the American ranks. He led a charge against a British artillery detachment, and though his men suffered terrible casualties, they ultimately took the position, fighting mostly at close quarters in vicious hand-to-hand combat. Scott's wounds were severe. He had two horses shot from under him and had to be carried from the field. Lundy's Lane is often classed as a British victory, but the Americans, under Scott's tutelage, had finally shown the mettle of an effective army.

Scott was brevetted to major-general in 1814. His fame stretched across the Atlantic. Though invalided by his wounds, he toured the United States and was honored for his heroism in every town he visited. Both the United States Congress and the State of Virginia awarded him medals, and the governor of New York presented him with a sword. The Society of the Cincinnati made Scott an honorary member. Had his career ended then, Scott would still be regarded as one of the greatest soldiers in American history, but there was more glory in store for "Old Fuss and Feathers."

The years following the end of the War of 1812 were a productive time for Scott. He married and wrote several books on military discipline, training, and tactics. His three-volume effort on tactics was the standard manual on the subject before the War Between the States. (On the issue that would divide the Union, Scott was an abolitionist; but he believed that slavery should not be addressed at the federal level.) Scott was a firm advocate of temperance. He once issued an order that any soldier found drunk had to dig his own grave so that he might contemplate his own demise. He expected much from his men, but also required much of himself. His men loved him, and his officers gained much from his guidance. He not only taught them the art of war but also insisted that they further their education and broaden their cultural horizons. Scott's memoirs contain references to poetry, philosophy, and literature, and he often cited Shakespeare, Aristotle, and Plato—not bad for a man with little formal education. Scott understood that civilized war required civilized men. Any brute can kill, but civilization requires rules on the battlefield, a gentlemen's code that Scott sought to follow.

One example of Scott's gentlemanly behavior occurred during the Black Hawk War of 1832. Scott was dispatched to Illinois with 950 men, but bad supply and worse conditions led to an outbreak of Asiatic cholera in his camp. Doctors warned him to avoid contact with his men, but Scott, ever the gentleman, was the only officer to stay behind and give aid and comfort to the stricken soldiers. He caught a mild case of the disease himself, but continued to nurse his men. Such dedication earned him the respect of his soldiers.

Later Scott displayed the same magnanimity when dealing with the difficult problem of the Indian Removal Act and the forced relocation of the Five Civilized Tribes of the South to the Oklahoma Territory. He issued an order that required the humane treatment of the Indians, went among the chiefs in an effort to gain compliance without bloodshed, and persuaded the tribes to accept vaccinations. Scott sympathized with the tribes, but he could not change the law, and his duty as a soldier compelled him to follow his orders. While the "Trail of Tears" was tragic for those involved, Scott's firm hand and his diplomacy with the tribes probably saved hundreds of lives.

Scott was sixty when the Mexican War began in 1846. His young man's dreams of military glory had long departed; because of his age, Scott preferred that younger men take the reins of battle in Mexico. But fate would intervene. Scott was sent to Mexico by President James K. Polk and commanded the southern arm of the two field armies. In 1847 he invaded Mexico at Veracruz—the first large-scale amphibious assault in American history, surpassed only by Operation Overlord (D-Day) in 1944. He punished the Mexican army and pushed quickly toward Mexico City. Scott was aided by the outstanding leadership of several subordinates, among them Robert E. Lee—Scott called him the finest soldier he had ever seen—and Thomas J. Jackson. Scott captured Mexico City within five months of landing on the

Mexico beaches. He had become the conqueror of Mexico and a household name in the United States.

Scott treated the Mexican people with respect, and they had as much reverence for the general as his fellow U.S. citizens did. Some Mexican leaders asked him to assume the dictatorship vacated by the deposed Antonio Lopez de Santa Anna. His benevolent treatment of the Mexicans mirrored his actions during the difficult period leading to the Trail of Tears. Keeping his men in line, however, was made difficult by politics in Washington and by the presence of raw recruits in the army in Mexico. Both threatened to undermine his authority. The Polk administration did not trust Scott (he was a Whig, while Polk was a Democrat), suspecting that his newfound fame would lead him to a presidential nomination in 1848. With help from Democrat generals, Scott was removed from command and returned to the United States under a cloud of suspicion. It was soon dispersed. Charges of misconduct were quickly dropped, and Scott received a hero's welcome. Congress gave him another medal and put forward legislation to promote him to lieutenant general. This was a tremendous honor, for no one since Washington had held that rank. Politics held up the legislation until 1855, but Scott eventually received his promotion.

An Army Forged in Battle

"Brave Rifles! Veterans! you have been baptized in fire and blood and have come out steel!"

—Winfield Scott, entering Mexico City and responding to his soldiers' cheers for him, which moved him to tears[2]

He was nominated for president by the Whigs in 1852, but a badly managed campaign ended in his defeat. In the months leading to the War Between the States, Scott urged the James Buchanan administration to reinforce the Southern forts and armories and crafted a plan that, should war come, would keep it as short and bloodless as possible. Though a native Virginian, he remained loyal to the Union, retained his command in the United States Army (and tried to persuade Robert E. Lee to do the same), and organized the defenses of Washington, D.C. After Abraham Lincoln was inaugurated in 1861, Scott advised against provisioning Fort Sumter in Charleston Harbor, South Carolina, insisting it would only result in war. Lincoln paid no attention to this warning and the war came. In the end, Scott's so-called "Anaconda Plan"—a blockade of Southern ports and an offensive down the Mississippi—ultimately won the war for the North. Scott was not popular with the Republican Party and was forced to retire in 1861. He was seventy-three, suffered from various ailments, and could not mount a horse. He died in 1866, regarded by many as a useless old man. The blatant popular disregard for one of America's greatest heroes is indicative of the partisanship of the dominant Republican Party at the time.

★ ★ ★ ★ ★ ★ ★ ★ ★ ★ ★ ★ ★ ★

A Wise Warning against a War of Subjugation

Scott cautioned the Lincoln administration against invading the South. In a short letter to Secretary of State William H. Seward, he outlined the North's four options during "Secession Winter." The only three that made sense, in his mind, were conciliation with the South, a blockade of the Southern states, or "Say to the seceded States, Wayward Sisters, depart in peace!"

"Old Blood and Guts"

Though from different eras, George Patton and Winfield Scott had much in common, both as men and as soldiers. Patton was born in 1885 in California. He was descended from a line of American soldiers, many of whom had won honor on the battlefield. His great-great-grandfather was Hugh Mercer, an American physician, friend of George Washington, and hero of the American War for Independence. Patton's grandfather and several great-uncles served with distinction in the Confederate army during the War Between the States. After his grandfather was killed at the Battle of Ope-quon in 1864, his grandmother moved her four children to California and married her husband's cousin. Patton's father followed the family tradition in attending the Virginia Military Institute, and then returned to California where he practiced law and became the first mayor of San Marino.

Young Patton spent most of his early days on the family ranch. He hunted, fished, sailed, and became an excellent horseman, but did not attend school until he was twelve. Patton was reared on the military achievements of his ancestors. He read history, principally Southern history, and admired men like Robert E. Lee, Thomas Jackson, Nathan Bedford Forrest, and J. E. B. Stuart. Though he lived in California, his heart was in Dixie. Patton eventually spent several years in a private academy and then enrolled at the Virginia Military Institute in 1903. He spent one year there before transferring to the United States Military Academy at West Point. He took five years to complete his studies after being derailed by the rigorous mathematics curriculum at West Point, but eventually he graduated in 1909 in the middle of his class.

Patton was a large, athletic man with tremendous energy and courage. It is difficult to find a picture of him without his trademark

Life Wisdom from General Patton

"By perseverance, study, and eternal desire, any man can become great."

"Moral courage is the most valuable and usually the most absent characteristic in men."

"If everybody is thinking alike, then somebody isn't thinking."

"A good solution applied with vigor now is better than a perfect solution applied ten minutes later."

"Success is how you bounce on the bottom."

—George S. Patton Jr.[3]

scowl—an indicator of his rigid determination and intensity. He could be pompous, intractable, and insensitive, and several contemporaries saw him as a glory-seeker, but he was also a visionary. He was a natural soldier and leader, and at one time was regarded as perhaps the best athlete in the army. He broke both of his arms playing football while at West Point, set a record in the 220-meter low hurdles, and participated in the first modern pentathlon at the 1912 Summer Olympics in Stockholm, Sweden. He finished fifth overall, placing seventh in swimming, third in cross-country riding, first in fencing, and fifth in the four-kilometer cross-country footrace. His poor showing in marksmanship—twenty-seventh—was due to his use of a .38 caliber pistol instead of the .22 caliber weapons used by other competitors. Patton had set a world record the day before the competition and scored all tens and nines on the day of the event, except when the judges gave him one miss, probably because an earlier shot from his .38 caliber weapon had completely torn out the bulls-eye. Without modern measuring devices, the judges were unable to find enough evidence that the later shot had gone through the target. Had that shot counted, he would have finished first and probably would have earned a medal in the pentathlon. Patton, however, refused to complain or challenge the result. He was a good sportsman, a great competitor, and most important a firm adherent of the soldiers' creed that forbade complaint. After World War II, he met with several of his former opponents from the 1912 games again in Sweden and scored higher than he had during the pentathlon. Patton proved his point, though without the pageantry and fanfare of the Olympics.

Patton eventually learned to fly and bought an airplane (crashing it twice). He studied navigation and bought a sloop he named *Arcturus*. Patton loved adventure and lived life to its fullest. He cheated death as a soldier, a pilot, and sea captain and once saved three boys in a severe gale off the Massachusetts coast by swimming out three separate times and bringing each boy back to safety on his boat. This feat earned him the Congressional

Lifesaving Medal. For a man who is often regarded as a natural killer and who had no remorse in taking life in the line of duty, Patton relished and respected life. That dichotomy in a soldier's character is often hard to grasp. It is their familiarity with death that often drives soldiers to live life with relish.

Patton loved the cavalry. Mobile warfare was in his blood. He was the United States Army's first "Master of the Sword" for his skill in fencing and horsemanship and rewrote the cavalry training manual. He also redesigned the cavalry saber in 1913, making it the thrusting instrument we know as the Patton Saber, rather than a "curved hacking tool," as Patton called the earlier weapon.

Patton quickly realized, as did every cavalryman who saw combat around this time, that the horse was no match for the modern machine gun. And Patton got some early experience in mechanized assault. In 1916, Patton was assigned to General John J. "Black Jack" Pershing as an aide-de-camp during an American expedition into Mexico to apprehend "Pancho" Villa in May 1916. In what has been called the first mechanized action in American military history, Patton used three Dodge touring cars in May to surround and then kill Mexican bandit Julio Cardenas. Patton and his men strapped the bodies of Cardenas and two other men to the hoods of their Dodge cars as trophies and rode triumphantly through town. As a result, Pershing called his aide-de-camp his "Bandito," and Patton became a household name across the United States. He put two notches

---

★ ★ ★ ★ ★ ★ ★ ★ ★ ★ ★ ★ ★ ★

Patton on the Proper Conduct of an Officer and a Gentleman

"We as officers of the army, are not only members of the oldest of honorable professions, but are also the modern representatives of the demi-gods and heroes of antiquity.

"In the days of chivalry—the golden days of our profession—knights-officers were noted as well for courtesy and gentleness of behavior, as for death-defying courage.... From their acts of courtesy and benevolence was derived the word, now pronounced as one, Gentle Man.... Let us be GENTLE. That is, courteous and considerate of the rights of others. Let us be MEN. That is, fearless and untiring in doing our duty as we see it."

on the handle of one of his famous ivory-handled .45s and told his wife that "I feel about it just as I did when I got my first swordfish, surprised at my luck."[4]

Patton became perhaps the greatest and most innovative proponent of mechanized warfare in the United States in the period leading up to World War II. After the United States entered World War I, Pershing assigned Patton the task of developing an American armor school. Tank warfare had only recently been invented, and Pershing, knowing and respecting Patton's ability, wanted the United States to learn as much as possible about this new form of combat and considered Patton the best man for the job. At this point, tanks were seen mostly as mobile artillery, but there were several British military strategists who saw greater potential for them. Patton agreed. Tanks, he thought, could be used in the same way horse cavalry had been used before the machine gun—as infantry support, and also to mount independent attacks with speed, mobility, and surprise. A well-trained and well-outfitted regiment of tanks could quickly smash the enemy and inflict terrible damage as the final shock in an assault. Patton saw the tank as the modern-day heavy cavalry. He was ahead of his time, but World War II ultimately proved him correct.

Patton was wounded and almost killed leading a tank and six men into combat during the late stages of World War I. He was promoted to colonel and received the Distinguished Service

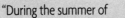

Moral Courage

"During the summer of 1914, I happened to be the only officer on duty at Fort Riley, Kansas, when one of the colored soldiers was accused of having raped a white girl in the neighboring town. It was rumored that the inhabitants intended to lynch this man. Naturally I am opposed to rape. However, I felt it was my duty as an officer to see that the soldier of the United States Army was not lynched. I, therefore, informed the leading citizens that, if any such attempt were made, it would be over my dead body. As a result of my stand, the man was not lynched, and, later, was proven not guilty."

—George S. Patton Jr.[5]

Cross, the Distinguished Service Medal, and a purple heart for his actions on the battlefield. He was thirty-three, and though he had seen combat, he had yet to achieve the battlefield glory he desired.

The interwar years saw Patton pressing for more funding for, training in, and emphasis on armored warfare. He was largely ignored and ultimately transferred back to horse cavalry. He was stationed at Hawaii where he organized the defenses of the islands and continued to develop a theory of amphibious and mechanized warfare, despite the fact that, as he wrote, "The theory of the necessity of hand-to-hand fighting" was still "so completely accepted."[6] Patton's writings display a remarkable knowledge of military history and strategy. He was a student of battle and often applied classical examples to modern problems. In his mind, warfare had changed little. Though the weapons had changed (and were about to change again, dramatically), men were still men.

Two Books You're Not Supposed to Read

The Patton Papers 1885–1945, ed. by Martin Blumenson (New York: Houghton Mifflin, 1972–74), 2 vols.

War As I Knew It by George S. Patton Jr. (Boston: Houghton Mifflin Company, 1947).

There are dozens of biographies on General Patton, but if you want to know what Patton thought, go to the source.

Shortly before the outbreak of World War II, the American military brass finally saw a need for an effective mechanized arm of the army. As the most vocal proponent of tank warfare for the previous two decades, Patton was promoted to major general in 1941 and put in command of the 2nd Armored Division and later the Third Army at Fort Benning, Georgia. The Third Army was then transferred to California, where Patton trained his men hard in desert warfare. They would spearhead Operation Torch, the invasion into Africa in 1943. Patton thought the punishing climate and geography of the southern California desert provided a suitable preparation for the conditions his men would face in North Africa. He was right.

Patton found his glory in Africa and Europe during World War II. After being promoted to lieutenant general in command of the Second Corps, he outsmarted and outmaneuvered the brilliant German general Erwin Rommel in Tunisia, and then, as commander of the Seventh Army, helped liberate Sicily in 1943. His nickname, "Blood and Guts," served him well during these early campaigns. He implored his men to fight hard and punish the enemy. The German and Italian defenders, he said, deserved no quarter. Patton was perhaps too zealous. In what has been called the "slapping incident," he publicly berated and then slapped a soldier who may have been suffering from "battle fatigue," now known as post-traumatic stress disorder. Patton didn't believe the man was ill; he had reports that men were shirking their responsibilities at the hospital. The soldier later reported that he had malaria. This incident almost ended Patton's career, but Dwight Eisenhower and the War Department knew they needed the hard-charging Patton in the final push against Germany and refused to dismiss him from the army.

Shortly after the invasion of Normandy in 1944, Patton was again placed in command of the Third Army and charged with organizing part of the offensive known as Operation COBRA, a plan designed to break the Americans out from the beaches of Normandy and into German-occupied territory. He handled the operation brilliantly. With an effective combination of armor, air power, and infantry, Patton quickly pushed the Germans back to the Belgian border. Patton wanted to invade Germany, but his ambition was checked when he ran out of fuel. Patton was forced to wait for orders and supplies. In the meantime, the Germans used the respite to prepare for their last great offensive of the war, the famous "Battle of the Bulge."

The American response highlighted Patton's strategic genius. He quickly broke off six divisions from his Third Army and relieved the surrounded and fatigued 101st Airborne in Bastogne, Belgium. This depended on a superb mastery of logistics, and even Eisenhower was surprised at how rapidly Patton was able to respond. Patton, however, had planned ahead of time. He told General Omar Bradley that the Germans were in the meat grinder and he had the handle. There has long been a debate as to who saved the army during the Battle of the Bulge. The 101st held on in Bastogne with little supply or ammunition, but Patton relieved them, halted the German advance, and in so doing checked and demoralized the German army. Both can claim credit. Patton called it his greatest battle, and it was, but without the hard-fighting men of the 101st, Belgium would have fallen before Patton arrived.

The rest of the war was virtually clean-up. Patton continued pursuing the German army through Belgium and in spite of efforts to cut his gasoline supplies, advanced across the Rhine and into Germany in early 1945. He was promoted to a four-star general in 1945 in recognition of his efforts in Normandy and Bastogne. Patton is regarded as the greatest American field general of the war, a man who fought like Stonewall Jackson and Nathan Bedford Forrest, his boyhood heroes. Several historians, most conspicuously the famous Southern historian Douglas Southall Freeman, have argued that Patton waged war like William T. Sherman during his march through Germany. He was as relentless as Sherman, but nowhere near as destructive—except to the Germany army.

As a man with Southern roots who had heard of the horrors of Reconstruction, Patton recognized the effect an invading and occupying army could have on the civilian population and the government of a conquered nation. He recommended treating German civilians liberally, and—in a controversial move which ultimately led the American brass to relieve him of his command of the Third Army—advocated keeping many former Nazi party members in administrative positions. This, he said, would avoid a potential power vacuum and thwart a pending communist takeover of Germany. He also argued against gutting the American military at the end of the war. Patton believed that America should "keep our boots polished" and stop Soviet expansion in Eastern Europe. No one listened, but his plan could conceivably have made the Cold War far less frigid. While on a hunting trip in late 1945, Patton was involved in a minor car accident. No one appeared hurt, but Patton, sitting in the back of the car, had rammed his head against the front seat and in the process damaged his spinal cord. He was paralyzed from the neck down and died a few weeks later of a pulmonary embolism. The invincible man was mortal after all.

Patton and Scott personified the American officer. They were daring, heroic, dedicated, firm, and principled. As professional soldiers, they recognized the responsibility that came with their status. There are still men of this caliber to be found in America, but Scott and Patton should be revered as a distinctly Western, and American, type of man—a type that is fast disappearing. Perhaps their kind of American heroism can be salvaged, if Americans are taught not to fear or denigrate toughness in the face of danger. If not, we are doomed to be led and governed by a class of men who can't pull their own weight—who don't have the intestinal fortitude for the painful decisions necessary to get America back on the right path.

Chapter 12

AVIATORS

Charles Lindbergh and Buzz Aldrin

No men have seized the American imagination as aviators have. Since Wilbur and Orville Wright made history in Kitty Hawk, North Carolina, in 1903, Americans have been captivated by flight. For many it is a romantic passion, inspired by tales of heroism, death-defying feats, freedom, science, engineering, and man's possibilities—and his limitations. Some of the great aviators in American history are household names: Armstrong, Yeager, Glenn, the Tuskegee Airmen, Earhart, Boeing, Doolittle, Bong, and Shepard. The Mercury Seven, the first American astronauts, were called heroes by the American press, and those with distinguished military careers, such as Richard Bong, the highest scoring American ace in World War II, and Charles Yeager, the famous American test pilot, made front page news with their exploits.

It appears, however, that Americans have lost interest in the art of flight, particularly in the modern age when each new technological feat is quickly surpassed by another. Man has already conquered air and space. The novelty has worn off. But there are two American pilots who stand out from the others, both for their careers in aviation and for their public

Did you know?

★ Charles Lindbergh learned to drive at the age of 11, chauffeured his father to campaign events, and regularly skipped school to go hunting

★ Lindbergh had to stay alert for 33 hours straight on his famous solo flight from New York to Paris

★ Before becoming an astronaut, Buzz Aldrin flew 66 combat missions in the Korean War

positions on controversial issues—Charles Lindbergh and Buzz Aldrin. They are heroes for their courage, both in the cockpit and in the public arena.

The Lone Eagle

Charles A. Lindbergh Jr. was born in Detroit, Michigan, in 1902, the only son of the prominent Republican congressman and lawyer Charles Augustus Lindbergh and his second wife Evangeline Land, a high school teacher. The marriage was an unhappy one, and Lindbergh's parents lived essentially separate lives. His father had moved the family to Minnesota, and young Charles spent much of his time in the woods, hunting, fishing, watching the logs roll down the Mississippi—anything to get away from formal education. Though his father and mother were both well read, Lindbergh did not care much for books. His world was adventure.

A Book You're Not Supposed to Read

Forgotten Conservatives in American History by Brion McClanahan and Clyde Wilson (Gretna, LA: Pelican, 2012). The book contains a chapter on the Lindberghs of Minnesota.

Lindbergh had much in common with his father. Both men had fierce independent streaks; both men loved and respected the wilderness; and both men believed in an America defined by the spirit of the frontier. Lindbergh had the opportunity to run the family farm as a teenager, a job he relished, but the rapid progress of technology in the early twentieth century really piqued his interest. He learned to drive the "horseless carriage" at eleven and even served as his father's chauffeur during his long political campaigns in the wilds of Minnesota. That would be unthinkable today—it alone would land both father and son in jail, not to mention the fact that the pre-teen Lindbergh often skipped school to go hunting and paraded around with a Colt .45 strapped to his hip in "cowboy" fashion.

At his parents' request, Lindbergh put his nose to the grindstone, polished his academic skills, and passed his college entrance exams in 1920. He enrolled at the University of Wisconsin in 1920—not for its academic reputation but "because of its lakes"—to study civil engineering. Lindbergh was considered an awkward young man. He was shy around women and considered his fellow college students to be nothing more than children who cared too much for dancing and booze. Lindbergh did not drink or smoke. Further complicating the course of his higher education was his fascination with flight. By 1920, news of the daredevil exploits of World War I pilots had become fireside stories in the United States, and Lindbergh wanted to fly. He quit school after one year, against his parents' wishes, and moved to Lincoln, Nebraska, to take flying lessons.

He participated in the barnstorming fad of the 1920s Midwest as "Daredevil Lindbergh," wing-walking and parachuting, but he wanted a plane of his own and the chance to fly solo. He scraped up enough money to buy a 90 horsepower hunk of junk in 1922. The plane looked terrible but flew well, and Lindbergh honed his skills as a pilot flying all over the West and paying for his wandering ways by offering rides for $5. He did not have a change of clothes and kept only a razor and a toothbrush on hand, but he was free and living a dream, no pilot's license required.

Barnstorming pilots were like rock stars in the 1920s, but Lindbergh preferred talking weather and crops with local farmers to availing himself of the wine and women in town. He was diffident, and feared he was not skilled enough to qualify for his dream job, commercial airline pilot. In 1924, at the insistence of a friend, he enlisted in the United States Army, ultimately graduating at the top of his class in flight school and receiving his commission as a second lieutenant. This training opened several doors to Lindbergh. Though he had always been a bad student—shiftless, distracted, and bored—he excelled in aviation. Lindbergh had found his calling, and he made the most of it.

In 1925 he took a job flying airmail. This gave him the chance to earn some money and maintain his required flight time for the Army Reserve. In the meantime, Lindbergh became interested in long-distance flight. This was a relatively new idea, particularly since technology had not quite caught up with the dreams of the pilots. In 1919 a Frenchman named Raymond Orteig had offered $25,000 to anyone who could fly solo nonstop from New York to Paris, a trip of 3,600 miles. No one pulled it off, and Orteig renewed his offer in 1926.

Like many other daredevils, Lindbergh knew of the offer. He worked out the logistics in detail in his mind and then later in several plans—including designs for a plane that he knew could make the trip. Lindbergh had never been a salesman, but he had to learn salesmanship in order to raise the capital for the venture. This would be no easy task. There were no government science grants, no federal stimulus or education packages to pull from, no government aid or loans for venture capital. Lindbergh was on his own. Of course the best ideas and endeavors in American history have almost all

Die with Your Boots On

"Any coward can sit in his home and criticize a pilot for flying into a mountain in fog. But I would rather, by far, die on a mountainside than in bed. Why should we look for his errors when a brave man dies? Unless we can learn from his experience, there is no need to look for weakness. Rather, we should admire the courage and spirit in his life. What kind of man would live where there is no daring? And is life so dear that we should blame men for dying in adventure? Is there a better way to die?"

—Charles A. Lindbergh Jr., 1938

been brought to fruition in the private sector (and those with government funding could probably have been accomplished more efficiently without it). Lindbergh's crowning achievement was no different.

He had contacts with several prominent St. Louis businessmen through flying lessons he had given. He went to each with a rehearsed sales pitch in an attempt to gain a dollar or two. He received much more than that. In short order, Lindbergh had raised $15,000, a sum he was convinced would purchase a plane to his specifications for the flight. His backers were as energetic and convinced as he was that Lindbergh was the man to accomplish the task. It took several months to find a suitable airplane. The breakthrough came in the form of an upstart aircraft company willing to build a plane to Lindbergh's designs, and on a shoestring budget. This was private enterprise at its best.

The end result of the collaborative effort was the *Spirit of St. Louis*, a single-engine monoplane (in contrast to the standard bi-plane of the day), completed in 1927. Lindbergh knew that there were several competitors for the Orteig prize, both in America and Europe. Several had already tried and failed, with a number of men having died in the attempt. Lindbergh and his backers understood the risks. Finally, after several months of construction and testing, Lindbergh was ready for a series of flights that changed history.

In May 1927, he flew from San Diego, California, to St. Louis, reaching speeds of over 100 miles per hour. That was unheard of in 1927. Then, two days later, he flew solo from St. Louis to New York in twenty-two hours, a new record. For a week he waited for the proper weather conditions to make the flight to Paris. On May 20, 1927, in the early morning hours, Lindbergh took off from New York on a barely usable, muddy runway in a fierce headwind. He headed north and skirted the coast of North America before turning over the Atlantic toward the British Isles. Fog and storms greeted him in the North Atlantic, and though Lindbergh had already flown for twenty-two hours nonstop, this flight was eleven hours longer. Fatigue was perhaps his most dangerous enemy. Finally, at 10:24 p.m. Paris time on May 21, 1927, Lindbergh landed at Le Bourget Airport in Paris. He had achieved what many thought was impossible.

When news reached Britain and Paris that Lindbergh was in the final stages of the flight, 100,000 people rushed to Le Bourget to greet him. In a little over one day, he had become the most famous man in the world, "the Lone Eagle." Newspapers in both Europe and America splashed the story across their front pages. He was honored across France, Belgium, and England. President Calvin Coolidge ordered that Lindbergh's plane be carried back to the United States by the Navy. When he reached home, Lindbergh was treated as a hero. The army promoted him to colonel and awarded him the Distinguished Flying Cross. President Coolidge awarded him the Medal of Honor. He was treated to a ticker tape parade in New York that attracted four million people, and later Lindbergh traveled across the United States and Latin America, being greeted by similar levels of adulation wherever he went.

★ ★ ★ ★ ★ ★ ★ ★ ★ ★ ★ ★ ★ ★

The Personification of America

After Lindbergh landed in Paris, American Ambassador Myron T. Herrick telegraphed the following to the United States: "IF WE HAD DELIBERATELY SOUGHT A TYPE TO REPRESENT THE YOUTH, THE INTREPID ADVENTURE OF AMERICA... WE COULD NOT HAVE FARED AS WELL AS IN THIS BOY OF DIVINE GENIUS AND SIMPLE COURAGE."[1]

Lindbergh attempted to live a normal life. In 1927 he married Anne Morrow, the daughter of a wealthy American banker who was U.S. ambassador to Mexico, and settled down in New Jersey on a private, gated compound reminiscent of his home in Minnesota. The press continued to hound Lindbergh, and he became increasingly hostile to their constant prying. Lindbergh attempted to shield his private life from the attention that his fantastic public accomplishments had attracted, but with little success. His wife had become part of the adventure. They flew across the globe together, and their stories later became part of her best-selling books. In the meantime, they had a son, Charles, and were awaiting the birth of another when tragedy struck. In 1932, twenty-month-old Charles was kidnapped and killed. "The Crime of the Century" again made Charles Lindbergh front page news. Lindbergh, in fact, blamed the press for the tragedy.

The couple fled the United States and lived in England until 1939. This is where Lindbergh made the transition from beloved hero to controversial and at times vilified public figure. While in Europe, he was asked by the Franklin D. Roosevelt administration to observe the capabilities of the Germany *Luftwaffe*. He was able to fly several German aircraft and gleaned important technical data on others. Lindbergh informed the American government that Germany was behind the United States in technology, but he suggested it would catch up by 1941 or 1942. And he was impressed with the resolve, spirit, and leadership of the German people. He thought Hitler a fanatic, but he did have some positive things to say about the German people. He observed the effect the Hitler regime had had in stabilizing the political and economic situation in Germany. Lindbergh worried about a potential war and believed that since the Western powers had allowed the Germans to begin rearming after World War I, the only choice they now had—short of losing millions of men in a war—was to allow Germany to continue with rearmament and regain some of its former strength.

Before 1938, the American public paid little attention to Lindbergh's European adventures. He had traveled not only in Germany, but also in Soviet Russia. Lindbergh despised communism and feared the effect a powerful Soviet Union would have on Europe. Thus he believed the Germans and the United States had a common enemy; however, he became increasingly worried about the Nazis, as did the American public. In the meantime, the German government presented Lindbergh with a medal. Lindbergh was unaware the German government intended to do so, as were the other Americans present, including several members of the Roosevelt administration. Lindbergh accepted the medal, and in the days after the event little was said about it. That soon changed.

The incident of the medal did not sit well with Harold Ickes, Roosevelt's Secretary of the Interior. He began using the resources of the federal government to publicly fillet Lindbergh, particularly after the Nazis ramped up their attacks on Jews in 1938. Lindbergh was shocked. He wrote a strong letter to Roosevelt insisting that he was innocent of any wrongdoing. He had, after all, received the award in the presence of officials of Roosevelt's own administration. Accepting a medal, he insisted, did not mean he supported the Nazis. He had, in fact, become worried about the now very real prospect of war in Europe—a war that he believed would wipe out Western civilization. Lindbergh worked for peace, but at the same time urged America to take seriously the threat of impending war by building up its own armed forces, including its air force.

Lindbergh returned to the United States only a few months before Germany invaded Poland in 1939. Between the beginning of the war and Pearl Harbor more than two years later, he became the most famous opponent of American involvement in World War II, but not because he wanted the limelight. On the contrary, Lindbergh questioned whether he should get involved at all. He was convinced to change his mind after Germany unleashed the Blitzkrieg in Poland and England declared war on Germany. "I do not intend," he wrote in his journal on September 7, 1941, "to stand by and see this country pushed into war if it is not absolutely essential to the future welfare of the nation. Much as I dislike taking part in politics and public life, I intend to do so if necessary to stop the trend which is now going on in this country."[2]

He became the most famous noninterventionist in America, at great expense to his reputation and peace of mind. He was called a Nazi and an anti-Semite, neither of which charge was true, and he was again hounded by the press. This made him uncomfortable, but Lindbergh accepted the hazards of public life as a cross he had to bear for the good of America. The Roosevelt administration made him public enemy number one. This was unprecedented in American political life. Long before Nixon had his personal enemies lists, Roosevelt had his. For a time, the noninterventionists were able to retard the mobilization for war, but their efforts proved to be too little, too late. After Japan attacked the United States at Pearl Harbor, Lindbergh and others conceded that war could no longer be avoided. Hostilities had come to American soil.

Lindbergh offered to serve in the U.S. Army, which at that time included our air forces. Though he was a decorated pilot and perhaps the best-known American aviator in the world, the Roosevelt administration refused. So Lindbergh signed on to serve as a consultant with the Ford Motor Company. He flew bombing runs in Asia as a private citizen and even shot down a Japanese fighter craft. Not bad for a man who supposedly favored American defeat. Not many men would have volunteered for combat duty *without* joining up. Lindbergh did. He used his talents to help improve American technology against the Axis powers, particularly Germany. Lindbergh was a war hero, but not just a war hero. He also did a great deal outside of combat to improve American chances for victory.

America First

"Lindbergh did not like Hitler or Nazism. He did not favor a Nazi dictatorship either for Germany or for the United States.... Whatever one may think of his views, Lindbergh formulated them in terms of his own judgment of what was best for the United States and for Western civilization. He thought the United States should not be guided in its conduct of foreign affairs by the wishes of any foreign government (German, British, or Russian) but, rather, by what Americans thought best for the United States."

—Wayne S. Cole[3]

After the war, Lindbergh worked for Pan American Airways, and with his reputation partly restored during the war, President Dwight D. Eisenhower made him a brigadier general in the Air Force Reserve. In 1953 he wrote a Pulitzer Prize-winning autobiography, *The Spirit of St. Louis*, and the book was made into a popular movie the following year starring Jimmy Stewart. Lindbergh died in 1974, his sterling early reputation damaged by what he still thought had been the proper course to take in the years leading up to American involvement in World War II. He never repudiated his positions, and though the attacks on his character have mostly (it does have to be admitted that he was not a faithful husband) proved unfounded, they still persist. Perhaps if Americans took the time to understand the stellar accomplishments and dauntless determination of Charles Lindbergh, he would be elevated again to the heroic status he rightly deserves.

Man on the Moon

Too often our "heroes" are those who merely do something first. Others with accomplishments no less remarkable, but second in time, are left languishing in the shadows. Until recently, such was the plight of Buzz Aldrin, "the second man to walk on the moon"—a designation that suggests that being first is the only thing that matters. As a matter of fact, Aldrin was first at many things. He was the first man to prove that extended spacewalking was possible, he held the record for most accumulated EVA (extra-vehicular activity) time until the Apollo 14 mission, he held the first religious service on the moon, and he has formulated a plan for continual manned missions to Mars—the "Aldrin Mars Cycler." His personal life has been, at times, fodder for supermarket tabloids, but Aldrin has overcome personal struggles to become a prominent activist—to call him outspoken on this subject would be an understatement—for continued American space exploration. He has also taken several "politically incorrect" stands on current issues, most importantly anthropogenic global warming.

Aldrin was born Edwin Eugene ("Buzz" was a nickname given by his sisters; he legally changed his name in 1988) Aldrin Jr. in 1930 in Glen Ridge, New Jersey, the son of a professional soldier and a homemaker. He finished high school in 1946 and turned down a full scholarship offer from the Massachusetts Institute of Technology (MIT) to enroll at the United States Military Academy at West Point. He was graduated in 1951 with a degree in mechanical engineering, third in his class. Aldrin immediately shipped off for Korea as a second lieutenant in the United States Air Force. This was the height of the Korean War, and Aldrin served with distinction. He flew sixty-six combat missions and had two confirmed kills, one of which was featured in the June 8, 1953, issue of *Life* magazine.

Following the war Aldrin served as an aerial gunnery instructor in Nevada and then as the aid to the dean of faculty at the United States Air Force Academy. He finished a doctorate in astronautics at MIT and then worked at the Air Force Space Systems Division. Aldrin had been angling for a career in space exploration for several years, and when an opportunity for selection into the astronaut program arose, he quickly signed up.

From the beginning of the space program, American astronauts were always selected from the ranks of test pilots, who were considered the most daring (perhaps the craziest) and skilled men in the United States military. The early phases of the American space program have been masterfully chronicled in Tom Wolfe's *The Right Stuff.* Aldrin was a great fighter pilot, a skilled engineer, and a dedicated Air Force officer, but he had never been a test pilot—and thus could not serve as an astronaut. But in 1963 the space program finally opened the doors to non-test pilots. Aldrin was in the first class selected under the new rules (the third class of American astronauts overall) and was immediately assigned to the Gemini program, the precursor to the more famous Apollo program.

Aldrin was the pilot assigned to the Gemini 12 launch, the last of the Gemini missions and the last chance that NASA had to prove the viability of EVA (Extra-Vehicular Activity by astronauts). Ed White had performed the first American spacewalk during the Gemini 4 mission, but his time in space was short (twenty-three minutes), and subsequent EVA attempts had shown little promise. The pressurized space suits proved difficult to maneuver, and working with small tools was nearly impossible. NASA had not developed an adequate training program for spacewalking. Zero-gravity test flights were too short to give astronauts the time to work on detailed small-motor-skill activities. Aldrin changed that. He is credited with formulating a simulation program which involved underwater training for spacewalks. This allowed the time necessary to prepare for the extended tasks he would perform in space.

Aldrin and James Lovell launched aboard Gemini 12 on November 11, 1966. On the second day of the mission, Aldrin suited up and performed the first extended spacewalk in American history, culminating in a cleaning of the command pilot's window. Afterwards, Lovell asked, "Hey, would you change the oil, too?" The "air in the tires" was "A-OK."[4] Aldrin had over five hours of EVA time on the mission and became the recognized expert on EVA tactics at NASA. Aldrin wrote in his autobiography, "My five-and-a-half hour spacewalk on Gemini 12 had been thrilling, and had set a world record for spacewalking in large part thanks to being the first astronaut to train underwater using scuba gear, and the first to use a system of greatly improved fixed hand and foot restraints I had suggested for the exterior of the Gemini spacecraft."[5] Gemini 12 proved that a planned moon mission was possible—at least with regard to extended time on the lunar surface.

Just three years later, Aldrin was selected for the Apollo 11 mission, the first attempt at a manned moon landing. This was a great honor that proved NASA considered him to be one of the best astronauts in the program. He was the lunar module pilot and because of his position in the vehicle could not be the first to step out of the craft. That task went to mission commander Neil Armstrong. No matter. Aldrin would walk on the moon.

The mission captivated the American public. The world was watching. Aldrin and the other two members of the mission, Armstrong and Michael Collins, would be immortalized. They knew it and trained hard to ensure the mission's success. All three had been to space before, but as Aldrin recounted, they gave each other nervous smiles before launch. Even heroes get jitters. They launched on July 16, 1969, for an eight-day mission to the moon and back, three days out, two days around and on the moon, and three days back. Aldrin said they were over 90 percent confident that they would get home safely, but less than 70 percent confident they could land on the moon. They were the explorers of the twentieth century, not unlike fifteenth- and sixteenth-century Europeans such as Columbus, Magellan, Drake, and Balboa, or American pioneers like Smith, Boone, and Crockett. Success was never guaranteed, but to them the value of the mission outweighed the dangers. Most Americans at the time would probably not have been willing to take the risk. That made them heroes.

Aldrin admitted that the moon landing was tense; after two computer malfunctions, they almost aborted the mission. When they finally touched down with just seconds of fuel remaining, Aldrin reported feeling a sense of relief and amazement. The trip to the surface, he said, was "the most intense, exciting ride in my life."[7] "For the rest of my life," he wrote, "I would remember those few seconds after we saw the contact button light up when the first probe on one of the *Eagle*'s legs touched the surface of the moon."[8]

The Future of Space Travel

"I believe that space travel will one day become as common as airline travel is today. I'm convinced, however, that the true future of space travel does not lie with government agencies—NASA is still obsessed with the idea that the primary purpose of the space program is science—but real progress will come from private companies competing to provide the ultimate adventure ride, and NASA will receive the trickle-down benefits."

—Buzz Aldrin[6]

Aldrin's first act after landing on the moon and accomplishing routine systems checks was nothing short of heroic, particularly in an era—the 1960s—when Americans seemed to be abandoning religion and becoming secular. He gave himself communion. This was controversial. NASA was already being sued by an atheist because the Apollo 8 astronauts had read from the Bible on their space flight, and the government did not want a similar controversy about this mission. Aldrin said he wanted "to do something positive for the world." He reached into his personal kit for the supplies provided by his Presbyterian church, poured wine into a cup and took communion, asking anyone listening "to pause for a moment and contemplate the events of the past few hours, and to give thanks in his or her own way." He read a Bible passage while he took communion and offered thanks and prayers for the mission and the gifts God had given him. Aldrin said later that looking back he might have done something differently, but his act is a fitting reminder that science and religion are not antagonists. Aldrin had seen the universe in a way few men had, and he was getting ready to set foot on the moon, the great object of man's curiosity since recorded history. That was enough justification for his short religious service. Thus before Neil Armstrong became the first man to walk on the moon, Aldrin gave proper thanks for their miraculous trip.[9]

★ ★ ★ ★ ★ ★ ★ ★ ★ ★ ★ ★ ★ ★

The Moon as a Symbol of Buzz Aldrin's Life

"Magnificent desolation," Aldrin said when he first set foot on the moon. This phrase became emblematic of his life, in both triumph and tragedy.

Armstrong was the first man to walk on the moon, but Aldrin was the first man to jog there. They spent twenty-one hours on the surface of the moon, and since their 1969 mission ten other Americans have made the trip. Aldrin wrote in his 1973 autobiography, "The manifest beauty of all that had been done lay in its precision and the ability of man to achieve the fulfillment of his dreams. If nothing else, our voyage was a tribute to man's restless imagination and creativity." He also realized that his view of earth had been altered. "We have seen it from space as a whole as bright and beautiful; we have seen it from the surface of the moon as not very large and somehow vulnerable."[10] These thoughts inspired by his travel in space—as well as the communion service he held on the moon—suggest that man is part and parcel of God.

Aldrin had a difficult time dealing with his newfound fame. He became an alcoholic, fought depression, and suffered through a divorce. He retired from the air force in 1972 and at one time was reduced to working as a used car salesman. He had not just returned to earth, he had hit rock bottom. He cleaned up his life, sought treatment for his personal problems, and remarried. In recent years Aldrin has revived his career, appearing on several cable news programs—and even a rap video with Snoop Dogg—to promote space exploration. That love, once buried under years of personal problems, has led him back to the top. No one is more interested in reclaiming American dominance in space than Buzz Aldrin (when asked on FOX Business Channel on June 6, 2012, which politicians were promoting a manned mission to Mars, Aldrin replied, "Buzz Aldrin").

> ## A Book You're Not Supposed to Read
>
> *The Politically Incorrect Guide™ to Global Warming (and Environmentalism)* by Christopher C. Horner (Washington DC: Regnery, 2007).

If nothing else, the septuagenarian should be admired for his willingness to physically defend his accomplishments. In 2002, Aldrin was confronted in Los Angeles by Bart Sibrel, a conspiracy theorist of the the-moon-landings-were-faked stripe. Sibrel called the then seventy-two-year-old Aldrin a coward and a liar—to which Aldrin responded with a right cross to the jaw. Footage of the incident went viral and again made Aldrin a national hero. When questioned about the moon landing hoax conspiracy theory, Aldrin blamed the media for leading "gullible" people astray, and asked the reporter if he had a better question. The right cross was the more appropriate response.

Aldrin has also taken aim at anthropogenic global warming advocates. In a 2009 interview with the UK *Telegraph*, Aldrin said, "I think the climate has been changing for billions of years. If it's warming now, it may cool off later. I'm not in favour of just taking short-term isolated situations and depleting our resources to keep our climate just the way it is today. I'm not necessarily of the school that we are causing it all, I think the world is causing it."[11] That makes him a so-called climate denier.

Both Lindbergh and Aldrin demonstrated that the impossible could be accomplished—and that taking a manly stand against popular opinion is, ultimately, heroic. They personify the American spirit of curiosity, of ingenuity, and of bravery in the face of seemingly insurmountable odds. They made the image of America great. If only their brand of American heroism could be bottled and given to future generations. Then, once again, America might be seen as a giant of technological achievements.

Part II

THE FRAUDS

Chapter 13

PROGRESSIVE FRAUDS

John Dewey and
Herbert Croly

No two individuals are more responsible for the rise of progressivism in America than John Dewey and Herbert Croly. Though all of the individuals in the next five chapters could be classified as "progressive," Dewey and Croly are the perfect representatives of the original Progressive Movement. Yet, outside of the academy, neither is a household name. Neither held political office, but their contributions in the realm of ideas have had enormous and lasting impact on the future of America. Woodrow Wilson and Franklin Roosevelt created the federal bureaucracy as we know it today—a real departure from the Constitution and the government of the founding generation. Dewey and Croly provided the intellectual muscle to make it stick, and in the process they transformed America. Americans are still influenced by their ideas on government and society. Most just don't know it. Exorcising their demons from the public education system and the political process would go a long way to restoring the federal republic of the founders.

Did you know?

★ John Dewey believed education should center on "the child's own social activities"

★ Herbert Croly used Alexander Hamilton and Thomas Jefferson to bolster a progressive ideology at odds with the thought of all the founders

★ Both Dewey and Croly tried to backpedal from their destructive progressivism late in life

The Educator

John Dewey is the more famous of the two. Born to a middle class family in Burlington, Vermont, in 1859, he attended the University of Vermont and was graduated in 1879. After teaching ("mostly everything" in his words) in the public schools of Oil City, Pennsylvania, he enrolled in the Ph.D. program in philosophy at Johns Hopkins University, ultimately receiving his degree in 1884. Dewey had a variety of interests, and while he was best known for his work on education, he actively studied and wrote about philosophy, psychology, government, ethics, religion, and law. In fact, Dewey would always classify himself as more of a philosopher than an educator. His goal was to use both philosophy and psychology to create a new educational environment that was ideal in its basic framework, its core curriculum, and its pedagogical methods. To accomplish all this, Dewey would need laboratories. Education was to become a science—and children, his lab rats.

After graduate school, Dewey accepted a job at the University of Michigan, then a pioneering institution in the new academic field of "education." It was here that Dewey began to develop the theories that would transform the American education system. He worked at Michigan for ten years and in 1894 accepted a position as chair of the department of philosophy, psychology, and pedagogy at the University of Chicago. One historian has called his arrival in Chicago "one of the most decisive events in American education."[1] Dewey formed a "Laboratory School" there to test his educational theories. In short order Dewey's educational theories were being spread throughout the United States, and not only by his growing catalog of educational writings. By the time Dewey moved on to Columbia University in 1904, he was the recognized "expert" on education in America, and his students, who numbered in the hundreds, were busily spreading his ideas to educational institutions across the country like bees carrying pollen from flower to flower. Actually, it was more akin to the spread of a cancer.

Every American parent who sees the problems in America's schools, who believes that the education system is corrupt and failing, can thank John Dewey. Dewey's supporters have long defended him against the charge that he is responsible for the disasters in modern education by contending that his ideas have been distorted and misunderstood. Dewey himself made the same suggestion. But while his writings are difficult to wade through and often vague, it's not hard to glean from them principles that were bound to transform American education (and ultimately damage American society)—in exactly the way it has been transformed, particularly where cultural norms and the family are concerned. As the great conservative philosopher Richard Weaver wrote, "ideas have consequences."

Dewey can be thanked for several innovations in education. Progressives were quite fond of scientific "experts." Forget parents, religious principles, and traditional culture tested by centuries of experience. Henceforth, educational experts would be responsible for shaping society according to new, scientific principles. Naturally Dewey was a committed proponent of the professionalization—and indoctrination—of teachers through "teacher education." What Americans used to call "teachers' colleges" are today integrated into

Quite an Exalted Role

"I believe… that the teacher is engaged, not simply in the training of individuals, but in the formation of the proper social life. I believe that every teacher should realize the dignity of his calling; that he is a social servant set apart for the maintenance of proper social order and the securing of the right social path. I believe that in this way the teacher always is the prophet of the true God and the usherer [*sic*] in of the true kingdom of God."

—John Dewey[2]

practically every university in America. "Educators" complete dozens of credit hours in "education" courses where they learn less about the subject matter they will be teaching than about "educational theory," the type of theory John Dewey pushed on his eager graduate students. These courses are more indoctrination than education. And it is only worse for advanced degrees. Often graduate students obtaining a master's degree or doctorate in education take few if any courses in any field outside of education. They write dissertations on classroom management, educational theory, student interaction, and educational statistics, and ultimately bloat public school systems' administrative rosters (and budgets) while offering "programs" to "fix" an educational system broken by their theories. It's a vicious cycle.

As a "pragmatist," Dewey believed in continually fixing things—that is, perpetually reforming the curriculum, the school environment, and so forth. In his philosophy newer is always better, and traditional methods of education never work. Pragmatists argue that a changing world necessitates changes in education. Their motto might be, *If the students ain't broke, government schools will fix them until they are.* Progressive education was and is an assault on traditional values in the name of change, and Dewey argued explicitly that tradition was the enemy of a proper education. Fixing education, according to him, required the "modification of traditional ideals of culture, traditional subjects of study, and traditional methods of teaching and discipline."[3] In other words, schools could teach new values to children and encourage them to reject traditional society and its cultural norms.

Innovations that Dewey made popular include the "child-centered" method of instruction, the "socialization" of children through the school, and the politically correct curriculum of the modern era. School, he believed, was "primarily a social institution" and should serve to stimulate the child's "social service." Education was "not a preparation for future living"; it was itself "a process of living."[4] Progressives knew that schools could become the ideal breeding ground for progressive ideas. And so they have been, ever since the Progressive Movement got control of them—just consider the inroads that feminism, Marxism, and environmentalism have made on the traditional history and science curricula. One of Dewey's disciples, George Counts, went so far as to advocate a new social order built by the public school system. Dewey rejected this idea late in life, but the acorn doesn't fall far from the tree.

While "socialization" in the schools has produced baneful effects on the nuclear family, "child-centered" education has ruined American school children. Dewey believed that education should be based on the norms and values of the children and that learning should be directed by them, not their teachers. In fact, Dewey railed against teacher-directed learning—that was traditional and authoritarian. Dewey's case for child-centered education has given rise to group projects focusing on "hands-on" learning, the abandonment of traditional rote memorization (of everything from the Declaration of Independence to the times table), the relentless emphasis on social skills, social interaction, and "social responsibility," the loss of a healthy competitive environment in school, the proliferation of activities for building self-esteem, and the gradual eradication of the content of the traditional American education—everything from history that includes actual dates to math where the students actually learn to figure compound interest. Dewey is the culprit behind the dumbed-down education and the scandalous promotion of failing students in public schools. Children, left to direct their own education, will naturally gravitate to easier work, less challenging questions, and fewer memorization exercises. They want less bang for the buck. Dewey has made it possible for them to get just that from our schools.

Why the Public School System Budget Just Keeps Growing

"I believe that it is the business of every one interested in education to insist upon the school as the primary and most effective instrument of social progress and reform in order that society may be awakened to realize what the school stands for, and aroused to the necessity of endowing the educator with sufficient equipment properly to perform his tasks."

—John Dewey[5]

The results of Dewey's innovations are blatantly clear. Students are now "children" until twenty-five or thirty. Thrift, honesty, integrity, responsibility, and moral virtue have been replaced with selfishness, consumerism, and self-gratification. The latter are the traits of children—and the logical results of teaching children to act like children well into their early adult years, instead of doing the difficult work of teaching them to act like adults. Children expect to be cared for and coddled, and they demand attention. The actions and demands of the 1960s hippies and the "Occupy Wall Street" crowd are just two examples of how "child-centered" education extends childhood indefinitely. Dependency is being bred in American school systems. Dewey's theories—and progressive ideas in general—are the root cause.

Why Johnny Can't Find Europe on the Globe—but He Has 678 Facebook Friends

"I believe… that the true center of correlation on the school subjects is not science, nor literature, nor history, nor geography, but the child's own social activities."

—John Dewey[6]

The Utopian

Dewey captured the American educational establishment for progressive ideology. Herbert Croly infiltrated American political life, government, and history. What Dewey did to education, Croly did to American political theory. He transformed the way too many Americans thought about government, and he did so in a creative—not to say devious—way, distorting the works of America's founding generation in support of his wrongheaded and ultimately disastrous interpretation of American history.

Croly was born in New York in 1869, the son of two prominent American journalists. Little is known about his early life, but he attended the City College of New York for a year, enrolled in Harvard in 1886 and studied there off and on for several years. Because of various personal issues, he never finished his degree. Croly didn't really need to do much in life. His mother was one of the more famous (and wealthy) women in America, and his father was a well-established newspaperman. So Croly spent much of his time amusing himself with leisure activities and writing; he was a poster boy for the American intelligentsia.

From 1905 to 1910, Croly wrote his political "masterpiece," *The Promise of American Life*—a tome that made him famous around America, garnered him influence with several prominent American politicians, and codified the Progressive Movement in America. The book was in many respects more a work of history than philosophy or political economy. Croly dug to find examples from the history of the founding generation that would comport with his progressive ideology. In the process, he "rediscovered" Alexander Hamilton and Thomas Jefferson and combined the most progressive-friendly ideas of the two, creating a Frankenstein known today as the establishment Left. Croly is rightly called the Father of Modern Liberalism, but perhaps he should be known as the Father of "Guns and Butter." He believed in big, active government both at home and abroad.

Though Croly found Hamilton and Jefferson to be useful, he was really interested in America in the abstract. The traditional American response to problems, he thought, was ill-suited to the age of industrial capitalism and the modern democratic order. Croly loved an America that never existed: "The only fruitful promise of which the life of any individual or any nation can be possessed, is a promise determined by an ideal. Such a promise is to be fulfilled, not by sanguine anticipations, *not by a conservative imitation of past achievements*, but by laborious, single-minded, clear-sighted, and fearless work" [emphasis added].[7] In other words, forget the time-tested responses of past generations to the problems of man. (They have only worked for several thousand years.) Croly's ideal America required new solutions germinated in the far-reaching intellects of progressives and idealists. America was a concept that must be continually updated by each new generation—and the whole process must be done through government.

Croly fused Hamilton's belief in energetic government with Jefferson's democratic philosophy to concatenate a political philosophy no one in the founding generation would ever have subscribed to. It favored social welfare legislation and foreign adventurism. It rejected agrarianism and favored an essentially fascist economic program, including the nationalization of corporations and essential industries by a powerful central government. Croly believed that the American military should increase in size and power to take a larger role in world affairs; he wanted what he labeled a "national foreign policy." His plan foreshadowed Woodrow Wilson's League of Nations and Franklin Roosevelt's United Nations. Croly believed that America must make the world safe for democracy long before Wilson used that line as a justification for leading the country into World War I.

> **The Socialist Promise (Somehow Never Fulfilled): Equality, if You'll Just Give Up Your Freedom**
>
> "The Promise of American Life is to be fulfilled—not merely by a maximum amount of economic freedom, but by a certain measure of discipline; not merely by the abundant satisfaction of individual desires, but by a large measure of individual subordination and self-denial...."
>
> —Herbert Croly

The Promise of American Life argued that Americans should lose their individual identity in the name of a national collective—all in aid of a national purpose that bordered on utopian fantasy. Croly, like other progressives, began to equate reform with democracy and democracy with nationalism. The progressives saw the nationalist impulse—a departure from the decentralized spirit that had long characterized the United States—as modern and democratic. A people with one purpose unified behind strong central authority and strong leadership could achieve any reform, any program that constructive ingenuity could dream up. They could make the ideal reality.

Of course, all of this was unconstitutional, and Croly and the other progressives knew it. So they dusted off Hamilton's other contribution to American history—loose construction of the Constitution. Limited government and individual rights were incompatible with progressivism, so Croly devised a way to circumvent the potentially thorny issue of constitutionality. The Constitution, he argued, lived and therefore evolved with America. In practice, this meant the Constitution was a dead letter. The Constitution as ratified by the founding generation—the document that actually limited the powers of the federal government and guaranteed rights—no longer existed. The idea of a living, evolving Constitution has been an intellectual shredding machine. If for no other reason, Croly should be a despised figure.

Perhaps the most damning indictment of both Dewey and Croly can be found in their own repudiation of their own respective ideas late in life. Dewey emphatically denied that his theories had led to the disastrous policies of "child-centered" schools across the country and argued that he had been misunderstood from the beginning. The curriculum, he claimed he had intended all along, should not be reduced, but enhanced. He had never meant for students to be the inmates running the asylum. Dewey saw the writing on the wall and attempted to backpedal, but too late. And Croly wrote an entire book denouncing progressivism, but did not publish it, and much of the manuscript was destroyed. He too could see the societal destruction flowing from his own ideas. But Dewey and Croly were the mad scientists of progressivism. They had opened a Pandora's Box, created a super-virus that, once unleashed on the American people, could not be destroyed. It has been brought under control at times, but it always mutates into a more potent form—much to the detriment of the American people.

Chapter 14

DEMOCRATIC FRAUDS

Woodrow Wilson and Edward M. House

illions of people annually cross the Woodrow Wilson Bridge between Maryland and Virginia on their way to Washington, D.C. Probably very few of them think about Wilson, and even fewer know anything about him. Leftist history professors certainly admire him. He is typically put in the top group in any ranking of the presidents by historians. A recent PBS documentary on Wilson called him "an intellectual with unwavering moral principles [and] one of America's greatest presidents… [who] reluctantly led" America into World War I only to see his "far-sighted League of Nations" fall apart. One of the historians interviewed for the project, Wilson biographer John Milton Cooper, said, "Well I think there's no question that he was one of the five greatest Presidents in American history. He has that rare combination, which he shares with, certainly with Jefferson and with Lincoln. That is he was a tremendously effective, practical politician, and a very deep thinker."[1]

In Cooper's mind, then, Wilson is an American hero, and many academics share that view. In reality, however, Wilson is a fraud. His public image was buttressed by American success in World War I, but his policies, both foreign and domestic, dramatically altered the United States for the worse.

Wilson should never be considered "great" or a "hero." His bizarre relationship with behind-the-scenes adviser Edward M. House alone—in which Wilson lived out another man's ambitions for political revolution—should place him low in the esteem of Americans and near the bottom of any historical ranking, not the top.

The Idealist and the Conspirator

Wilson was born in 1856 in Staunton, Virginia, the son of a Presbyterian minister. His father was a chaplain in the Confederate army during the War Between the States, and Wilson lived in Columbia, South Carolina, during Reconstruction while his father taught at the Columbia Theological Seminary. He attended the University of Virginia for one year but returned to North Carolina to continue his studies because of frail health. He was eventually admitted to the bar in Georgia and practiced in Atlanta. Wilson earned a Ph.D. from Johns Hopkins University in history and government in 1886 and by 1902 was president of Princeton University. He later served as Governor of New Jersey, from 1911 to 1913.

Wilson was the first Southerner to be president of the United States since Andrew Johnson in 1865 and the first Southerner elected president since Zachary Taylor in 1848. His style of governance was uniquely influenced by his Scots-Irish and Southern roots, but more importantly by the evolution of his political philosophy in the years during and after his graduate work at Johns Hopkins. Wilson personified and implemented the "democratic" progressivism that had been pushed by Herbert Croly.

The story of Wilson's presidency cannot be told without the inclusion of "Colonel" Edward Mandell House, Wilson's most trusted adviser and presumably the driving force behind many of Wilson's policy decisions. House was born in Texas in 1858, the son of a wealthy businessman who was mayor of Houston. He was educated in New England and New York, and he made his fortune in banking and cotton. Like his father, House was always interested in politics. He was a recognized kingmaker in Texas, helping four men reach the governor's office between 1892 and 1902. Each time, House served as an unofficial adviser, the same role he would later fill in the Wilson administration. Texas Governor James Hogg gave House what became his familiar title, "Colonel," after the 1892 election. House had never served in the military, but he was without question the tactical genius behind several successful politicians in the progressive era.

House and Wilson became friends in 1911, and House, sensing that a larger political stage than Texas awaited him, helped propel Wilson to the 1912 Democratic nomination. When Wilson won, he offered House his choice of

> ## A Book You're Not Supposed to Read
>
> *Philip Dru: Administrator: A Story of Tomorrow, 1920–1935*, published anonymously by Edward M. House (New York: B. W. Huebsch, 1912).

any position in the cabinet except secretary of state. House declined, instead preferring to be an unofficial adviser, the same role he had had in Texas. He was even given a room in the White House and was privy to classified information. House didn't need a title, as he had the president's ear on all questions. Even foreign dignitaries would consult with House before making a pitch to Wilson in person.

Before assuming office in 1913, Wilson spent several weeks in Bermuda reading a little novel penned anonymously by Edward House entitled, *Philip Dru: Administrator: A Story of Tomorrow, 1920–1935*. Wilson knew House had written it, but not many others did, and though it was not a strong seller (or readable, for that matter), the book served as the blueprint for Wilson's "New Freedom" agenda as president and is thus worth analyzing.

The character Philip Dru was House's alter-ego. Dru is a West Point-educated revolutionary who is too ill to continue to serve in the army. As a result, he leads a political revolution in the United States to scrap the

Woodrow Wilson and Edward House: Administrators

Edward House, concealing his identity as the author of *Philip Dru*, once wrote, "It was written by a man I know.... My friend—whose name is not to be mentioned—told me... that Philip *was all that he himself would like to be but was not*" [emphasis added]."[2] As president, Wilson became everything that House wished he himself could be.

Constitution and replace it with a Marxist utopia. The key to the accomplishment of his ambitions is a massive world war in which the "democratic" West squares off against the "plutocratic" East. Dru then becomes the dictator of the United States, a savior of the American nation and the American people, only to relinquish his power once a truly "democratic" order has been crafted on the ruins of the old Constitution. The novel would seem far-fetched if Wilson had not lived out much of its plot as president.

Take for example Dru's political agenda: the nationalization of the telegraph and railroads, a graduated income tax, universal suffrage, a central banking system, reduction in the tariff, national economic planning, the nationalization of the government through the abolition of the states, and a foreign policy managed by an "international coalition." This sounds eerily similar to the "New Freedom" agenda that Wilson ran on in 1912 and his better-known "Fourteen Points" for making peace at the end of World War I.

Wilson pushed for tariff reform, the Federal Reserve System (a central bank), a fiat currency (paper money), a graduated income tax (with the ratification of the Sixteenth Amendment to the Constitution), women's suffrage (with the Nineteenth Amendment), and the direct election of United States senators (with the Seventeenth Amendment, which curtailed the states' influence in the federal government). And during World War I he outright nationalized the railroad industry and controlled production and consumption through various government "boards." If Wilson was not a *de jure* domestic dictator he was certainly one *de facto*. He was not the first president to abuse the Constitution, but he was certainly the most flagrant up to that time in his disdain for the federal republic of the founding generation.

Wilson's famous "League of Nations" mirrored the proposals set forth by House in *Philip Dru*—the novel's author was even sent to Europe to craft much of Wilson's "Fourteen Points for a Lasting Peace." The two men had a falling-out in 1919 after Wilson came to believe that House had been too conciliatory with the Europeans, but the framework that House had put in place for Wilson's administration remained intact. Wilson's dream of an international community to "make the world safe for democracy"—not to mention his "nation building" in Yugoslavia and Czechoslovakia—was recognized as a sham in America, and Congress refused to ratify the Treaty of Versailles. Wilson ultimately had a stroke trying to defend it and was incapacitated during the later months of his administration.

Of course, to suggest that Wilson was nothing more than House's puppet is to ignore his own political philosophy, developed as a graduate student and later as a progressive governor. Wilson believed that the president was the political leader of the nation and argued that he should take a greater role in the legislative process. The president, Wilson thought, should be more like a "prime minister," and he actively fought for parliamentary reform in the United States. He actively initiated legislation, became the first president since John Adams to deliver the State of the Union address in person to Congress—a move he hoped would spur them to action—and often acted as if the president were part of the legislature, rather than the head of a separate branch of government.

Books You're Not Supposed to Read

The Creature from Jekyll Island: A Second Look at the Federal Reserve by G. Edward Griffin (New York: American Media, 2010).

End the Fed by Ron Paul (New York: Grand Central, 2009).

These books make up a double-barreled assault on the unconstitutional Federal Reserve System.

The Evolving Constitution

Wilson's magnum opus, *Constitutional Government in the United States*, contains his assessment of American politics and his prescriptions for reform. This book, born from his lectures on government at Princeton, showcases Wilson's progressive attitude and principles. In it, Wilson suggested that the Constitution as originally ratified unjustly hindered the president from acting as "the leader of his party and the guide of the nation in political purpose, and... in legal action." In short, he was complaining that the president could not legislate. Yet Wilson had hope because in his mind the living, "organic" nature of government—he called it a "vehicle of life"—meant that over time, the form of government established by the Constitution had already morphed into a different system, a "practical" system of government built on circumstance and experience: "There can be no mistaking the fact that we have grown more and more inclined from generation to generation to look to the President as the unifying force in our complex system, the leader both of his party and of the nation. To do so is not inconsistent with the actual provisions of the Constitution; it is only inconsistent with a very mechanical theory of its meaning and intention. The Constitution contains no theories. It is as practical a document as Magna Carta."[3]

Wilson also was also interested in reforming the relationship between the states and the central government. The old relationship between federal and state governments had been made obsolete, Wilson opined, by the changing nature of government in the United States. What the Constitution needed was an injection of pure democracy. Wilson had no problem with the fact that Washington had usurped power from the states without the benefit of

A Book You're Not Supposed to Read

Who Killed the Constitution? The Federal Government vs. American Liberty from World War I to Barack Obama by Thomas E. Woods Jr. and Kevin R.C. Gutzman (New York: Three Rivers Press, 2008).

constitutional amendment. In a "living" government, that was perfectly natural. So Wilson saw no need for substantial legal reform. It had already taken place organically. Translation: Forget the Constitution. It is old, undemocratic, rigid, and ill-suited to the needs of twentieth-century American society. We are smarter than the founding generation and have made worthwhile changes. Reform under this illegal method can continue because the central government, and by default the American people, have deemed it acceptable. Wilson did not just think this dangerous nonsense, he governed this way.

This way of governing may seem proper to modern Americans, but Wilson was busily transforming the executive branch into the thing the founding generation feared most—a pseudo-monarchy with control over the purse, the sword, and the legislative process. As the *New York Times* noted in 1913, Wilson drove the legislative agenda—by driving Congress "pitilessly."[4] He kept them in session for over a year and hammered them until they bent to his will. Executive leadership took on new meaning under his administration.

> ## A Book You're Not Supposed to Read
>
> *Woodrow Wilson and the Roots of Modern Liberalism* by Ronald J. Pestritto (Rowman & Littlefield, 2005).

As a result of Wilson's aggressive "leadership," all the many legislative and foreign policy disasters of his administration can be traced directly or indirectly back to his desk. Take, for example, the infamous Sedition Act of 1918. Designed in concert with his Committee on Public Information, the Sedition Act was an outgrowth of concern about popular unrest after the United States entered World War I. The law authorized a stiff fine and imprisonment for publishing anything "abusive" about the government or Constitution of the United States. (The Committee on Public Information ensured that the "correct" version of the War was presented to the public and preserved for posterity.)

The Sedition Act helped foster a general climate of hostility toward German-Americans during the War. Americans of German extraction were required to kiss the United States flag, buy extra war bonds, and cite the Pledge of Allegiance—and even then they could face violence, even death, if their accusers were not satisfied of their sincerity. Wilson, of course, never advocated mob violence, but his war to make the world "safe for democracy" made America unsafe for some people.

And then there are the terrible results of Wilson's personal plan for "democracy" and "peace" in Europe. The "brilliant" Wilson did not foresee the effects a dictated peace would have on Germany—the destruction of the German economy and the rise of Adolf Hitler—nor fear the effects of his "democratic" stabilization of Europe—the rise of Benito Mussolini—nor foresee the outcome of a politically redrawn Europe—the ethnic wars in a "unified" Yugoslavia during the 1990s. Wilson believed in experimentation, at home and abroad, and both the United States and Europe suffered from his experiments.

Wilson and House hid their agenda behind the cloak of "democracy" and reform. Neither cared for the Constitution as written and ratified; both favored the type of executive action Americans have become accustomed to in the last one hundred years. Every time an American complains about executive overreach, he can thank Woodrow Wilson. Wilson had a legislative agenda, and like a prime minister, he expected Congress to follow it; beginning with his tenure in office, the legislative branch has been too willing to defer to the executive. Wilson also believed that the president

---

★ ★ ★ ★ ★ ★ ★ ★ ★ ★ ★ ★ ★ ★ ★

"He Kept Us Out of War"?

Wilson lied to the public during the 1916 presidential campaign; he had no desire to keep the United States out of war. He was already privately pushing American involvement in World War I—to the degree that his anti-interventionist secretary of state, William Jennings Bryan, resigned *before* the 1916 election because he could not stand Wilson's bald-faced duplicity with the American people.

did not need much political experience, just the right "particular qualities of mind and character" to do the job. You might call that "democratic," but in practice it meant relying on the advice of the utopian political insider and thug who has often been dubbed his co-president, "Colonel" House. Together, Wilson and House systematically planned for a complete transformation of the American system, and unfortunately succeeded. Their "reforms"—from a scheme to centralize the American banking system, to a pre-meditated plan to involve America in a massive world war while deceiving the public about it, to the usurpation of the legislative process by the executive branch—were not really democratic. That makes them both "democratic frauds," and they should be remembered as such.

Chapter 15

FASCIST FRAUD

Franklin D. Roosevelt

“"hen the war drums rolled a great golden veil came down upon the American scene through which its actors would be viewed. Behind it they postured—statesmen and generals and admirals—in the role of heroes. And lifted above them all, posing in the full glory of the stage lights, decorated by propaganda with the virtues of a national god, was the figure of the Leader."[1] So wrote journalist John T. Flynn about Franklin D. Roosevelt in 1948—though his words sound more appropriate for Adolf Hitler or Benito Mussolini. That was the point. To Flynn and many other Americans in the 1930s and 1940s, Roosevelt was the American version of a European-style dictator. He used crises to build his political career on the blood, toil, and hardships of the American people and was nothing more than a demagogue, an opportunist. But this is not the image most Americans have of the thirty-second president.

Leftist historians love him, and for every negative account of his career, personality, programs, and foreign policy, there are shelves of books in his defense. Roosevelt is inevitably in the top three of any "historical ranking" of the presidents, is viewed as the man who "saved America from the Great Depression" and "liberated Europe" from totalitarian fascism, and is seen

Did you know?

★ FDR refused to help Herbert Hoover ameliorate the Great Depression, and then his own New Deal made it worse

★ Roosevelt admired Mussolini

★ Before Pearl Harbor, Roosevelt's Secretary of War wrote about maneuvering the Japanese into "firing the first shot"

★ By the end of World War II a quarter of Americans depended on government for some income

as a hero for the common American. He deserves none of this. Roosevelt should not even sniff the top half of presidential rankings. The New Deal made the Great Depression worse, and Roosevelt's foreign policy went from devious manipulations to get America into World War II to embroiling the United States in a decades-long Cold War with the Soviet Union. He was a notorious philanderer and duplicitous showman. There needs to be a serious historical correction about Franklin Roosevelt.

Books You're Not Supposed to Read

The Roosevelt Myth by John T. Flynn (New York: The Devin-Adair Company, 1948).

The Politically Incorrect Guide™ to the Great Depression and the New Deal by Robert Murphy (Washington DC: Regnery, 2009).

The People's Pottage by Garet Garrett (Caldwell, OH: The Caxton Printers, 1953).

The American Aristocrat

Roosevelt was born in 1882 in New York. His family was one of the oldest and most prominent in American history, having been in New York since the days of early Dutch settlement. One ancestor fought in the American War for Independence, and the family had made millions in real estate and trade. As a result, young Roosevelt led a charmed life, one that most Americans cannot relate to. He traveled Europe and attended the finest schools. His undeserved image as a hero of the common man hardly jibes with his aristocratic lineage. We are perpetually reminded of the privileged background of almost every other wealthy American—particularly the Founding Fathers—but Roosevelt gets a pass.

Roosevelt was never considered to be much of a thinker, but he was a superb politician, and he expertly used his family name and connections to advance his political career. He served as state senator, assistant secretary of the navy, and governor of New York. At each stop, Roosevelt built his political empire and waited for an opportunity to shine on the grand American political stage. He was a showman who loved the spotlight and craved attention. Women flocked to him. Roosevelt married his fifth cousin Eleanor Roosevelt in 1905 and had six children, but that did not stop him from seeing other women. In fact, his long-term mistress Lucy Mercer, not his wife, was with him the day he died in Georgia in 1945. That was the most conspicuous affair, but there were others. Roosevelt was no model of marital fidelity.

Roosevelt was nominated for president in 1932 during one of the worst economic crises in American history. He had the support of Joe Kennedy and several other prominent Democrats. His election was assured, but Roosevelt had no interest in saving the American economy—at least not before becoming president. The outgoing president, Herbert Hoover, contacted Roosevelt weeks before his inauguration in 1933, begging him to work with the Hoover administration to solve the banking crisis. Roosevelt stuffed the private note in his pocket and showed it to his political advisers only as a way of showing up Hoover. What Roosevelt wanted was to be seen as the savior of the American people, the knight in white armor riding in to Washington, D.C., in March 1933. Meanwhile, Hoover could go down in flames, and the American economy with him. Roosevelt didn't care, as long as he could be the one to provide the solutions—solutions he unfortunately stole from… Herbert Hoover. As Barack Obama's henchman Rahm Emanuel said in 2008, "Never let a good crisis go to waste." Decades earlier, Franklin Roosevelt was already acting on that principle.

The American Dictator

In his Inaugural Address, Roosevelt promised to circumvent Congress if they failed to act in accord with his wishes. "I shall not evade the clear course of duty that will confront me," he thundered. He bullied Congress to change the Constitution without the benefit of amendments, arguing that the "emergency" of the Great Depression made emergency measures necessary. So Congress usurped power from the states, and Roosevelt in his turn from Congress. The end result was a centralization of American political and economic life unprecedented in American history. If the federal republic was not dead before 1933, it certainly died a swift death in the "First Hundred Days" of Roosevelt's administration. He was nothing short of an American dictator.

Roosevelt's blatantly unconstitutional actions during the "First New Deal" are legendary. He signed into law a "bank holiday" whereby all banks in the United States were shut down and then re-opened backed by the full faith and credit of the United States. No one could find the authority for a "bank holiday" in the Constitution, but Roosevelt declared one anyway, of course with the blessing of his tame Congress. That made it acceptable. His New Deal programs, notably the National Industry Recovery Act (NIRA) and the Agricultural Adjustment Administration (AAA), co-opted the American economy through central economic planning, price fixing, wage controls, and slash-and-burn agricultural policies. Americans were forced to pay more for industrial and agricultural goods at a time when over twenty million people were unemployed. Even President Jimmy Carter, no conservative, recalled in his book *An Hour Before Daylight* that the AAA did serious damage to farmers across the South when they had to slaughter pigs and plow under crops to keep prices artificially high; he lived through the New Deal as a boy in rural Georgia.

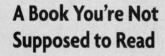

A Book You're Not Supposed to Read

America's Great Depression by Murray N. Rothbard (Auburn, AL: Ludwig von Mises Institute, 2000). A superb dissection of the causes of the Great Depression and the idiotic "solutions"—which actually made it worse—offered by state planners like Roosevelt.

Roosevelt continued the irresponsible policies of the 1920s by signing mountains of legislation that increased the federal debt tenfold. Ultimately, the value of the dollar was cut in half. He signed unconstitutional legislation to seize private gold reserves in the United States, making it a crime for private citizens to own gold. He spent wildly, trying to revive the economy by "priming the pump." All the while, unemployment remained above 14 percent for his entire first two terms in office. When the economy dipped again in 1936, Roosevelt and his economic minions simply called it a "recession"—a much softer term than depression—insisting that the economy would rebound. Roosevelt's policies were failing, and

he knew it. He attempted to pack the Supreme Court with sycophantic judges in 1937 in order to ram unconstitutional legislation through the judiciary review process. The court-packing plan crashed and burned, but

not without giving Roosevelt the moniker "King Franklin." What he needed was another good crisis.

Roosevelt believed he was greater than any man who had ever served as president—better than George Washington or Thomas Jefferson. How do we know that? In 1939, Roosevelt decided to break the long-standing precedent established by George Washington and run for a third term in the 1940 election. Roosevelt

claimed that the military "crisis" in Europe made this necessary. He alone was best equipped to deal with a supposed threat from Germany. No matter that Roosevelt had been conciliatory toward Hitler throughout the 1930s, that Mussolini had been admired within the Roosevelt administration (the

A Play You're Not Supposed to See

Knickerbocker Holiday by Maxwell Anderson and Kurt Weill. This play, which hit Broadway in 1939, was a thinly veiled attack on Roosevelt—comparing him to fascist dictators Hitler and Mussolini—using early New York history as a backdrop.

A Book You're Not Supposed to Read

Three New Deals: Reflections on Roosevelt's America, Mussolini's Italy, and Hitler's Germany, 1933–1939 by Wolfgang Schivelbusch (New York: Metropolitan, 2006).

president himself had spoken of Il Duce as "that admirable Italian gentleman" to a reporter, and Roosevelt adviser Rexford Tugwell had called Mussolini's Italy "the cleanest... most efficiently operating piece of social machinery I've ever seen. It makes me envious."),[2] or that his economic plan mirrored much of what Hitler and Mussolini had done in Germany and Italy respectively. Roosevelt needed a way to stay in power, and World War II offered that opportunity.

Heil Roosevelt!

"[I am] in accord with the President in the view that the virtue of duty, readiness for sacrifice, and discipline should dominate the entire people. These moral demands which the President places before every individual citizen of the United States are also the quintessence of the German state philosophy, which finds its expression in the slogan 'The Public Weal Transcends the Interest of the Individual.'"

—Adolf Hitler, in a 1933 message to Franklin Roosevelt[3]

The Warmonger

Roosevelt began preparing for war with Germany long before 1941, though most Americans were unaware of his plans. Through legislation, Roosevelt began arming the United States and her eventual allies, quietly building up the American military while American banks became actively involved in helping fund the war for the British. By diplomatic channels, he was privately pushing the notion that the United States should serve as the driving force in a "one world" peace arrangement. That dream had been alive since World War I, but as in World War I, the United States had no dog in this fight, save for what Churchill would later call our "special relationship" with the British. Germany had no interest in invading the United States, and with a large ocean between Germany and America's shores, many Americans were asking what the United States had to fear. If Germany could not even conquer England, a close neighbor, by air power, how was it conceivable that Germany could attack the United States by air? And after

Hitler violated his non-aggression pact with the Soviet Union in 1941, a full six months before the bombing at Pearl Harbor, many asked whether it might not be better to let the two dictators slug it out in Europe. Roosevelt thought not, but he needed a kick, something to wake the Americans out of their anti-war slumber. Japan provided that impetus.

Secretary of War Henry Stimson wrote in his diary on November 25, 1941, that "the question is how we should maneuver them [Japan] into the position of firing the first shot without allowing too much danger to ourselves."[4] That diary entry, less than two weeks before the attack on Pearl Harbor, showed that the United States had been deliberately provoking the Japanese into war. By the end of November, the Roosevelt administration had given up attempting to find a peaceful solution to the problems with Japan—problems the United States had helped create in the first place.

Earlier in 1941, Cordell Hull, Roosevelt's secretary of state, had drawn up ten demands that he knew the Japanese would reject, sat back, and waited for the inevitable. Unfortunately the administration's preparations for the inevitable did not include warning the United States Pacific Fleet that the Japanese planned to attack. A week before Pearl Harbor, American listening stations in Hawaii had intercepted messages from the Japanese navy detailing a planned attack on Hawaii, and on December 4, 1941, just three days before Pearl Harbor, these same listening stations identified the code word for war. If Pearl Harbor was a surprise attack, as Roosevelt insisted, it sure wasn't a surprise to him, his administration, or possibly even his military advisers. But there were no preparations made to ramp up American defenses. Roosevelt knew what he was doing. According to reports he was as calm as a summer breeze in the days leading up to the attack and even more so on the day of the attack, sitting in his study with *all incoming phone calls cut off*, studying his stamp album—not his usual habit.

In fact, warnings were delayed and the proper protocols ignored when messages relating to the attack began filtering into Washington. George C.

Marshall, Roosevelt's army chief of staff, was unreachable when attempts were made to contact him on December 7. The historian Charles Tansill, at a great cost to his career, wrote about this in 1952 with his typical wit and humor: "General Marshall… for some strange reason, suddenly decided to go on a long horseback ride. It was a history-making ride. In the early hours of the American Revolution, Paul Revere went on a famous ride to warn his countrymen of the enemy's approach and thus save American lives. In the early hours of World War II, General Marshall took a ride that helped prevent an alert from reaching Pearl Harbor in time to save an American fleet from serious disaster and an American garrison from a bombing that cost more than two thousand lives."[5] The rest is history.

Tansill asks, "Was the preservation of the British Empire worth the blood, sweat, and tears not only of the men who would die in the agony of Pearl Harbor but also of the long roll of heroes who perished in the epic encounters in the Pacific, in the Mediterranean area, and in the famous offensive that rolled at high tide across the war-torn fields of France?"[6]

Of course, Roosevelt used this new crisis to his advantage. While the New Deal centralized the American economy, World War II gave the government real teeth. Several new government boards were created to manage production and consumption. If the Supreme Court could knock down the NIRA, then Roosevelt would simply use the war to circumvent the judicial branch. The War Production Board (WPB)—created unconstitutionally by a Roosevelt executive order—placed all industrial production under the supervision of the government. Certain products, such as major appliances, were prohibited from being produced, as metal, plastics, and even paper and gasoline were being rationed by the government for the war. People who voted for Roosevelt to end bread lines

A Book You're Not Supposed to Read

Back Door to War by Charles C. Tansill (Chicago: Henry Regnery Company, 1952).

in 1932 now had to wait in line for sugar. Inflation and government spending increased during the war, and the government-mandated wage and labor controls were in part a nod to Roosevelt's support for the mass unionization of American workers. Big government now became a leviathan—and not by accident.

And that was only part of the mess Roosevelt left in the wake of the war. His negotiations with Joseph Stalin set the table for the Cold War, and his insistence on a replacement for the useless League of Nations saddled the United States with the prospects of a "world government" under the United Nations. It has been argued that the UN has prevented World War III, but this has not stopped American soldiers from dying in several wars after the end of hostilities in 1945. Arlington National Cemetery is full of dead heroes who perished since the establishment of the United Nations. As the historian Philip Bobbitt illustrated in his *Shield of Achilles*, World War II was simply part of a larger war that began in 1914 and ended only with the fall of communism in 1990. Woodrow Wilson and Franklin Roosevelt are responsible for hundreds of thousands of American lives snuffed out in that seventy-year period.

Roosevelt did not save or preserve anything in the United States, and he created only chaos in foreign policy. By the end of the war, one quarter of the American people were dependent on the government for some type of income. The debt had skyrocketed, and though Roosevelt never publicly advocated tax increases, the American people were saddled with new taxes from Social Security—and of course the hidden taxes of inflation, as the dollar lost half its value in this period. The United States economy has remained a wartime economy since. Progressives love "Guns and Butter." Perhaps it would be better to say fascists love them. Roosevelt fits that description nicely. The fact that Roosevelt is classified as a great president means that Americans have lost all connection with the founding generation. That is what the progressives always wanted.

Chapter 16

FEMINIST FRAUDS

Betty Friedan and Margaret Sanger

Feminist "heroes" are now enshrined in the pantheon of American greats. Like other "champions of the oppressed," they are given special honors in today's politically correct version of American history. America was unfair. America reneged on its promise of "liberty and equality" (when actually the idea of putting "equality" on the same plane with "liberty" came out of the French Revolution, not the American War of Independence). America was a place where only white males could succeed. Feminists came to the rescue and helped women begin to achieve equal dignity and opportunities—but their work is still not finished. (One wonders, when will it ever be? They've done quite an impressive amount of damage already.)

Long before modern feminism, there were women who believed in the intellectual equality of the sexes, and rightly so. Three of them are included among the American heroes in this book. But these women also recognized that traditional gender roles had worked well for thousands of years, producing generations of successful statesmen, soldiers, husbands, fathers, mothers, wives, farmers, lawyers, businessmen, doctors, philanthropists, inventors, and teachers. The moral values and traditions of earlier generations are a testament to the effectiveness of traditional motherhood. Traditional women, however brilliant their achievements in the wider world, believed in selfless devotion to family and society and thought that a well-educated woman was an asset to her husband, family, and community regardless of whether she had a successful "career." Even early feminists like Elizabeth Cady Stanton thought that a woman's primary role was wife and mother, and that large families were a blessing rather than a curse.

But beginning in the late nineteenth and early twentieth centuries, these positions were challenged by a new wave of feminists uncomfortable with women's traditional role in society. Out in front were Margaret Sanger and Betty Friedan, two women considered to be heroes by many on the Left.

The Birth Control Crusader

Margaret Sanger was born Margaret Higgins in New York in 1879 to Catholic parents. She was the sixth of eleven children and spent much of her early life caring for her family. Sanger attended boarding school for two years as a teenager but returned home to care for her sick and dying mother. With the help of some affluent friends, Sanger enrolled in nursing school near the turn of the century, a move that eventually led to her more famous career as a political activist.

Sanger married in 1902 and had three children. Her youngest child, Peggy, died in 1915, just shy of her fifth birthday, a painful loss that had a terrible effect on Sanger. She had recently been estranged from her husband and was working as a nurse in the slums of Manhattan. The suffering she witnessed her mother endure as a child, the loss of her own child, and the plight of poor mothers in Manhattan convinced Sanger that women were "enslaved" by childbirth. To Sanger, childbirth and large families were a curse rather than a blessing, particularly for women who could not afford to feed and care for multiple children.

She founded the modern birth control movement to alleviate this suffering. Sanger began her crusade in 1912 by publishing the articles "What Every Girl Should Know" and "What Every Mother Should Know" in a socialist New York newspaper. Two years later she launched a newsletter titled *The Woman Rebel*. It was here, and in collaboration with various progressive leaders, that she created the term "birth control," a softer and more palatable term than "family limitation," which she had used earlier.

But even this term was offensive in the moral and religious America of her day. Disseminating literature that contained contraceptive information was against federal law. Sanger openly flaunted her illegal promotion of birth control, and she had to flee to Europe in 1915 under an alias to avoid arrest. In the meantime, she was sentenced to thirty days in jail for distribution of illegal literature.

Clarence Darrow offered to serve as her counsel, but after she returned to the United States the charges were dropped, presumably because of substantial public pressure against her arrest in and around New York, particularly from the "muckraking" intellectual crowd led by Upton Sinclair of *The Jungle* fame.

In defiance of the law, Sanger opened a birth control clinic in New York in 1916. It was shut down in a little over a week and Sanger

A Cure Worse than the Disease

"The most merciful thing that the large family does to one of its infant members is to kill it. The same factors which create the terrible infant mortality rate, and which swell the death rate of children between the ages of one and five, operate even more extensively to lower the health rate of the surviving members."

—Margaret Sanger[1]

Hear Me Roar

Long before the 1972 Helen Reddy hit "I Am Woman" there was Margaret Sanger.
She urged women to "look the whole world in the face with a go-to-hell look in the eyes; to have an ideal; to speak and act in defiance of convention."[2]

was arrested. This time she did not flee, hoping for a public trial. She got her wish and was sentenced to thirty days incarceration. Two years later, in appeals, a New York judge ruled that contraception could be legally distributed by a physician. Thus began the medical birth control phenomenon in the United States, much to the consternation of the orthodox Christian churches, who at the time were universally opposed to contraception. But Sanger, putting it mildly, didn't care what the Christian churches had to say about birth control.

In 1920, Sanger published *Woman and the New Race*, a frontal assault on traditional society and on Christian morals in particular. Here she expanded on her thesis that women are "slaves" in traditional society and that only through control of reproduction can they gain true liberty. The norms of traditional society had been imposed upon women by men and the Church, because woman, Sanger argued, "since time immemorial... has sought some form of family limitation."[3] In Sanger's estimation, the traditional family was never in line with true femininity; it was only the creation of some misogynist who wanted to keep a "slave" in the household to mop up after him and birth and rear his children. Creation and biology had nothing to do with traditional gender roles, which were a social construct.

Sanger takes this line of argument further in a chapter entitled "Women and the New Morality." She calls feminine purity a "bugaboo," argues that traditional morality is based on "ignorance and submission," classifies marital intimacy as nothing more than "legal rape," and opines that children born out of "accidents" are condemned to misery and hardship because their mothers did not want them and have no time or energy to love and care for them. Sanger insists that at the heart of this oppressive traditional morality is fear inculcated by Christian clerics— reproductive freedom was the last chain holding women in "intellectual darkness," a darkness that could be enlightened by the accepted truths of science and most importantly evolution.[4] She was firing both barrels at Christianity, supposedly misogynistic "Dark-Ages" clerics, and their purportedly brainwashed followers.

Sanger's life at this point was definitely not that of a traditional woman. While she wrote as an advocate for mothers and children, her own personal life was a wreck. She was estranged from her husband, had affairs with high-profile progressives, and ultimately divorced in 1921, only to remarry the following year, to wealthy oil magnate J. N. Slee. Slee's money helped fund Sanger's social activism and birth control programs for the next two decades.

To Sanger, birth control represented a higher calling, the ability to create a new and improved race of people—literally. She dabbled in eugenics and at one time appointed well-known eugenicist and white supremacist Lothrop Stoddard to the board of her American Birth Control League, founded in 1921. His book *The Rising Tide of Color Against White World-Supremacy* was written *before* his appointment to the League; the work had been well received by one of Sanger's lovers and confidants, Havelock Ellis (Ellis had written the introduction to her *Woman and the New Race*). While Sanger never openly embraced the very worst of the eugenics movement, which would soon be made infamous by the Nazis, she did

A Book You're Not Supposed to Read

Margaret Sanger's Eugenic Legacy: The Control of Female Fertility by Angela Franks (New York: McFarland Press, 2005).

at one point run the slogan: "Birth Control: To Create a Race of Thoroughbreds" on the cover of her magazine, *The Birth Control Review*.

And then there is the Klan. Sanger wrote in her *Autobiography* that it was "one of the weirdest experiences I had in lecturing," but the fact is, she accepted an invitation to speak to a women's Ku Klux Klan rally in Silver Lake, New Jersey, in the mid-1920s because "any aroused group was a good group." Her lecture bore fruit. In her words, "the conversation went on and on until the late hours of the night" and her appearance inspired "a dozen invitations to speak to similar groups...."[5] Sanger's desire to reach any audience is understandable, but the fact that she accepted an invitation to speak at a Klan rally raises questions about Sanger's racial beliefs and her enthusiasm about birth control for the minority population. She did, in fact, believe that white people were racially superior, and though she never advocated the extermination of black Americans, as some have suggested, she was very interested in curbing pregnancies in that minority population

Sanger's crowning achievement was the formation of the Planned Parenthood Federation of America in 1942 as part of an international attempt to push birth control and combat legislation outlawing it. Her birth control clinics had been in operation since the early 1920s, but now Sanger focused her time, money, and energy on legal challenges to the Comstock Laws, which forbade the dissemination of birth control. Planned Parenthood has since become the recognized arm of the pro-abortion wing of the "women's movement" in America. To give her credit where credit is due, Sanger denounced abortion; actually, she originally became interested in birth control to limit the practice, but like John Dewey in education and Herbert Croly in progressive ideology, she had opened a Pandora's Box.

Sanger died in 1966, just one year after the Supreme Court made birth control legal for all

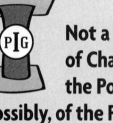

Not a Big Fan of Charity to the Poor—nor, Possibly, of the Poor Themselves

"The effect of maternity endowments and maternity centers supported by private philanthropy would have, perhaps already have had, exactly the most dysgenic tendency.... It encourages the healthier and more normal sections of the world to shoulder the burden of unthinking and indiscriminate fecundity of others; which brings with it, as I think the reader must agree, a dead weight of human waste. Instead of decreasing and aiming to eliminate the stocks that are most detrimental to the future of the race and the world, it tends to render them to a menacing degree dominant."

—Margaret Sanger[6]

married couples in America, and six years before the Supreme Court applied that ruling to all women. She has since been called one of the hundred most important women in history. Awards are given annually in her name. Perhaps if more Americans understood Sanger's checkered life, her disdain for Christianity, and her connections to the Klan and other white supremacists, they would have a different opinion of the "hero" of the modern birth control movement. One can only hope.

The Feminist

Whether most Americans realize it or not, Betty Friedan has changed the way we think about femininity and the family. She is, without question, one of the most important "heroes" of the Left, and her career is still shaping the way women on both the Left and the Right view family and career. If Sanger changed the size of the American family, Friedan changed the role of wife and mother in the family, the role of women in society at large, and the way the debate over "women's issues" has been framed in the media.

Friedan was born in Illinois in 1921. Her father owned a jewelry store and her mother was a traditional housewife. After her father became ill, her mother began working outside the home, a transition that Friedan said left her mother more satisfied. This memory stuck with Friedan for the rest of her life.

She was an avowed Marxist who had been engaged in left-wing politics both before and during college. She attended the all-female Smith College

This Land Is Her Land

"The woman is not needed to do man's work. She is not needed to think man's thoughts. She need not fear that the masculine mind, almost universally dominant, will fail to take care of its own. Her mission is not to enhance the masculine spirit, but to express the feminine; hers is not to preserve a man-made world, but to create a human world by the infusion of the feminine element into all of its activities."

—Margaret Sanger [7]

where she earned a bachelor's degree in psychology. She took graduate courses in psychology at the University of California at Berkeley for one year before leaving the program, because—she claimed—her boyfriend had pressured her to do so (blame it on the man).

For the next twenty years, Friedan worked as a journalist and freelance writer for various left-wing publications and acted as a community organizer. She was a sixties radical before the term existed and readily embraced—or rather, helped pioneer—sixties leftism.

Then she struck gold. After attending a college reunion in 1957, Friedan "discovered" that she, along with many of her fellow graduates, had become discontented with the traditional "housewife" role supposedly imposed on them by a male-dominated society (blame it on the man). She decided to write a book that detailed women's collective experiences and to show

A Book You're Not Supposed to Read

Betty Friedan and the Making of "The Feminine Mystique": The American Left, the Cold War, and Modern Feminism by David Horowitz (University of Massachusetts Press, 2000).

how men had shaped the role of women to their own liking in an effort to keep them at home, repressed, stupid, barefoot, and pregnant. Friedan's arguments were a major impetus for what has been labeled "Second Wave Feminism" in the United States.

The Feminine Mystique, published in 1963, became the bible of feminism. Friedan's perhaps-not-so-exhaustive research focused on narratives of several of her socialite friends' lives, the highly selective use of magazine advertisements, and her own life experience—which would hardly qualify as "traditional" in any sense of the word. The first chapter—"The Problem That Has No Name"—opens with this iconic paragraph:

The problem lay buried, unspoken, for many years in the minds of American women. It was a strange stirring, a sense of dissatisfaction, a yearning that women suffered in the middle of the twentieth century in the United States. Each suburban wife struggled with it alone. As she made the beds, shopped for groceries, matched slipcover material, ate peanut butter sandwiches with her children, chauffeured Cub Scouts and Brownies, lay beside her husband at night—she was afraid to ask even of herself the silent question—"Is this all?"[8]

For the next three hundred pages, Friedan proceeds to take apart American society by... blaming everything on the man. Women were unsatisfied as housewives, and they had been forced into that role by men. Women who tried to break the chains of housewife slavery were smacked down by men returning home from World War II. Women could not cope with the drudgery of housewife hell, so they turned to other things—affairs for example—to satisfy their unmet needs. Women's magazines focused on women almost exclusively as cooks, housekeepers, and mothers rather than as real, creative beings, and of course these advertisements were created by—wait for it—*men*. Housewives were trapped by their own biology, forced to look pretty to please men, act a certain way to please men, and believe that the only satisfaction in life came from being a wife and mother—a lie perpetuated by, of course, men. A woman's life revolved around men and children, if she had any, and her schooling only reinforced this idea.

The book became a bestseller. Friedan, an abrasive, egotistical, and mean-spirited person prone to screaming fits, was now the leading figure in the "women's rights" movement. She founded the National Organization for Women (NOW) in 1966 and began using legal challenges to push a feminist agenda. This suited her personality and her career path to that point. Her Marxist past made it natural that she should pursue legal and political "solutions" to perceived societal "problems," and that she should assume that strong central government was needed to enforce those solutions.

Friedan, however, did not always get along even with other feminists. She was unceremoniously dumped as president of NOW in 1969, and by the 1970s her movement had been hijacked by Gloria Steinem and other even more radical feminists. Though Friedan was a cutting-edge Marxist, she was not radical enough for the pro-abortion, pro-lesbian crowd that followed in her wake.

The tragedy is that American women were persuaded to throw traditional womanhood away by a case that was full of holes. Friedan's book purported to be based on historical scholarship, but there have been several challenges to both her research and her credibility. The historian Joanne Meyerowitz took Friedan apart in a 1993 article entitled "Beyond the Feminine Mystique" in the *Journal of American History*. Friedan, Meyerowitz demonstrated, had been quite selective in her research. In fact, many magazines had shown women as *both* housewives and employees; they had presented a much more robust and complex image of woman than Friedan had allowed in her work. They were feminine, yes—but also crafty, intelligent, and supportive figures, not downtrodden slaves, beholden to men.

Furthermore, the historian Daniel Horowitz, at one time a Friedan supporter, has illustrated that Friedan's credentials as a "housewife" were suspect. She worked for pay, had maids to do her housework, and was married to a man who actually gave up his career to support Friedan and their children (and who did not in fact beat her, as she later claimed, and then denied)—all during the period Friedan was supposed to be the trapped housewife slave in the "comfortable concentration camp." And she had always been an activist. In short, Friedan could not be trusted. She had no real "street cred." Friedan craved the spotlight and got it. She used a fictional narrative of her own life (she had never even worked a washing machine) to buttress her claims of feminine woes. If she was duplicitous about her own marriage, how could anyone trust the other elements of her case against traditional womanhood? Friedan was simply guilty of the same type of power lust that many people in society—men and women alike—have today: she was willing to lie, if necessary, to become famous. How can that be classified as heroic?

Regardless, Friedan has become a hero to millions of American women. Traditional images of women have been replaced by a sexless ideal. Gender roles are blurred (of course Friedan blamed this, too, on men in one of her chapters), and the traditional housewife is now scorned rather than applauded. Refreshingly, a growing number of women today are confronting this paradigm shift head-on, doing their best to revive the traditional womanhood that feminists trashed in the sixties and seventies. But they have a long, steep battle ahead of them—made more difficult by the fraudulent work of Sanger and Friedan.

Chapter 17

FAMILY FRAUDS

Camelot and the Kennedy Clan

No image from American politics shines brighter than that of the Kennedy Clan and Camelot. According to the establishment they are America's royalty, a tragic set of men who were doomed by their own success. "Handsome," "brilliant," "dashing," and "charming" have all been used to describe the four titans of the clan—Joe Kennedy, John F. Kennedy, Robert F. Kennedy, and Edward Kennedy. The terms "thug," "adulterer," and "swindler of the American people" would be more accurate. The clan was all image and no substance from the beginning—and they brought their flashy, fraudulent style into the political world at the highest levels. Americans have been fooled ever since.

Jack, Bobby, and Ted were the products of their environment, and the three sons learned almost everything about life from their father, Joe. Perhaps they can be excused, at least in part, for inheriting the sins of their father. When a man finds it so easy to cheat both his family and the system, it is hard to see how his sons are going to learn to behave any differently. Still, as adults—particularly as powerful members of the federal government—they had a duty to behave in an honorable manner. That is what heroes and statesmen do. The Kennedys were neither.

Did you know?

★ Joe Kennedy opposed U.S. entry into World War II out of anti-Semitism

★ Cheating on pregnant wives was a Kennedy family tradition

★ JFK accepted a Pulitzer Prize for a ghostwritten book and never credited the real author

229

The Sins of the Father

Joe Kennedy was born in Boston in 1888. His father, P. J. Kennedy, was a hard-nosed political knee-capper who made his fortune first in the liquor business as a bar owner, then as a political thug who specialized in graft. He learned whom to know and whom to intimidate, traits that served his son, grandsons, and other members of his extended family well.

Joe Kennedy was never much of a student. He did poorly in school and was admitted to Harvard only because of family influence. He liked baseball and was a crafty businessman, even in his younger days. What he could not earn honestly, he cheated to get. For example, he "earned" a letter in baseball at Harvard by weaseling his way onto the field for the final outs of the last game of the season—and then refused to give the game ball to the winning pitcher. He put it in his pocket. He learned to shark money from unsuspecting saps who took the bait in crooked business deals. When his shady deals didn't work out, he relied on his daddy to bail him out or get him a job. Kennedy loved money and power, but what he loved most was women. And the combination of the three was a drug he couldn't refuse.

★ ★ ★ ★ ★ ★ ★ ★ ★ ★ ★ ★ ★ ★ ★

Family Tradition

"Mort [Morton Downey] did him favors in the department Joe liked best—girls." Downey typically passed along the gorgeous women of Hollywood to the married father of nine, and his sons naturally followed in his footsteps.[1]

Joe married Rose Elizabeth Fitzgerald, the daughter of powerful Boston mayor John "Honey Fitz" Fitzgerald, in 1914. Joe may or may not have loved Rose, but she made a perfect political ally. The union merged the two most powerful and corrupt families of Boston into a potent political force. Joe and Rose had nine children, though Joe was never faithful, even in the early years when the two were dating. Rose once caught him with a couple of college buddies and some girls, but Joe talked his way out of it. She should have known then. In his later years, Joe made it a habit never to lie about his extra-marital affairs, but he often left his pregnant wife alone while cavorting with other women on the West Coast and elsewhere. That habit became a Kennedy family trait.

After Joe was graduated from Harvard, P. J. procured him a job as a state bank examiner. He used the skills he learned in that job to rip off dozens of banks and businesses in his long business career. Joe also mastered the art of "insider trading" during his brief stint in the banking business. Because of such insider information, Joe was able to acquire—by borrowing money from family members, money that he never repaid—a struggling bank in 1913 for pennies on the dollar. His initial $45,000 investment netted him millions. At twenty-five, at least according to Joe, he became the youngest bank president in the country. No one knows if that claim is true, but Joe said it, so the press believed it. That became one of his most valuable skills—fabricating stories for the press.

Joe's success in banking and his high-profile marriage to the daughter of Boston's political boss enabled him to skip World War I. All of his friends out of college joined the fight in Europe, but not Joe. When his draft registration put him on a list of highly probable draftees, his father-in-law pulled some strings and got him a job as a shipbuilder in Boston with a contract for building Navy destroyers. This job let him escape the draft entirely while earning a nice paycheck for doing nothing. He quit the job just a few months after peace in Europe, when he no longer needed it to keep him out the war. (Joe didn't need Woodrow Wilson for that. He had his father-in-law.)

> ★ ★ ★ ★ ★ ★ ★ ★ ★ ★ ★ ★ ★ ★
>
> ## "I'd Rather Have a Bottle in Front of Me than a Frontal Lobotomy"
>
> Joe had a hand in both. In 1941, he had his oldest daughter, Rose Marie, lobotomized in a controversial move to "cure" her mental problems. Many think Rosie suffered from mental retardation and was not a good candidate for the procedure, which was used to treat mental illness.

Joe took advantage of the "roaring twenties." He dabbled in the stock market, made a small fortune on "short selling"—a practice he later helped make illegal during his time as the first chairman of the Securities and Exchange Commission under Franklin Roosevelt—and became a prominent bootlegger. Joe put the glamor in organized crime. He bought and sold liquor illegally, and his buddies in crime bragged that they made him rich. (Joe's connections in the criminal world later served his son Jack well in the 1960 presidential campaign. They helped bankroll it.) Miraculously, Joe avoided the stock market crash of 1929, perhaps because he knew it was coming. He switched his investments to real estate, gobbled up distressed properties, and by 1935 had increased his net wealth by forty-five times. He would be a billionaire today. And Joe used his power and influence in the government to choke out other investors. Kennedy personified crony capitalism.

He later became involved in movie production and bedded several "A-list" actresses. Joe worked hard to remove Jews from the business side of Hollywood. He despised Jews, so much so that as ambassador to Great Britain he diligently worked to keep the United States out of World War II. In contrast to Charles Lindbergh, who wished to avoid war because he believed the United States was unprepared, Joe Kennedy wished to keep the United States out of the war because he did not want to benefit Jews. His private correspondence is littered with racial slurs and derogatory comments about Jewish people. Because of his opposition to the war, his public influence gradually waned, but Joe never gave up hope that one day a Kennedy would assume the highest political office in the United States. He had dumped thousands into Franklin Roosevelt's campaigns. By 1960, Joe thought he deserved a little political payback.

A Book You're Not Supposed to Read

The Sins of the Father: Joseph P. Kennedy and the Dynasty He Founded by Ronald Kessler (New York: Warner Books, 1996).

Though all three of Joe's high-profile children are regarded by the Left, and even by some on the Right, as great men, they shouldn't be. All three boys (they could not be called responsible men) lived in a perpetual pseudo-college fraternity. They never grew up. They were terrible with money—Joe had a standing order that no Kennedy was to discuss finances, and thus all spent more than they made and lived off their father's generosity—drank heavily, used drugs, and philandered like Hugh Hefner. Responsibility was not a word the Kennedy boys knew or understood, at least not in their private lives, and their private lives often spilled over into their public roles.

Jack

John F. Kennedy is the most conspicuous of the three boys, mostly because he was elected president in 1960 and later assassinated in 1963. His untimely death may be the reason he is so highly regarded today. The scandals and misadventures of his administration never saw the light of day until after he was dead and buried, and by that point his legacy had reached almost mythical proportions. Kennedy himself wondered aloud if his legacy, like Abraham Lincoln's, would not be solidified by an assassination. Assassinated presidents are often given a pass by the American people for their "sacrifice." But Jack left a trail of seedy escapades in his wake.

Born in 1917, the second son to Joe and Rose, Jack was not supposed to be the standard-bearer for the Kennedy clan. His older brother Joe, who died in a wartime accident in 1944, was pegged by their father to be the first Catholic president of the United States. Jack had to do instead, but because he was never groomed for the role, Jack spent his youth in lazy debauchery.

> **A Book You're Not Supposed to Read**
>
> *The Dark Side of Camelot* by Seymour M. Hersh (Boston: Little Brown and Co., 1997).

Like his father, he was never considered much of a student, and he partied with his daddy's money like a spoiled child. He drove his convertible all over the United States and Europe, and in the process picked up every girl he could, from the students at Radcliffe to the California girls he met on the West Coast during his one-year stint at Stanford Business School. He got a tan—and a case of gonorrhea. Jack supposedly became a much more serious student in his final year at Harvard, but he never had much interest in a real career, and though he attended business school, he didn't learn much.

Because of a chronically bad back, Jack was disqualified from serving the army when the United States entered World War II. He got a commission in the navy instead and because of family connections was able to secure the command of a patrol boat—PT 109. He was never considered a good skipper and avoided commanding "by the book." His unorthodox methods led to his boat being cut in half by a Japanese destroyer in 1943. Later investigations revealed that he could have avoided the collision. But rather than destroy his career, the disaster and his saving several sailors on his crew after it happened made him a war hero, in large part because of the public relations skills and connections of his father in the United States. The newspaper magnate William Randolph Hearst was a close Kennedy friend, and he worked tirelessly to craft the heroic image of John F. Kennedy, both during and after the war. Jack, in fact, worked for Hearst after being discharged from the navy in 1944.

Jack thought a career as a journalist might suit him, but with his brother Joe's death, their father insisted that Jack become a politician. Joe Senior forced out the incumbent in the Massachusetts 11th Congressional district and inserted his son as the Democratic candidate. Jack won easily and served in the United States House of Representatives for six years. He won a United States Senate seat in 1952 and held that office until shortly after he was elected president in 1960.

His domestic and foreign policy accomplishments are well known, and though there is some speculation that the concoction of drugs he was taking for his back pain dulled his senses and perhaps diminished his mental acuity during serious negotiations with foreign governments, Kennedy is often considered a great president. He did have his problems. Kennedy was engaged in several illegal attempts to kill Cuban dictator Fidel Castro, was seen as a blundering novice in regard to foreign policy by many astute observers, and could have pulled the United States out of Vietnam in 1961 but chose not to. Contemporaries remarked that his administration was noted for its laxity and unprofessionalism. Kennedy was still a playboy, except now the White House served as the backdrop.

He had married Jacqueline Bouvier in 1953 and eventually had three children with her, but that did not stop his extracurricular activities with the opposite sex. His conquests are now well known, from celebrities such as Marilyn Monroe and Marlene Dietrich to interns such as Mimi Alford. Kennedy had an insatiable appetite for women. He once complained that if he went three days without a woman he had headaches. If Jackie wasn't around, any woman would do. He attended parties that involved illegal drugs and celebrities and slept with prostitutes.

He also lied about his famed literary accomplishments. He had ghost writers for his books, though he never mentioned it when he accepted the Pulitzer Prize for *Profiles in Courage* in 1955. His father ensured that his books would reach best-seller status by buying thousands of copies and storing them, just to up book sales numbers. Jack was just as duplicitous as his father Joe—except he never got caught.

A Book You're Not Supposed to Read

Once Upon a Secret: My Affair with John F. Kennedy and Its Aftermath by Mimi Alford (New York: Random House Books, 2012).

Bobby

Like his brother, Robert Kennedy appeared in public to be the perfect husband. He had eleven children with his wife Ethel, but like the other men of the Kennedy family, Bobby loved power and women and did not let marriage vows hinder his promiscuity.

Bobby, born in 1925, was the seventh child of Joe Kennedy and spent most of his youth in New York after the family moved there in 1927. He attended several different private and boarding schools, and by 1944 enlisted in the naval reserves. Two years of training and a brief stint on the destroyer USS *Joseph P. Kennedy Jr.*, named in honor of his older brother at his father's behest, accounted for his military career. He enrolled in Harvard and was graduated in 1948. He went to law school at the University of Virginia and after passing the bar in 1951 spent time traveling like his brothers.

A Book You're Not Supposed to Read

The Kennedy Men: Three Generations of Sex, Scandal and Secrets by Nellie Bly (New York: Kensington, 1996).

Bobby lived his public life in his brother Jack's shadow. He dabbled in politics, mostly at his father's insistence, and even worked for Republican senator Joe McCarthy, a close friend of the family. When Jack was elected president in 1960, Bobby was appointed United States Attorney General. He made headlines in his crusade for civil rights—one Southern senator called him an anti-Southern bigot—and worked closely with Jack on several policy decisions, both foreign and domestic. He was one of his brother's closest advisers. After his brother was assassinated, Bobby was elected United States Senator from New York in 1964 and then decided to run for president in 1968. In 1968 he was cut down by an assassin's bullet like his brother, and as with his brother, his image received a public boost from the event.

Bobby had several high-profile affairs during his time in Washington politics, and like his father, kept his often pregnant wife at home while he philandered across the globe. He and Jack shared Marilyn Monroe (and may have had a hand in her death), and he was attached to several socialites, but the affair that was buried from everyone but family and close friends was the four-year relationship with his sister-in-law Jackie that began shortly after Jack was assassinated in 1963. Ethel would leave the room whenever Jackie came to visit, and Jackie and Bobby were often seen together in intimate embrace. As per custom, Ethel was pregnant three times during the affair. That never stopped a Kennedy. Bobby told others that he wanted to leave his wife for Jackie. The two only ended the affair when Bobby decided to run for president. It was Jackie, in fact, not his wife, who ordered that Bobby's life support system be turned off after he was shot in 1968.

Teddy

With the premature deaths of both Jack and Bobby, Teddy became the most visible member of the Kennedy clan, and because he lived to old age, had years to make his two brothers look like choir boys. Teddy, born in 1932, was the last of Joe's nine children. Like his brother Bobby, he kicked around from school to school and, also like his brothers and father, was never a good student. He was expelled from Harvard in 1951 for cheating, joined the army but avoided the Korean War by means of his father's influence, and eventually re-enrolled in Harvard in 1953. After being graduated, he attended law school at the University of Virginia, where he was an average student, and helped Jack with his re-election bid

A Book You're Not Supposed to Read

Senatorial Privilege: The Chappaquiddick Cover-Up by Leo Damore (Washington, DC: Regnery, 1988).

for the Senate in 1958. Like his brothers, Teddy chose politics—and women—as a career.

He married the beautiful Virginia Joan Bennett in 1958 and had three children with her, but Teddy did not consider wedding vows a binding contract of fidelity. During their almost thirty years of marriage, Teddy was as well-known for his marital indiscretions as his "career" as a United States senator from Massachusetts. The most infamous example of his playboy behavior (rising to criminality in this case), often called the "Chappaquiddick Cover-Up," took place in 1969.

After partying with several drinking buddies and their girlfriends at Chappaquiddick Island in 1969, Kennedy, probably drunk, drove his car off a bridge, killing his passenger Mary Jo Kopechne. Teddy did not report the accident until the next day, *after her body was found*, and though he expressed "deep remorse" for the accident, he was never punished. Rumors swirled about their relationship, including speculation that Kopechne was pregnant and was killed to cover up the embarrassment.

For the next ten years, Teddy continued to drink and cavort, so much so that *Time* magazine actually reported on his activities in 1979. Teddy became a better politician than his father and a more prominent "stud" than his brothers. He attempted a run for the Democratic nomination for president in 1980 against the struggling incumbent Jimmy Carter, but lost. By 1982 he had given up his hopes for the White House and was facing a nasty divorce. His wife finally left him—with a $4 million settlement. Teddy kept being Teddy. Now free from the "bondage" of marriage, Kennedy became fodder for the tabloid press. He usually did not disappoint, with either his drinking or his indulgences in "free love."

★ ★ ★ ★ ★ ★ ★ ★ ★ ★ ★ ★ ★ ★

Helping Maintain the Dignity of the Senate

In 1989, the paparazzi caught Ted cavorting with a young woman in a boat while vacationing in Europe. When the photos went public, Alabama Senator Howell Heflin remarked that he was glad "Kennedy has changed his position on offshore drilling."

Teddy finally "settled down" in 1992 when he married Victoria Reggie. He was sixty, she was thirty-eight. When he died in 2009, the press treated him as the last of a dynasty and seemed to forget his checkered past. Like his brothers, Teddy was hailed as a great statesman who had worked tirelessly for the American people and endured tremendous tragedy to reach the heights of political greatness. Teddy was none of that, and like his father and brothers should be remembered as he was—a serial philanderer, a man of poor morals, and a career political thug.

The Kennedys were a dynasty—yes—but a sharp departure from the great early American political families. They achieved their success through back-room deals, convenient marriages, a public image crafted by their own narrative, and a self-serving lust for the public eye. Consider, in contrast, such American dynasties as the Adamses of Massachusetts and the Bayards of Delaware. Those two families were even more influential than the Kennedys. Between them they count among their members two presidents of the United States, six members of the United States Senate, several judges, signers to the United States Constitution and the Declaration of Independence, several prominent members of the American military, and dozens of state and local elected officials. The Adamses and the Bayards shared a moral republican patriotism that grew out of a keen understanding of history—and the historians among them did not have to employ ghostwriters. They were great because of who they were and what they accomplished, not because of a popular image.

Certainly, members of both families could be petty and partisan, but no one ever credibly accused a Bayard or an Adams of being dishonest or immoral. They were disinterested statesmen who resolutely defended American principles. As Senator James A. Bayard the younger once said about political popularity, the "candle wasn't worth the wax." Unlike the Kennedys, the Adamses and the Bayards made political decisions without thought of personal gain, never campaigned for office, and never sought the spotlight. These families, not the Kennedys, are our great political dynasties.

John F. Kennedy has been called one of the three greatest people of the twentieth century, along with Martin Luther King Jr. and Mother Teresa. He doesn't deserve it. Both he and Bobby have been honored with awards, buildings, bridges, and street names. Teddy was made a knight by the Queen of England. The image of the handsome, brilliant Kennedys, born to lead, so carefully crafted by Joe during his family's rise to fame and fortune, has seduced Americans into their current love affair with this notorious and seedy family. Rescuing the American collective conscious from their clutches would go a long way toward improving American political life. Thankfully, none of the other Kennedys has been as politically successful as Joe and his sons. As morally corrupt, yes—but as long as they stay in the tabloids and out the of statehouses, America will be a better place.

CONCLUSION

The famous rock star Alice Cooper once said, "If you're listening to a rock star in order to get your information on who to vote for, you're a bigger moron than they are." True enough. And the same could be said for virtually every "celebrity" in the United States today. Yet the exploits, misdeeds, and musings of musicians, actors and actresses, and athletes have not only become fodder for American tabloids, they actually shape public discourse and opinion in America. The Dixie Chicks made headlines when they famously ranted about George W. Bush in Europe. A sane response would have been, "Who cares what the Dixie Chicks think? We pay to hear you sing, not wax philosophical about American politics." The story should have been buried, never to see the light of day, but Americans—particularly young Americans—eulogize and lionize these people, and so their opinions hold weight. That has to change.

Having a shared set of heroes forges an identity, a common culture that transcends section, race, class, sex, or occupation. Americans need heroes in the traditional sense, men and women with noble qualities we can aspire to. The common man and woman, working to rear a family, put food on the table, save a little for their future, buy a house, and leave a legacy for posterity can learn more from John D. Rockefeller, Robert E. Lee, Mercy Otis Warren, or Booker T. Washington than from the entire lot of leftist "heroes" and modern celebrities.

All of the real heroes in this book exemplify at least several of the attributes Americans should emulate: courage, charity, industry, thrift, independence, honor, virtue, sacrifice, faith, manliness, selflessness, ingenuity, and hard work. These were the traits that made America a unique and shining vessel of liberty and prosperity in the world. None of these heroes were politicians, at least not in the modern sense; power, prestige, and the spoils of office were not more important to them than statesmanlike responsibility. To men like George Washington and John Dickinson, political office was a sacred trust held for the benefit of the public, not a chance to fill their own coffers. The quiet and determined faith of men like Thomas J. Jackson and Joshua Chamberlain and heroines like Augusta Jane Evans sustained them in difficult times. They understood that sacrifice could bring as much glory as pain and that the reward may not be in this world. To the early explorers and frontiersmen like Captain John Smith, Daniel Boone, and David Crockett and "underdogs" like Booker T. Washington and S. B. Fuller, independence meant something. They didn't turn to government as a source of a "handout," or even a "hand up." They, in fact, saw too much government as a hindrance to success. In their eyes, prosperity was self-reliance.

Certainly all of these characters have their faults, but none equal to those of the frauds we too often mistake for heroes today. Leftist "heroes" like Franklin Roosevelt and the Kennedys tend to have more personality flaws, seedy histories, and moral shortcomings than the genuine American heroes. And it makes sense that they do. The Left has always been interested in waging war on traditional American values in the name of "equality," "justice," "democracy," and "fairness." It has taken only about a hundred years to destroy the bonds of civilization that it took centuries to forge—all in the name of "progress" and "modernity." If we seek to save America, we must first reconnect with the values and principles that made America great. Yet simply knowing these great men and women is not enough. We must all learn to follow in their footsteps on our own steam—to be independent. That is real American heroism.

NOTES

Introduction

1. Sam Wineburg and Chauncey Monte-Sano, "Famous Americans: The Changing Pantheon of American Heroes," *Journal of American History* 94 (March 2008): 1186–1202.

Chapter 1
Explorers

1. William Gilmore Simms, *The Life of Captain John Smith: The Founder of Virginia* (New York: A.L. Burt Company, 1902), 142.

2. Ibid., 371.

3. Avery Craven, *The Coming of the Civil War* (Chicago: University of Chicago Press, 1957), 3.

4. Quoted in John Filson, *The Adventures of Daniel Boone & the Discovery, Settlement and Present State Of Kentucke* (1784), 53.

Chapter 2
Founders

1. Letter of Instructions to the Captains of the Virginia Regiments.

2. "George Washington to Robert McKenzie," October 9, 1774, George Washington Papers, Library of Congress, http://memory.loc.gov/cgi-bin/query/r?ammem/mgw:@field%28DOCID+@lit%28gw030177%29%29 (accessed January 3, 2012).

3. Journals of the Continental Congress, June 16, 1775,

http://memory.loc.gov/cgi-bin/query/r?ammem/hlaw:@field%28DOCID+@
lit%28jc00237%29%29 (accessed January 3, 2012).

4. "George Washington to the Continental Congress," December 23,
1783, http://gwpapers.virginia.edu/documents/revolution/resignation.
html#2 (accessed on January 3, 2012).

5. "George Washington to Henry Knox," April 1, 1789, http://
memory.loc.gov/cgi-bin/query/r?ammem/mgw:@field%28DOCID+@
lit%28gw300225%29%29 (accessed January 3, 2012).

6. Paul Leicester Ford, ed., *The Writings of John Dickinson* (Philadelphia: The Historical Society of Pennsylvania, 1895), I: 324.

7. Ibid.

8. Paul Leicester Ford, ed., *Pamphlets on the Constitution of the
United States* (Brooklyn, NY, 1888), 208.

9. Quoted in Brion McClanahan, *The Politically Incorrect Guide™ to
the Founding Fathers* (Washington, DC: Regnery, 2009), 227.

10. John Dickinson, *The Political Writings of John Dickinson* (Wilmington, DE: Bonsal and Niles, 1801), I: 199.

Chapter 3
Sailors

1. Quoted in *Willis J. Abbot, The Naval History of the United States*
(Charlestown, South Carolina: BiblioBazaar, 2012), 114.

2. R. C. Sands, *Life and Correspondence of John Paul Jones* (New York:
1830), 27.

3. A. S. Mackenzie, *The Life of John Paul Jones* (Boston: 1841), I: 205–6.

4. Quoted in *A. S. Mackenzie, Life of Stephen Decatur,* 34–36.

5. Ibid., 369.

6. Ibid., 293.

7. Ibid., 295.

8. Ibid., 354–55.

Chapter 4
Frontiersmen

1. John S. C. Abbott, *David Crockett: His Life and Adventures* (New York: Dodd Mead and Publishers, 1874), iii–iv.

2. Quoted in ibid., 37.

3. David Crockett, *A Narrative of the Life of David Crockett, of the State of Tennessee* (Philadelphia: E.L. Carey and A. Hart; Boston: Allen and Ticknor, 1834), 145.

4. Ibid., 75.

5. Ibid., 68.

6. Ibid., 85.

7. Abbott, *David Crockett*, 285.

8. Crockett, *A Narrative of the Life of David Crockett*, 206.

9. Abbott, *David Crockett*, 269.

10. Quoted in Edward Sylvester Ellis, *The Life of Colonel David Crockett* (Philadelphia: Porter and Coates, 1884), 148.

11. Quoted in William Garrott Brown, *Andrew Jackson* (Boston: Houghton, Mifflin and Company, 1900), 72.

Chapter 5
Southerners

1. Quoted in James I. Robertson Jr., *Stonewall Jackson: The Man, The Soldier, The Legend* (New York: MacMillan, 1997), 26.

2. Quoted in Douglas Southall Freeman, *R. E. Lee* (New York: Charles Scribner's Sons, 1934), I: 8.

3. Ibid., I: 32–33.

4. Ibid., I: 122.

5. Ibid., IV: 147.

6. Quoted in Frank E. Vandiver, *Mighty Stonewall* (College Station, Texas: Texas A&M University Press, 1988), 250.

7. Quoted in Harry Crocker, *The Politically Incorrect Guide™ to the Civil War* (Washington, DC: Regnery, 2008), 226–27.

8. Quoted in John Selby, *Stonewall Jackson As Military Commander* (Barnes & Noble, 2000), p. 25.

9. Quoted in Mary Anna Jackson, *Memoirs of Stonewall Jackson* (Louisville, KY: The Prentice Press, 1895), 100.

10. Quoted in Robertson, *Stonewall Jackson*, 169.

11. Mary Anna Jackson, *Life and Letters of General Thomas J. Jackson* (1891), 429.

12. Frank E. Vandiver, *Mighty Stonewall* (1957), 250.

13. Quoted in Robertson, *Stonewall Jackson*, ix.

14. Robertson, *Stonewall Jackson*, xvii.

15. Ibid., xviii.

16. Ibid., IV: 484.

17. Letter to Lieutenant Colonel Charles Marshall, quoted in Freeman, *R.E. Lee*, IV: 483.

Chapter 6
Northerners

1. "Joshua Chamberlain to Israel Washburn Jr.," July 14, 1862, available at http://www.maine.gov/sos/arc/sesquicent/transcpt/jcvolunteer.html (accessed June 12, 2012).

2. Quoted in James M. McPherson, *For Cause and Comrades: Why Men Fought in the Civil War* (New York: Oxford University Press, 1997), 65.

3. Thomas Desjardin, *Joshua Chamberlain: The Life and Letters of a Great Leader of the American Civil War* (New York: Osprey Publishing, 2012), 185.

4. Ibid., 190.

5. Quoted in McPherson, *For Cause and Comrades*, 6.

6. Ibid., 170.

7. Quoted in James M. McPherson's introduction to Joshua Chamberlain, *The Passing of the Armies: An Account of the Final Campaign of the Army of the Potomac* (New York: Bantam Books, 1993), 5.

8. Quoted in Evan S. Connell, *Son of the Morning Star: Custer and the Little Bighorn* (San Francisco: North Point Press, 1984), 111.

9. Ibid., 112.

10. Quoted in Connell, *Son of the Morning Star*, 411.

11. Abraham Lincoln, quoted in Ibid., 115.

Chapter 7
Traditional Women

1. The Massachusetts Historical Society, eds., *Warren-Adams Letters Being Chiefly a Correspondence between John Adams, Samuel Adams, and James Warren* (Boston: Massachusetts Historical Society), II: 380.

2. Alice Brown, *Mercy Warren with Portrait* (New York: Charles Scribner's Sons, 1896), 245.

3. Massachusetts Historical Society, eds., *Warren-Adams Letters*, 241.

4. Ibid., 242.

5. Ibid., 241.

6. Ibid., 235.

7. Mercy Otis Warren, *History of the Rise, Progress, and Termination of the American Revolution Interspersed with Biographical, Political and Moral Observations* (Boston: Manning and Loring, 1805), III: 362. I have supplied a quotation mark omitted in the original.

8. Augusta Jane Evans, *Macaria; Or, Altars of Sacrifice* (Richmond, VA: West and Johnson, 1864), 416.

9. Augusta Jane Evans, *St. Elmo* (New York: Grosset & Dunlap, 1866), 404.

10. Ibid., 453.

11. Juliette Gordon Low, *How Girls Can Help Their Country* (1916), 134.

12. Ibid., 8.

13. Girl Scouts of the USA, "Girls Speak Out: Teens Before Their Time: Executive Summary," 19, http://www.girlscouts.org/research/pdf/teens_before_time.pdf (accessed July 2, 2012).

14. Low, *How Girls Can Help Their Country*, 10.

15. Ibid., 9-10.

16. Ibid., 13.

17. Ibid., 106.

Chapter 8
Captains of Industry

1. Quoted in Bertie Charles Forbes, *Men Who Are Making America* (New York: B.C. Forbes Publishing, Inc., 1922), 297–98.

2. Quoted in Ron Chernow, *Titan: The Life of John D. Rockefeller* (New York: Vintage Press, 2004), 55.

3. Quoted in Forbes, *Men Who Are Making America*, 297.

4. John D. Rockefeller, *Random Reminiscences of Men and Events* (New York: Doubleday, Page, and Co., 1913), 20.

5. Andrew Carnegie, "Wealth," *The North American Review* 148: 391 (June 1889), 656.

6. Ibid., 663–64.

7. Andrew Carnegie, *Autobiography* (London: Constable and Co., 1920), 265.

Chapter 9
Inventors

1. Quoted in Quentin R. Skrabec Jr., *George Westinghouse: Gentle Genius* (New York: Algora, 2007), 19.

2. Quoted in Francis Ellington Leupp, *George Westinghouse: His Life and Achievements* (Boston: Little, Brown, and Co., 1918), 277.

3. Ibid., 149.

4. Ibid., 255.

5. Quoted in Marc J. Seifer, *Wizard: The Life and Times of Nikola Tesla: Biography of a Genius* (New York: Citadel Press, 1998), 53.

6. *New York Times*, July 11, 1935.

Chapter 10
Underdogs

1. Booker T. Washington, *Up From Slavery: An Autobiography* (New York: Doubleday, Page, and Co., 1907), 12.

2. Ibid., 14.

3. Ibid., 32.

4. Ibid., 53.

5. Ibid., 39.

6. Ibid., 217.

7. Ibid., 221–22.

8. Quoted in Thomas E. Woods Jr., *33 Questions About American History You're Not Supposed to Ask* (New York: Three Rivers, 2007), 247.

9. Luke Skyfreeper, "It's Not Racial Barriers That Keep Blacks from Prospering," including the text of S. B. Fuller's 1963 speech to the National Association of Manufacturers, reprinted from *Issues & Views* (Summer 1991), http://www.freerepublic.com/focus/f-news/1029516/posts (accessed on June 21, 2012).

10. Ibid.

11. David Bieto, "S. B. Fuller Centenery," HNN (George Mason University's History News Network), http://hnn.us/node/12280 (accessed on June 21, 2012).

Chapter 11
Soldiers

1. Charles Jacobs Peterson, *The Military Heroes of the War of 1812 with a Narrative of the War* (Philadelphia: William A. Leary and Co., 1849), 152.

2. Orville James Victor, *The Life and Military and Civic Services of Lieut-Gen. Winfield Scott Complete up to the Present Period* (New York: Beadle and Company, 1861), 106.

3. From the website owned and operated by the Patton Estate at http://www.generalpatton.com/quotes/index.html (accessed on July 2, 2012).

4. Martin Blumenson, ed., *The Patton Papers 1885–1945* (New York: Houghton Mifflin, 1972–74), I: 336.

5. George S. Patton Jr., *War As I Knew It* (Boston: Houghton Mifflin Company, 1947), 368.

6. Blumenson, ed., *The Patton Papers*, I: 832.

Chapter 12
Aviators

1. Quoted in Leonard Mosley, *Lindbergh: A Biography* (New York: Doubleday and Company, 1976), 115.

2. Wayne S. Cole, *Charles A. Lindbergh and the Battle Against American Intervention in World War II* (New York: Harcourt Brace and Javanovich, 1974), 72.

3. Ibid., 152.

4. Barton C. Hacker and James M. Grimwood, *On the Shoulders of Titans: A History of Project Gemini Published* as NASA Special Publication (4203 in the NASA History Series, 1977), available at http://www.hq.nasa.gov/office/pao/History/SP-4203/ch15-5.htm (accessed on June 11, 2012).

5. Ken Abraham and Buzz Aldrin, *Magnificent Desolation: The Long Journey Home from the Moon* (New York: Three Rivers Press, 2010), 12.

6. Ibid., 307.

7. Ibid., 15.

8. Ibid., 13.

9. Ibid., 16.

10. Edwin E. "Buzz" Aldrin Jr. and Wayne Warga, *Return to Earth* (New York: Random House, 1973), 242.

11. Richard Alleyne, "Buzz Aldrin calls for manned flight to Mars to overcome global problems," U.K. *Telegraph*, July 3, 2009, http://www.telegraph.co.uk/technology/5734525/Buzz-Aldrin-calls-for-manned-flight-to-Mars-to-overcome-global-problems.html (accessed on June 11, 2012).

Chapter 13
Progressive Frauds

1. Martin S. Dworkin, ed., *Dewey on Education: Selections with an Introduction and Notes* (New York: Teachers College Press, 1959), 8.

2. Ibid., 33.

3. John Dewey, *Democracy and Education* (New York: Macmillan, 1963), 135.

4. Dworkin, ed., *Dewey on Education*, 22.

5. Ibid., 31.

6. Ibid., 25.

7. Herbert Croly, *The Promise of American Life* (Boston: Northeastern University Press, 1989), 6.

Chapter 14
Democratic Frauds

1. "Woodrow Wilson: The Film & More," PBS, http://www.pbs.org/wgbh/amex/wilson/filmmore/index.html (accessed on June 18, 2012).

2. Quoted in Alexander L. George and Juliette L. George, *Woodrow Wilson and Colonel House: A Personality Study* (New York: Dover Publications, 1964), 131.

3. Woodrow Wilson, *Constitutional Government in the United States* (New York: Columbia University Press, 1908), 60.

4. Quoted in Alexander, *Woodrow Wilson and Colonel House*, 133.

Chapter 15
Fascist Fraud

1. John T. Flynn, *The Roosevelt Myth* (New York: The Devin-Adair Company, 1948), 413.

2. Quoted in Wolfgang Schivelbusch, *Three New Deals: Reflections on Roosevelt's America, Mussolini's Italy, and Hitler's Germany, 1933–1939* (New York: Metropolitan Books, 2006), 31–32.

3. Ibid., 19–20.

4. Quoted in Charles C. Tansill, *Back Door to War: The Roosevelt Foreign Policy, 1933-1941* (Chicago: Henry Regnery Company, 1952), viii.

5. Ibid., 651.

6. Ibid, 652.

Chapter 16
Feminist Frauds

1. Margaret Sanger, *Woman and the New Race* (New York: Brentano's, 1920), 63.

2. Margaret Sanger, *The Woman Rebel*, quoted in Wendy Martin, ed., *The American Sisterhood: Writings of the Feminist Movement from the Colonial Times to the Present* (New York: Harper and Row, 1972), 235.

3. Sanger, *Woman and the New Race*, 11.

4. Ibid., 167–85.

5. Margaret Sanger, *An Autobiography* (New York: Dover Publications, 2004), 366–67.

6. Margaret Sanger, *The Pivot of Civilization* (New York: Brentano's, 1922), 115–17.

7. Quoted in Martin, *The American Sisterhood*, 238.

8. Betty Friedan, *The Feminine Mystique* (New York: W.W. Norton and Company, 1963), 15.

Chapter 17
Family Frauds

1. Ronald Kessler, *The Sins of the Father: Joseph P. Kennedy and the Dynasty He Founded* (New York: Warner Books, 1996), 45.

INDEX

A

Adams, Abigail, 102

Adams, John, 27, 102, 104, 105, 201, 239

Adams, John Quincy, 68, 239

Adams, Samuel, 102

Addison, Joseph, 27

Agricultural Adjustment Administration (AAA), 210

air brake system for railroad cars, 132

Alamo, 53, 59–60

Aldie, Battle of, 96

Aldrin, Edwin Eugene Jr. "Buzz", 5, 170, 178–84

Alford, Mimi, 235

Alfred, USS, 41

Alliance, USS, 43

alternating current versus direct current, 133–34

American Birth Control League, 221

American War for Independence, 19, 21, 26, 28, 32, 34, 40–42, 44–45, 54, 62, 72, 74, 80, 88, 102, 104, 154, 160, 208, 214, 217

An Hour Before Daylight (Carter), 210

"Anaconda Plan," 159

Anthony, Susan B., 2–3

anthropogenic global warming, 178, 184

AOL, 2

Apollo 11 mission, 180–83

Appomattox Courthouse, 78–79

Aristotle, 156

Arlington National Cemetery, 215

Armstrong, Neil, 169, 180–82

Articles of Confederation, 29, 35

B

Baden-Powell, Agnes, 111–12

Baden-Powell, Sir Robert, 111–12

Balboa, Vasco Núñez de, 181

Bank of the United States, 68

Barbary Pirates, 45–47, 48, 49

Barry, John, 45

Bayard, James A., 239

Bee, Bernard, 84

Bennett, Virginia Joan, 238

Benton, Thomas Hart, 63–64, 67

Betsey (ship), 41

Bill of Rights, 23, 105

birth control, 218–23

The Birth Control Review, 221

Black Hawk War of 1832, 153, 157

Blue Back Speller (Webster), 143

Blue Licks, Battle of, 21

Bobbitt, Philip, 215

Boeing, William, 169

Bolshevism, 149

Bonaparte, Napoleon, 83

Bong, Richard, 169

Bonhomme Richard, USS, 41, 42–43, 44

Boone, Daniel, 1, 2, 3, 9, 16–22, 181

Bouvier, Jacqueline, 235, 237

Bowdoin College, 88–89, 90, 93

Boy Scouts, 111

Braddock, Edward, 17

Bradley, Omar, 166

Brandywine, Battle of, 35

Brown, Harold P., 133–34

Bryan, William Jennings, 197, 204

Buchanan, James, 158–59

Bulge, Battle of the, 165–66

Bush, George W., 241

Byron, 6th Baron (Lord Byron), 16

C

Carden, John Surman, 48

Cardenas, Julio, 153, 162

Carnegie, Andrew, 5, 116, 122–27, 149

Carnegie Hall, 126

Carnegie Hero Fund, 126

Carnegie Steel Company, 124, 127

Carter, Charles "King," 73

Carter, Jimmy, 210, 238

Castro, Fidel, 235

Cato, 105

celebrities, heroes versus, 2, 241

The Century, 138

Chamberlain, Joshua, 87–94, 100, 153, 242

Chancellorsville, 77, 85

"Chappaquiddick Cover-Up," 238

Chapultepec, 81

Chippewa, Battle of, 155

Churchill, Sir Winston, 212

Cincinnatus, 23, 27

City College of New York, 192

Clarke, George Rogers, 21

Clausewitz, Karl von, 84

Clay, Henry, 61, 67–68

Cold Harbor, 78

Cold War, 167, 208, 215

Cole, Thomas, 16

Collins, Michael, 181

Columbia Theological Seminary, 198

Columbia University, 188

Columbus, Christopher, 39, 181

Committee on Public Information, 203

Common Sense, 33

communism, 175, 215

Comstock Laws, 222

Congress of Racial Equality, 151

Congress, USS, 47

Connell, Evan, 100

Constitution, 4, 29, 35, 36, 74, 76, 104–5, 187, 200–1, 209–10, 239

Bill of Rights of, 23, 105

Franklin Roosevelt's actions without authority of, 209–12

obsolete per Woodrow Wilson, 197, 202–205

Sixteenth, Seventeenth, and Nineteenth Amendments to, 200

Constitution, USS, 47

Constitutional Government in the United States, 202

contraception, 219–20

Coolidge, Calvin, 174

Cooper, Alice, 241

Cooper, James Fenimore, 16

Cooper, John Milton, 197

Cotton States and International Exposition in Atlanta, Booker T. Washington's speech at, 146, 150

Craven, Avery, 17

Crazy Horse, 100

Creek Indians, 56, 63–65

Creek Red Stick Indians, 67

Creek War of 1813–1814, 56–57

Crockett, David "Davy," 1, 2, 5, 53–60, 62, 69, 181

Crockett, John, 54

Croly, Herbert, 187, 192–95, 198, 222

Cruise, Tom, 2

Custer, George Armstrong, 5, 87, 94–100, 153

Custis, George Washington Parke, 74–75

Custis, Mary Anna Randolph, 74

D

Daniels, Jeff, 88

Darrow, Clarence, 219

Davis, Jefferson, 83

Dazed and Confused, 3

Decatur, Stephen, 1, 39, 45–51

Declaration of the Causes of Taking up Arms, 34

Declaration of Independence, 23, 35, 71, 73, 239

Democratic Party, 98, 158, 199, 234

Democratic-Republican Party, 74–75

Dewey, John, 2, 4, 40, 187, 188–92, 195, 222

Dickinson, Charles, 63

Dickinson, John, 23–24, 27, 32–38, 102, 242

Dietrich, Marlene, 235

direct current versus alternating current, 133–34

Discovery Channel, 2

Dixie Chicks, 241

Dogg, Snoop, 183

Doolittle, Jimmy, 169

Downey, Morton, 230

Drake, Sir Francis, 181

Dubois, W.E.B., 150–51

Duras (ship), 42

E

Eagle (ship), 181

Earhart, Amelia, 3, 169

Edison, Thomas, 3, 129, 132–34, 136–37

education
  "child-centered," 4, 187, 191–92, 195
  "multi-cultural," 3
  Progressive Movement and, 187–95, 222

Einstein, Albert, 3, 138

Eisenhower, Dwight D., 165, 177–78

electric chair, 129, 133–34

Elizabeth II, 240

Ellis, Havelock, 221

Emanuel, Rahm, 209

Endymion, HMS, 49

Enterprise, USS, 46

entertainers, heroes versus, 2, 241

eugenics, 217, 221

Evans, Augusta Jane, 101, 102,
105–10, 114, 242

F

Fairfax, George William, 25

FBI, 129, 139

Federal Reserve System, 200

Federalist Papers, 36

Federalist Party, 31, 37, 74–75

The Feminine Mystique, 224–25

Finley, John, 17

First Continental Congress, 26,
34

Fitzgerald, John "Honey Fitz,"
230–31

Fitzgerald, Rose Elizabeth, 230–
31, 233

Five Civilized Tribes of the South,
157

Flagler, Henry, 118

Flynn, John T., 297

Ford, Henry, 3

Ford Motor Company, 177

Forrest, Nathan Bedford, 160, 166

Fort George, recapture of, 155

FOX Business Channel, 183

Franklin, Benjamin, 2, 3, 40, 42

fraud(s). *See also* heroes,
fraudulent
democratic, 197–205
family, 4, 229–40, 242
fascist, 4, 207–15, 242
feminist, 4, 217–27
progressive, 187–95, 198

Fredericksburg, Battle of, 77, 85,
90–91

Freeman, Douglas Southall, 166

French and Indian War, 17, 18, 26

French Revolution, 217

Friedan, Betty, 217–18, 223–27

Fuller Products, 149, 152

Fuller, Samuel B., 141, 148–52

G

Garvey, Marcus, 151

Gates, Bill, 140

*The Generall Historie of Virginia,
New England, and the Summer
Isles*, 13, 15

George III, 29, 34

Gerry, Elbridge, 102

Gettysburg, Battle of, 77–78, 85–88, 91, 97

Girl Guides, 111

Girl Scouts, 101, 111–14

Glenn, John, 169

Godkin, E. L., 79

Gordon, John B., 93

Gordon, William Washington, 110

Grant, Ulysses S., 78–79, 92–93, 98

Great Depression, 4, 149, 207, 210, 297–98

The Greatest American, 2

H

Hamilton, Alexander, 31, 36, 187, 193–95

Hampton Normal and Agricultural Institute, 144

Harrison, William Henry, 65–66

Harvard University, 192, 230, 234, 236–37

Hays, Samuel, 72

Hearst, William Randolph, 234

Heflin, Howell, 238

Hefner, Hugh, 2, 233

Henry, Patrick, 2

Hermitage, 63, 67–68

heroes
attributes of, 5, 241–42
aviators as, 169–84
captains of industry as, 115–27
celebrities and entertainers versus, 2, 241
explorers as, 9–22, 242
founders as, 23–38, 242
fraudulent, 2. *See also* fraud(s)
frontiersmen as, 53–69, 242
inventors as, 129–40
Northern, 87–100, 242
sailors as, 39–51
soldiers as, 153–67
Southern, 1, 71–86, 242
traditional women as, 101–14, 217–18, 242
underdogs as, 141–52, 242

Herrick, Myron T., 174

Hewes, Joseph, 41

Higgins, Margaret. *See* Sanger, Margaret

hippies of 1960s, 192

History of the Rise, Progress, and Termination of the American Revolution, 104

Hitler, Adolf, 175, 177, 204, 207, 211–13

Hogg, James, 199

Hoover, Herbert, 207, 209

Horowitz, Daniel, 226

Horseshoe Bend, 65

House, Edward Mandell
"Colonel," 197, 198–201, 204–205

How Girls Can Help Their Country
(Low), 112–14

Hull, Cordell, 213

Hume, David, 103–4

I

Ickes, Harold, 176

Indian (ship), 42

Indian Removal Act, 157

Intrepid, USS, 46–47

J

Jackson, Andrew, 53, 58–69

Jackson, Mary Anna, 82

Jackson, Michael, 2

Jackson, Thomas J. "Stonewall," 1, 5, 71–72, 77, 79–86, 153, 157, 160, 166, 242

Jamestown, 12–15

Jefferson, Thomas, 3–4, 23, 37, 46, 63, 75, 81, 102, 105, 187, 193–94, 197, 211

Jobs, Steve, 140

Johns Hopkins University, 188, 198

Johnson, Andrew, 98, 198

Johnson, Robert Underwood, 138

Johnston, Joseph E., 76–77

Jones, Allen, 41

Jones, John Paul, 39–45, 48, 50

Jones, Willie, 41

Joseph P. Kennedy, Jr., USS, 236

Josephson, Matthew, 115

Journal of American History, 226

The Jungle, 219

K

Kemmler, William, 133–34

Kennedy clan, 2, 4, 229–40

Kennedy, Edward "Ted" "Teddy," 229, 237–40

Kennedy, Ethel, 236–37

Kennedy, Jacqueline Bouvier
"Jackie," 235, 237

Kennedy, John F. "Jack," 4, 229, 232–37, 239–40

Kennedy, Joseph P., Jr., 233–34

Kennedy, Joseph P., Sr. "Joe," 4, 209, 229–36, 239–40

Kennedy, P. J., 230–31

Kennedy, Robert F. "Bobby," 229, 236–37, 239–40

Kennedy, Rose Elizabeth Fitzgerald, 230–31, 233

Kennedy, Rose Marie, 231

Kennedy, Victoria Reggie, 238–39

Kennedy, Virginia Joan Bennett, 238

Keystone Bridge Company, 123

Killer Angels, 87–88

King George (ship), 41

King, Martin Luther, Jr., 2, 150, 240

King's Mountain, Battle of, 54

Kinzie, Eleanor, 110

Klein, Calvin, 3

Knox, Henry, 102

Kopechne, Mary Jo, 238

Korean War, 169, 179, 237

Ku Klux Klan, 4, 217, 221–23

L

Land, Evangeline, 170

League of Nations, 194, 197, 201, 215

Lee, Ann Hill Carter, 72

Lee, Henry "Light-Horse Harry," 28, 72–75

Lee, Robert Edward, 1, 2, 3, 5, 61, 71–79, 80–83, 85–86, 92–93, 153, 157, 159–60, 241

Leonidas I, 153

Letters from a Farmer in Pennsylvania to the Inhabitants of the British Colonies, 33

Lexington and Concord, Battle of, 41

libraries, 125

Life, 179

Lincoln, Abraham, 96, 123, 159, 197, 233

Lindbergh, Anne Morrow, 174–75

Lindbergh, Charles (kidnapped and murdered son of flyer), 175

Lindbergh, Charles A., Jr., 1, 3, 170–78, 184, 232

Lindbergh's solo New York to Paris flight, 169, 173–74

Lindbergh, Charles Augustus, 170

Little Bighorn, 87, 94, 99–100

Little Round Top, 87–88, 91

Livingston, Robert, 63

Longstreet, James, 77

Louis XVI, 43–44

Low, Juliette Gordon "Daisy," 101–2, 110–14

Low, William Mackay, 111

Luftwaffe, 175

Lundy's Lane, Battle of, 155–56

M

Macaria: Or, Altars of Sacrifice, 106–7

Macedonian, HMS, 48

Madison, James, 36, 66

Madonna, 2

Magellan, Ferdinand, 181

Magna Carta, 202

Manassas, First Battle of, 83–84, 95

Marshall, George C., 213–14

Marxism, 149–50, 190, 200, 217, 223, 225–226

Massachusetts Institute of Technology (MIT), 179

Mayflower (ship), 39

Mayflower Compact, 12

McCarthy, Joe, 236

McClellan, George B., 95–96

McGraw, Phillip Calvin "Dr. Phil," 2

Meade, George, 97

Memoirs of the War in the Southern Department, 74

Mercer, George, 159–60

The Mercury Seven, 169

Mexican War, 71, 75–76, 81–82, 157–58

Mexico City, capture of, 157–58

Meyerowitz, Joanne, 226

Michigan, University of, 188

Monroe, James, 67

Monroe, Marilyn, 2, 3, 235, 237

Monte-Sano, Chauncey, 2–3

Montgomery Bus Boycott, 141, 150

moon landing, first (Apollo 11 mission), 180–83

Morris, Gouverneur, 36

Morris, Robert, 41

Morrow, Anne, 174–75

Mother Teresa, 240

Mount Vernon, 23–26, 28, 74

Muscoota, USS, 130

Mussolini, Benito, 4, 204, 207, 211–12

N

N.A.A.C.P., 150–51

Napoleon, 83

NASA, 179–82

National Association of
Manufacturers, 150

National Industry Recovery Act
(NIRA), 210, 214

National Negro Business League,
145

National Organization for Women
(NOW), 225–26

National Urban League, 151

Nazis, 3, 175–77, 221

Nelson, Horatio, 39, 47

New Deal, 210, 214, 297–98

New Orleans, Battle of, 66–67

New York Age, 149

New York Times, 203

Newport, Christopher, 14

Nineteenth Amendment, 200

Nixon, Richard, 177

Northwest Indian War, 30

O

Obama, Barack, 132, 209

"Occupy Wall Street" crowd, 117,
192

Olympics, 1912 Summer, 161

Opequon, Battle of, 160

Operation Overlord (D-Day), 157,
165

Orteig, Raymond, 172–73

Overland Campaign, 78, 92

P

Paine, Thomas, 33, 101–4

Pan American Airways, 177

Parks, Rosa, 2, 150

The Passing of Armies, 90

Patton, George S., 1, 5, 153, 159–67

Patton Saber, 162

Paul, John. *See* Jones, John Paul

Paul, William, 40

PBS, 197

Pearl Harbor, Japanese attack on,
4, 176–77, 207, 213

Pearson, Richard, 43–44

Peninsula Campaign, 95

Pershing, John J. "Black Jack,"
162–63

P.E.T.A., 57

Petersburg, Battle of, 78, 92

Philadelphia Convention, 29, 33,
35–37

Philadelphia, USS, 39, 46–47

philanthropy, 115, 120–22, 124–27

*Philip Dru: Administrator: A Story
of Tomorrow, 1920-1935*, 199–201

"Pickett's Charge," 78

Piqua, Battle of, 21

Pittsburgh Courier, 149

Planned Parenthood Federation of
America, 222

Plato, 156

Pleasanton, Alfred, 96

Plymouth, 15

Pocahontas, 13

*Poems Dramatic and
Miscellaneous*, 103

Polk, James K., 157–58

Poor Richard's Almanac, 42

Powhatan, 13

President, USS, 49

Princeton University, 198, 202

Profiles in Courage, 229, 235

Progressive Movement, 187–95,
198, 215, 222

The Promise of American Life,
193–94

prosperity, victimhood versus, 152

Providence, USS, 42

Pullman, George, 131

Q

Quasi-War, 45, 48

Queenstown Heights, Battle of,
155

R

Raleigh, Sir Walter, 39

Ranger, USS, 42

Reagan, Ronald, 2

Reconstruction, 98, 166, 198

"Red Summer" race riots of 1919,
149

Reddy, Helen, 219

Reggie, Victoria, 238–39

Republican Party, 98, 117, 151,
159, 170, 236

Revere, Paul, 2, 214

The Right Stuff, 179

*The Rising Tide of Color Against
White World-Supremacy*, 221

Robertson, James, 86

Rockefeller Foundation, 121

Rockefeller, Frank, 117

Rockefeller Institute for Medical
Research (now Rockefeller
University), 121

Rockefeller, John David, 3, 5, 116–
23, 126–27, 149, 241

Rockefeller, William, 118

Rodgers, John, 48

Rommel, Erwin, 165

Roosevelt, Eleanor, 209

Roosevelt, Franklin D., 2, 4, 175–
77, 187, 194, 207–15, 232

U.S. led into World War II by, 4,
207–8, 212–15
Ross, Betsy, 3

S

Sanger, Margaret, 4, 217–23, 227
Sanger, Peggy, 218
Santa Anna, Antonio López de,
60, 158
Schwarzenegger, Arnold, 2
Scott, Thomas A., 123
Scott, Winfield, 1, 81, 153–59, 167
"Secession Winter," 75, 83, 159
Second Continental Congress, 27,
34–35
Securities and Exchange
Commission, 232
Sedition Act of 1918, 203–4
Seminole Indians, 67
Serapis, HMS, 43
Seven Days Battles, 77
Seventeenth Amendment, 200
Seward, William H., 159
Shaara, Michael, 87
Shakespeare, William, 156
Shawnee Indians, 18–19, 20
Shepard, Alan, 169
Sheridan, Philip, 98, 99

Sherman Anti-Trust Act of 1890,
120
Sherman, John, 120
Sherman, William Tecumseh, 99,
110, 166
Shield of Achilles, 215
Sibrel, Bart, 183
Sinclair, Upton, 219
Sioux Indians, 99
Sixteenth Amendment, 200
Slavery, 71, 75–76, 82–83, 141–42,
156
Slee, J. N., 221
Smith College, 223–24
Smith, John, 1, 9, 10–16, 22, 181
Smith, William F. "Baldy," 95
Snoop Dogg, 183
Social Security, 215
Spanish-American War, 111
Spelman College, 121
Spirit of St. Louis (airplane),
173
The Spirit of St. Louis, 178
Stalin, Joseph, 215
Stamp Act Congress of 1765, 23,
33
Standard Oil, 115, 119–20, 122–23,
127
Stanford Business School, 234
Stanton, Elizabeth Cady, 218

Stars and Stripes, USS, 130

State of the Union address, 201

Station Camp Creek, 18, 19

Steinem, Gloria, 226

St. Elmo, 107–9

Stewart, Jimmy, 178

Stimson, Henry, 207, 213

Stoddard, Lothrop, 221

Stowe, Harriet Beecher, 90

Stuart, James Ewell Brown
   "J.E.B.", 97, 160

Susan Constant (ship), 39

T

Tansil, Charles, 214

Taylor, Zachary, 198

Telegraph (UK), 184

Teresa, Mother, 240

Tesla, Nikola, 129, 136–40, 149

Thornton, Billy Bob, 53

Time (periodical), 238

"Trail of Tears," 157–58

Treaty of Versailles, 201

Trust, 119–120

Tubman, Harriet, 2

Tugwell, Rexford, 212

Turner, Frederick Jackson, 1, 69

Tuskegee Airmen, 169

Tuskegee Institute, 125, 141, 145,
   148, 151

Twain, Mark, 115

Two Friends (ship), 41

U

UK *Telegraph*, 184

United Nations, 194, 215

United States Air Force Academy,
   179

United States Military Academy,
   72, 74, 79–81, 84, 94–95, 160–61,
   179

United States Naval Academy, 44

United States, USS, 45, 47–48

University of California, at
   Berkeley, 224

University of Chicago, 121, 188

University of Vermont, 188

Up From Slavery, 142, 146

V

Valley Forge, 64

Veracruz, amphibious assault at,
   157

vertical integration, 120, 123

victimhood, prosperity versus, 152

Villa, "Pancho," 162

Virginia Company of London, 12, 15

Virginia Military Institute, 82, 160

Virginia, University of, 198, 236–37

Voltaire, 103–4

W

War Between the States, 71, 74, 75–79, 81, 83–98, 100, 106–7, 110, 117, 123, 130, 142, 153, 156, 158–60, 198

War of 1812, 47–50, 63–64, 66–67, 75, 88, 154–56

War Production Board (WPB), 214

War with Tripoli, 45–49

Wardenclyffe Tower, 139

Warren, James, 102

Warren, Mercy Otis, 101–5, 114, 241

Washington, Ann Fairfax, 24

Washington, Augustine, 24–25

Washington, Booker Taliaferro, 141–52, 241

Washington College (now Washington and Lee University), 79

Washington, George, 2–5, 23–32, 34, 37–38, 61, 64, 69, 72, 74–77, 79–80, 153, 158, 160, 211, 242

Washington, Lawrence, 24–25

Washington, Mary Anna Randolph Custis, 74

Wayne, John, 53

Weaver, Richard, 189

Wellington, 1st Duke of, 153

West Point, 72, 74, 79–81, 84, 94–95, 160–61, 179

Western Union Telegraph Company, 137

Westinghouse Electric Company, 133, 137–38

Westinghouse Farm Engine, 131

Westinghouse, George, 129–38, 140, 149

Whig Party, 75, 158

White, Ed, 180

Wilderness, Battle of the
in 1755, 17–18
in 1864, 78

Wilderness Road, 19, 21

Wilkinson, James, 154

William and Mary College, 154

Wilson, James, 36

Wilson, Woodrow, 2, 149, 187, 194,
   197–205, 231

Wineburg, Sam, 2–3

Winfrey, Oprah, 3

Wolfe, Tom, 179

Woman and the New Race, 220–21

The Woman Rebel (newsletter),
   219

World War I, 149, 163–64, 171,
   175, 212, 231

World War II, 4, 163–66, 169, 176–
   78, 233–34
   U.S. led into by Franklin
      Roosevelt, 4, 207–8, 212–15

World's Columbian Exposition,
   134

Wright, Wilbur and Orville, 169

Y

Yeager, Charles, 169